THE NONVIOLENT
COMING OF GOD

THE NONVIOLENT
COMING OF GOD

James W. Douglass

*With a new Foreword by
Jonathan Wilson-Hartgrove*

Wipf & Stock
PUBLISHERS
Eugene, Oregon

Wipf and Stock Publishers
199 W 8th Ave, Suite 3
Eugene, OR 97401

The Nonviolent Coming of God
By Douglass, James W.
ISBN: 1-59752-611-8
Copyright©1992 by Douglass, James W.
Publication date 4/1/2006
Previously published by Orbis Books, 1992

To Archbishop Raymond Hunthausen
with gratitude and love

FOREWORD

On December 2, 2005, the fiftieth anniversary of Rosa Park's civil disobedience that started the Montgomery bus boycott, the state of North Carolina killed Kenneth Lee Boyd, the thousandth person to be executed in the United States since the death penalty was reinstated in 1977. Inspired by the witness of Rosa Parks, which reflected to us the nonviolent coming of God in Jesus, seventeen resisters approached the gates of Central Prison and told the police officers standing guard that we had come to stop the execution. We were resisting not only the murder of Mr. Boyd, but also the idolatry inherent in the sacrifice of a fellow human being to the god of security. After refusing to leave, we were arrested, to be released only after Mr. Boyd had been pronounced dead.

Later that day my wife, Leah, and I drove to Birmingham, Alabama, for the annual Advent retreat at Mary's House, the Catholic Worker where Jim and Shelley Douglass live and work. Recalling the events of our day that evening, I told Jim about the woman who had booked me at the police station downtown.

"What is your occupation?" she asked.

"Baptist minister," I said.

"My, my!" she exclaimed sympathetically, as only a Baptist could. "The good Lord Jesus is gonna have to come on back soon and put an end to all this killin'."

Jim did not miss a beat, excitedly interpreting her gesture toward the Second Coming. "Jesus is here!" he said pointing his finger around at us. "The kingdom is now! Did you invite her to join the movement?"

The book that you hold in your hands is unapologetically an invitation to join the movement. "The Palestinian Jew, Jesus of Israel, envisioned for his people, and strove to create, a nonviolent society based on faith, a reality which for us remains all but unthinkable," Jim writes. But a recovery of this vision "can mean our seeing for the first time the nonviolent coming of God, both now and then." Jim writes to open eyes and set feet in motion. So I'll offer a warning here at the start: this book could get you killed.

That is, of course, what happened to Jesus of Israel. And this book, of all Jim's writings on nonviolence, is his most sustained attempt to take seriously what the gospels say about Jesus. One of the most important contributions of the historical-critical study of the New Testament has been the reminder to Gentile Christians in the West that Jesus was, in fact, a Jew. As such, he suffered under the Roman Empire in first-century Palestine. That Jesus was ultimately executed by the ruling authorities indicates a tension between the kingdom he came preaching and the imperial order of his day. Jim's reading of the gospels in this book helps us to see how Jesus was offering a whole new way of life to a people living under occupation.

That new way was necessary because the violence and counter-violence of empire was about to destroy Israel in Jesus' day. This was what the prophets had been saying for centuries before him. To understand Jesus, Jim contends, we must hear the prophets—hear them name the destruction that is inevitable if we do not turn to follow the way of peace. "Jesus," Jim writes, "adopted [this] penetrating truth of judgment as the contingent prophecy it was and posed a total alternative to that judgment: the nonviolent coming of God."

It must be said, of course, that Jim is able to see what is happening in the gospels in part because he has read these texts in the prisons of another empire—what we today call "the world's last remaining super-power." And I, the Baptist preacher, must say that my Gandhian-Catholic brother has learned in those new monastic cells to read like a good Baptist. The twentieth-century Baptist theologian Jim McClendon wrote about how Baptists have always read the Bible with a "this is that" hermeneutic. This empire is that empire—this nonviolent coming that one. The world that Scripture describes is indeed the one we live in—even now for those who believe.

"Jesus is here! The kingdom is now!" As you read you should feel Jim pointing his finger at you. Are you ready to join the movement?

In the years that have transpired since *The Nonviolent Coming of God* was first published, many things in our world have changed. Most will not remember the white train that Jim and so many others worked to stop. But, again, this is that. This war on terror is that white train. This Gulf War is that one. This depleted uranium is that agent orange. The next execution is, once again, Jesus on the cross. This is that, we Baptists say. And the kingdom of God that Jesus came preaching is a way that we can walk in now.

I'm delighted that Wipf and Stock has decided to republish all four of Jim's fine books in this series. His words, like those of all prophets, were too often neglected in the century in which they were written. But, as Yeshayahu Leibowitz says at the end of this book, "Every prophecy deserves to happen—and it depends on humankind whether those things which deserve to happen will or will not happen." Dear reader, please allow this Baptist to end with an altar call: Are you ready to join the movement?

Jonathan Wilson-Hartgrove
Rutba House, 2006

CONTENTS

PREFACE

I first saw *Mother Intifada*, the painting on the cover of this book, in December 1989 as a poster on the wall of a United Nations clinic in Gaza. Its portrayal of the Palestinian uprising struck me immediately as a vision of the nonviolent coming of God. A Palestinian friend with whom I stayed for two transforming days in Beach Camp, Gaza, surprised me, upon my departure from his home, with a farewell gift of his copy of the poster. A few days later, through a providential introduction, the artist of *Mother Intifada*, Sliman Mansour, gave me permission to have his creation grace the cover of *The Nonviolent Coming of God*.

Today, as I look at *Mother Intifada* on our living room wall in Birmingham, Alabama, I see in it the Compassion of God giving birth to a new humanity. I believe Mansour has captured the essence of our hope, what Jesus meant by the kingdom of God. *Mother Intifada* represents the coming of that nonviolent kingdom, the birth of that new humanity of God which is now spreading around the world.

Yet there is also a question in *Mother Intifada*, as there is in the *intifada* itself. The new people being born in the dawn light from the womb of Mother Intifada, and approaching us at the bottom of Mansour's painting, are going in different directions. The beginning, nonviolent life of this revolution can turn in various ways. Will the children of Mother Intifada take only life-giving paths?

The question is addressed to us all, especially with the coming of the Persian Gulf War. Before that whirlpool of violence began to suck humankind into it, a nonviolent transformation of our world was more clearly visible. What the greatness of God had released through the lives of Mohandas Gandhi, Martin Luther King, and millions of other nonviolent practitioners in the world, could be seen transforming humanity. In our time of total destruction, the nonviolent coming of God was at hand. It is *still* at hand—a coming of God no farther away than the hands God has given us. Yet as the United States and its enemies threaten every conceivable violence on each other, annihilation also remains imminent. Set in the widening evil of the Persian Gulf War, the nonviolent transformation portrayed by *Mother Intifada* is far more than a tragically outdated vision. It is a prophetic imperative to us all: Be thus reborn as a global people by your Nonviolent God, or be annihilated by a desert storm beyond the imagination of presidents and generals.

We can live out the imperative of transformation by acting on a faith in the nonviolent coming of God. Being precedes action. Our Nonviolent God initiates the changes we have not yet fully chosen. Nothing is predetermined. Yet our transformation is underway; it is our deepest reality; it is beginning to surface in nonviolent movements everywhere. If we open our eyes, as Martin Luther King did, we can still see the beloved community coming into being. We can see peacemakers, justice-makers, giving their lives to God, in an earth-encircling Love that will transform even the carnage of the Persian Gulf War. We do have the capacity to destroy ourselves. But our very freedom is so profoundly an expression of Compassionate Love, as in the people born from Mother Intifada, that we can have faith in our ultimately choosing the beloved community. God's upside-down kingdom for the poor and the oppressed is at hand—a kingdom where we love our enemies and are saved by them as the Jew in the ditch, in Jesus' parable, was saved by the enemy Samaritan. In the nuclear age that kingdom where we resist evil nonviolently and realize transformation through our enemy, must come. It will come. It is coming now.

That was Jesus' faith, a faith in the ever-present power of God's nonviolent transformation of humanity. But Jesus also warned that destruction was imminent. The ultimate choice of transformation was in danger of postponement. Thus he proclaimed to his people, and to all people, a double prophecy, contingent in the choices it offered: the nonviolent kingdom of God *or* the destruction of Jerusalem, and ultimately of the world. The deepest implications of that contingent prophecy have been brought home finally by our nuclear age.

I believe a sea change is necessary in our understanding of the gospels if we are to understand Jesus and the prophetic choice he proclaimed. In his prophecies about Jerusalem and the world, Jesus predicted nothing as a predetermined future. Nor was he compelled by apocalyptic fantasies. Jesus proclaimed the urgent necessity of choosing collectively between a nonviolent humanity found in God and the looming alternative of self-destruction by violence.

In order to see Jesus' way of transformation, I have interpreted the scriptures in a way derived from his Hindu successor, Gandhi. *The Nonviolent Coming of God* is based on a Gandhian hermeneutic. Gandhi's life was a series of experiments in truth. The truth that concerns me here is Jesus' faith. I have written this book as an experiment in Jesus' faith, as seen in the synoptic gospels, viewed in turn in the light of contemporary, nonviolent struggles. The constant analogies to nonviolent movements, especially those I have experienced firsthand, are the conscious lens of interpretation. I believe in the nonviolent coming of God because I have seen it stop trains on their way to the end of the world and transform enemies into friends. Because a community of faith believed such events would happen, they did happen. Thus the community came to believe and act more deeply.

The Nonviolent Coming of God is the fourth in a series of books on the theology of nonviolence. *The Nonviolent Cross* was a theology of revolution and peace based on the Christic reality of suffering love. *Resistance and Contemplation* sought a theology of liberation through the yin and yang of a nonviolent way of life. *Lightning East to West* began the transformation hypothesis which is continued here, but seen there in more autobiographical terms. *The Nonviolent Coming of God* is about Jesus of Nazareth and his hope for transformation at the end of his and our worlds — an effort to discern Jesus' own eschatology of nonviolence.

ACKNOWLEDGMENTS

I wish to thank the friends who read earlier stages of the manuscript and shared their criticisms: Philippe Batini, Ann Berlet, David Batker, Philip Berrigan, Harry James Cargas, Joseph Cunneen, Ron Dart, Richard Falk, Rachelle Linner, A. G. Mojtabai, David Oliver, Laurie Raymond, and Victor Reinstein.

Herbert C. Burke, my teacher thirty-four years ago at Santa Clara University, has become my teacher again by his red-penned comments running across every page of the manuscript, mailed back from his home on Fuerteventura in the Canary Islands. There would have been no book at all had not Herbert introduced me in his English composition course, during that unforgettable spring of 1957, both to the discipline of writing and to the nonviolence of Dorothy Day (a story told in Chapter 4).

I have also had the invaluable aid of scripture scholars who challenged and helped clarify virtually every line of my first two drafts: Marcus Borg, John Pairman Brown, John R. Donahue, George Edwards, Lloyd Gaston, Walter Harrelson, Ched Myers, Charles H. H. Scobie, and Walter Wink. The years I have spent studying the works of Jesus scholars, then assimilating their criticisms, have been a thoroughgoing education on what I do not — and never will — know about Jesus.

Lloyd Gaston wrote the extraordinary book that began my journey into Jesus' cry for Jerusalem, *No Stone on Another*. I am also grateful to Lloyd for his patient responses to my late-evening phone calls seeking new leads, which he often provided.

The two years of research and writing done while I was a hermit in the Similkameen Valley of British Columbia would have been impossible were it not for the librarians of Vancouver School of Theology. Elizabeth Hart, Ruth Forrest, Anne McCullum, and Sheila Pelto-McLane succeeded in finding and mailing to me at Hedley, B.C., almost every book and article I requested. The final year's research, at Shelley's and my new home in Birmingham, was facilitated by the thoughtful assistance of Denise Gyauch at the Kesler Circulating Library of Vanderbilt Divinity School.

The backyard Birmingham office where the book was completed was built through the love and labor of a host of friends: Claire Feder, Ernie Goitein, Nick DeRocher, Wayne Schucker, Konomu Utsumi, Tom Gagnon, Helen O'Brien, Robert O'Brien, Bill Bates, Carolyn Beighle, Carl Lemp, Tim Herring, and the many other friends from Habitat for Humanity and elsewhere who pitched in their energy at late hours and on weekends.

Through her faith, friendship, and generosity, Nancy S. Nordhoff made possible the continuous work on the book in Hedley, B.C., and Birmingham.

The Epilogue is based on a transforming experience in Israel and the Occupied Territories in December 1989 with a Middle East Witness delegation led by Scott Kennedy and Deena Hurwitz.

The prayers of many people sustained me through periods of darkness. I mention only the one whose prayer I have been most conscious of: my mother, Madalin Douglass. Her letters with their recurring words, "May the Holy Spirit inspire you," were themselves an inspiration.

Our Ground Zero community, while taking up the slack when I retreated from the Trident campaign, continually encouraged my writing based on that experiment in truth.

Shelley's and my life together is the immediate context for everything said in the book. We continue to seek together, in love, the way of Jesus' kingdom of God, believing everything else we need will be given us as well.

Robert Ellsberg is as patient and thoughtful an editor as any writer could hope for. His enduring faith in this often-delayed project has been a sustaining force every step of the way.

I dedicate this work to a friend whose life has been a revelation of the nonviolent coming of God in our time: to Archbishop Raymond Hunthausen, with gratitude and love.

BEGINNING AT THE END
OF THE LINE

I have experienced the end of the world hundreds of times.

Approximately once a week, for seven years, our house begins to shake. By that shaking I know that the end of the world is coming. As the shaking increases, I walk out the door onto our porch and look down on railroad tracks, sixty-five feet below the hill on which our family lives. A train whistle sounds, approaching from the right. The shaking of the porch beneath my feet merges into a rumbling presence. The train rolls into view from beyond our trees. The engineer glances up from the cab of the engine and waves, aware that the people in the house respect him, but hate what he is doing.

We and other members of our community have sat in front of his train and been arrested many times.

After the engine and a buffer car pass beneath me, the Defense Department flatcar appears. Locked onto it is the silver boxlike shape of the Rio Grande container with its bright orange "EXPLOSIVES A" placard, confirming its contents. We know these to be one hundred thousand pounds of solid fuel propellant which, when ignited, will send a Trident missile with eight hydrogen bombs far above its submerged submarine and four thousand miles around the globe. Praying against that prospect, I write down the container identification numbers for future train tracking. The train continues past our house and enters the Trident base.

I have seen another train to the end of the world. May God forgive and transform all of us for the sake of life itself.

I remember a man whose story haunts me. During World War II, he was the traffic superintendent of the Treblinka village railway station in occupied Poland. This traffic supervisor, who was also a member of the Polish underground, counted the cattle cars filled with Jewish victims being shuttled to the Treblinka extermination camp. On each car the Nazis had written in chalk the number of Jews inside. From July 1942 through August 1943 this man counted 1,200,000 Jewish victims in the trains passing him.

Then the trains stopped. They had accomplished their task. There were no more Jews to be sent to Treblinka.[1]

As I write down the numbers on Trident missile shipments rumbling past our house, I wonder how long this process can possibly continue before it concludes in a global fire.

The train that shakes our house at the end of the line is one of many such trains crisscrossing the country. They pass your home as well as ours. Day and night these trains with cargoes for annihilation slice across the United States like assassins' knives on a victim's flesh. We have absorbed these trains into our nation and our unconscious. Yet they are trains to the end of life itself. Their whistles sound a final warning. Whenever you hear a train whistle, remember that these trains to the end of the world are sounding that warning to all of us.

JESUS' PROPHECIES: THE NONVIOLENT COMING OF GOD OR THE END OF THE WORLD?

The end of the world, for Jesus, was both a warning and the point of departure for his good news.

The gospels present Jesus' public life as beginning with his baptism by John and his identification with John's message, a warning of destruction. Following the tradition of his precursor prophets, John the Baptist warned of a divine judgment to be visited upon his own people. Like the prophets before him, he said that if his people did not change, they would experience a fiery judgment in history. In the past such prophetic judgments had usually come in the form of disastrous wars for Israel. John used the images of God's judgment employed earlier by Isaiah, Jeremiah and other prophets: the burning of the chaff after harvest, and a fire consuming the trees of an orchard. He proclaimed the need for repentance in the face of annihilation: "Already the ax is laid at the roots of the trees: and every tree that fails to produce good fruit is cut down and thrown on the fire" (Luke 3:9).

John, like all the great prophets, was speaking about a historical event toward which he saw the Jewish people moving. He was warning his people that they were headed toward a catastrophe. John's prophecy was adopted by Jesus. In passages scattered throughout the gospels Jesus warns that Jerusalem will be destroyed in a war with Rome. Mark's gospel places this prophecy of destruction in the context of a disciple's awe at the massive stones of the Temple:

As he was leaving the Temple one of his disciples said to him, "Look at the size of those stones, Master! Look at the size of those buildings!" And Jesus said to him, "You see these great buildings: Not a single stone will be left on another: everything will be destroyed" (Mark 13:1-2).[2]

But it need not happen. As we shall see, Jesus identified the threatened destruction of the Temple system with its current injustice to the poor of Israel. Jesus' prophecies are warnings of a terrible violence, to which he poses an alternative: the nonviolent kingdom of God, an upside-down kingdom whose first citizens are the poor and the starving (Luke 6:20-21). He also identifies that transforming alternative as a divinely revolutionized humanity, the Human Being. His prophecies of the Jewish-Roman War are contingent prophecies. Nonviolent transformation and the threat of destruction are concrete alternatives, dependent on the people's choice of action. In his prophecies concerning Jerusalem's destruction Jesus was not predicting an inevitable event, any more than he was doing so by proclaiming his alternative vision of God's kingdom. The two were mutually exclusive possibilities contingent on the people's decision: their conversion to a nonviolent society following the laws of God, an upside-down kingdom which would serve the poor, or their suicidal encounter with their own violence and the imperial violence of Rome.

Jesus' repeated warnings that Jerusalem would be destroyed by Roman legions thus reveals not only an over-all historical context for his mission, but also the specific point of departure for his proclamation of the kingdom of God. The beginning point in his public life was his prophetic recognition, with John the Baptist, that a violent historical crisis was imminent. His people were threatened by internal forces—exploitation, violence, and counter-violence—precipitating that crisis.

Following the prophetic tradition, Jesus used the imagery of the end of the world to warn of the end of the autonomous city-state, Jerusalem, by Roman forces. The power of his insight, and of the symbol itself, carries beyond Jerusalem's end to a planetary end now threatened through our own global exploitation and nuclear technology. Jesus' language thus has two points of reference, the end of Jerusalem and the prophetic myth of the world's end, which we have been forced by our own violence to understand concretely:

> The New Testament myth of the end of the world is a true foreshadowing of demonic technology; it sees the destruction of the physical environment as a direct consequence of social violence. . . . Jesus validates ethics by eschatology; ours is the first generation where the truth of his words has emerged from faith into history.[3]

For our generation the symbol has become reality through the exploitation of millions of people, the rape of the earth, and a final judgment that will come from the spread of nuclear technology. For the Jewish generation in Palestine after Jesus' death, the truth of his words "emerged from faith into history" at the critical historical junction leading to the Roman annihilation of Jerusalem. The creative tension of Jesus' words is that they point simultaneously to the end of Jerusalem and to the end of the world. Both were and are threatened by the same cause, human injustice and violence. The ever-present alternative to such an end is the non-violent coming of God in the new humanity of God's kingdom.

To understand this continuous choice in history, as it was posed by Jesus, we shall have to confront a terrifying mistake made by the early Christian church. That mistake was the profoundly violent separation of Jesus from his Jewish people in the growth of Christian belief. The separation of Jesus from Israel is already underway in the gospels and the writings of Paul; thus began the thinking of Christianity. Without attributing our own evils to our forebears, we must recognize that their displacing Jesus from Israel was a first step toward Auschwitz. The path is long and twisting, but as we shall see, the Holocaust had its sacred sources.

That fatal separation of perspective in the early church, divorcing the man from his people, leads also to Hiroshima. For it destroys in our sources Jesus' historical vision of the transforming, nonviolent alternative posed within, not over against, his own people—and thus within every people. The Jew, Jesus, envisioned and tried to create with his people a reality which is for us the unthinkable: a nonviolent society based on faith in the power of truth and love. That still unrecognized and unfulfilled vision is the nonviolent coming of God. Its alternative is the end of the world.

THE PEOPLE AT THE END OF THE LINE

In the nuclear age we all begin at the end of the world. But it may take us a while to realize where we are. Some situations bring home that truth in ways we cannot avoid.

For Shelley and me, the end of the world has been the end of the line where the Burlington Northern Railroad tracks enter Naval Submarine Base Bangor, the West Coast Trident base. This is where our home is located. Our home brought it all home. When we crossed the tracks every day to get the newspaper, pick up our mail, and walk our dogs, we were reminded that hundreds of hydrogen bombs and missile propellant shipments had passed over those same steel rails in front of our house. Nuclear war was here, in our front yard. We could not ignore it. We were responsible for it. We were compelled to act on that responsibility. We therefore worked with our Ground Zero community and hundreds of church, peace, and justice groups at organizing the tracks campaign coast to coast, in resistance to the weapons trains.

In the late 1980s the missile propellant trains became less frequent. The more notorious White Train, which had appeared every six months with its nuclear warheads, had stopped coming altogether. Because of the thousands of people who lined the tracks of the White Train, and the hundreds who blocked it with their bodies, the Department of Energy had switched its nuclear warhead deliveries to trucks. It was not the tracks campaign, however, which had slowed down the missile propellant shipments. These were now going to a different destination, the new Kings Bay, Georgia, Trident submarine base. They had also become the parts of an even more destructive missile system: the Trident-2 (D5) missile, capable of destroying underground missile silos in a first strike. To get to Kings Bay, the Trident-2 missile propellants traveled on tracks through Birmingham, Alabama. With the support of our Ground Zero community, Shelley and I decided to move to Birmingham.

We now live one hundred feet from the railroad tracks in Birmingham, where again our lives are shaken every week by trains on their way to the end of the world. Trains with Department of Defense boxcars, carrying Trident-2 missile parts and displaying bright orange "EXPLOSIVES A" placards rumble past our Birmingham home twice a week. In our new house by the tracks, however, we are shaken not only by a future end of the world. More immediate to us is the end of the world *now*, in Birmingham, Alabama, for the people who live alongside the tracks.

We are the only white people in our neighborhood and in our church, the Catholic parish of Our Lady Queen of the Universe. When Shelley tells people the name of our parish, she smiles and says, "We begin at the top." We rejoice in the faith and friendships of our parish, but Our Lady Queen of the Universe is not really at the top of anything. Nor is the inner city of Birmingham. Like many cities in the United States, Birmingham has experienced white flight. Just over a small mountain beside Birmingham, there is a series of white, suburban communities, with pleasant, tree-lined streets and enormous shopping malls, and with a population that has grown as whites have continued to move out of the ever more predominantly black population of Birmingham.

Many of the African Americans who remain in the city live near railroad tracks. Birmingham is an old railroad town. The intersection of railroads created Birmingham a century ago. But the tracks which crisscross our city today no longer symbolize progress. The tracks pass by housing projects, where people without jobs and resources are in danger of being shot accidentally on their front porches by warring drug dealers. The tracks go near Cooper Green Hospital, the hospital for poor, mainly black people, where our friend and sister parishioner Suzie Walker was near death once her kidney stopped functioning. Thousands of African Americans such as Suzie Walker die prematurely every year from the combined force of poverty, illness, and the restricted treatment of public health hospitals deprived of funds that have gone instead into U. S. weapons systems.[4]

The tracks in Birmingham also go near the Catholic Center of Concern, where Shelley has taught a summer school class to first-graders who know far more about the streets of Birmingham than we do. This is what Shelley has written about her first-graders and the truth they brought home to her:

David is six. He stands about waist-high and has bright eyes, an engaging grin, a devil-may-care manner. Andrew is bigger; he comes nearly up to my shoulder. Andrew is slower, too, moving a little clumsily, but his grin is just as big as David's, his eyes just as bright. Quenton is another slight one, about David's size and also David's best friend. They play football and basketball together. David speaks with a slight lisp. Andrew draws his letters and numbers. Quenton reads only words he already knows, not knowing how to learn new ones. . . .

We began our religion studies in the prescribed way, talking about disciples. Our book had pictures of disciples, bearded men wearing bathrobes and walking around in sandals. The boys, however, knew a real disciple when they saw one. They knew the hand signals, the grafitti, and the threats that come with Disciples in their neighborhoods. They knew all about which colors it was safe to wear, and which words no one should ever say. Eyes big, they told me about a sister who went to the wrong corner and was threatened by a friend's older brother who belonged to a gang. Indeed, they knew all about disciples.

Each afternoon I would leave the boys and drive home to the little white house by the railroad tracks. Sometimes Jim and I would be receiving phone calls and watching out the window for the Trident trains to pass. As I watched the trains clatter by I thought frequently of Andrew, David, Quenton, and the other children in my class. Each of them was bright, capable of working up-to grade level and probably beyond. Why do they not know phonics? Why no basic arithmetic? Why do they live with constant threats to their lives, and why will some of them be killed before they reach their twenty-fifth birthdays?

Watching the trains, thinking of my young friends, I found the statistics taking on new meaning. The $155 billion being spent for Trident suddenly became tutors for each of my boys, smaller classes, better materials, maybe a way to create purpose in the lives of their older brothers who now find their purpose in the gangs. Passing before my eyes were boxcars carrying all these things, carrying them far away from the people who needed them, and transforming them into Trident missiles, loaded on subs to patrol the oceans. The passing of each train has become a very specific occasion for repentance and mourning for me, mourning for all the children I met this summer who do without, and will not be able to recoup what they have lost.[5]

For Shelley's students, Andrew, David, and Quenton; for the people who live in Birmingham's housing projects; for people like Suzie Walker in public health hospitals, the end of the world is now. On January 22, 1991, Suzie Walker, forty-nine years old, died on the same day on which the United States and its allies completed their ten-thousandth bombing run over Iraq and Kuwait in a six-days-old war. For the poor from Birmingham to Baghdad, who experience at first hand the effects of militarism, the end of the world is now.

ROMAN CRUCIFIXION AS DETERRENCE

Confronted by the end of the world, which is present in the cargo aboard the trains and already experienced by the people beside the tracks, we reach for a way to understand total violence. Seattle Archbishop Raymond Hunthausen once shared a symbol of total violence when he said in a speech at the University of Notre Dame: "Our nuclear weapons are the final crucifixion of Jesus, in the extermination of the human family with whom he is one."[6]

Archbishop Hunthausen chose his words carefully in using the present tense: Our nuclear weapons *are* the final crucifixion of Jesus in the humanity he shares with us all. Nuclear weapons not only will be that crucifixion if fired in omnicide. Their crucifixion of the poor is already happening. Archbishop Hunthausen has been clear in condemning the policy of nuclear deterrence and the global injustice it keeps in place. Our nuclear policy of threatening all life on earth to maintain a "new world order" in which forty thousand children die every day from want, hunger, and preventable disease is evil in a way that corresponds to the execution inflicted on Jesus by the Roman Empire. That analogy needs to be examined further.

Martin Hengel in his book *Crucifixion*[7] has provided the most extensive research on what crucifixion meant at the time Jesus received the death penalty. Crucifixion was a form of the death penalty which the Romans inflicted on the lower classes, in particular slaves, violent criminals, and the rebellious. Crucifixion had a political and military purpose: to silence and deter rebels. Jesus was one of those thousands of Jews executed publicly on crosses, because what they represented had to be suppressed in order to safeguard law and order in the Roman state. In the colonized world Rome controlled, crucifixion was seen as essential to a deterrent policy. The Roman state needed crucifixion to deter threats to its way of life whenever they arose in rebellious provinces. Rome therefore made its crucifixions as public and as horrible as possible to serve as more effective deterrents against rebellion. Rebels were stripped naked, tortured, and nailed alive onto crosses, which were then erected in prominent places in order to deter other rebels. It was a frequent practice to leave the rotting corpse unburied as food for vultures and wild animals and as an enduring humiliation of the victim.

The cross was a key to the security system of the Roman Empire. From the standpoint of Roman security, the choice was either to torture and crucify rebels one by one as a deterrent, or to carry out the ultimate threat by annihilating a whole population center, as Rome did in fact do at Jerusalem in 70 C.E.

In *The Jewish War* Josephus describes the mass crucifixions of captured Jews carried out during the siege of Jerusalem in 70 by command of the man who was to become the next Roman Emperor, Titus:

Scourged and subjected before death to every torture, they were finally crucified in view of the wall. Titus indeed realized the horror of what was happening, for every day five hundred — sometimes even more — fell into his hands. However it was not safe to let men captured by force go free, and to guard such a host of prisoners would tie up a great proportion of his troops. But his chief reason for not stopping the slaughter was the hope that the sight of it would perhaps induce the Jews to surrender in order to avoid the same fate.[8]

When Titus' mass crucifixions outside the walls of Jerusalem failed to force a surrender from within, the final step of the Roman security policy was taken. Jerusalem was overrun, destroyed, and its survivors enslaved.

Roman subjects knew well the deterrent philosophy of crucifixion. In John's gospel, Caiaphas, a high priest appointed by Rome, responds to the fear of other national leaders that, if they tolerate the growth of Jesus' movement, "the Romans will come and destroy both our holy place and our nation" (John 11:48). Following Rome's logic, Caiaphas tells them that by collaborating in the crucifixion of one rebel, they can avoid Rome's ultimate use of force: "You do not understand that it is expedient for you that one man should die for the people, and that the whole nation should not perish" (John 11:50).

To preserve the Roman way of life, Rome tried to deter its colonized peoples from rebellion, first with the threat of crucifixion, then with the annihilation of cities. Crucifixion was for Romans, and their client ruling classes, an unquestioned institution for the preservation of peace and security.

DETERRENCE FROM ROME TO WASHINGTON

United States military theorists have studied Rome's security system and have applied it to the deterrent policy of a modern empire. Edward N. Luttwak in his classic study *The Grand Strategy of the Roman Empire* shows that Rome understood the subtle nature of a deterrent policy: "Above all, the Romans clearly realized that the dominant dimension of power was not physical but psychological — the product of others' perceptions of Roman strength rather than the use of this strength."[9] Rome acted deliberately, calculating the political impact of its violence. A rebel's body nailed to a cross was a lesson in imperial politics. Rome regarded crucifixion as a discriminate deterrent, a prudent public notice that legions stood waiting behind that cross, prepared to level cities if a rebellion continued.

"Discriminate deterrence" has become a key term for United States theorists of power as they envision a perpetual deterrent strategy after the end of the Cold War.

In an important article in *Foreign Affairs*, "America's New Geostrategy," Zbigniew Brzezinski, President Carter's former national security advisor, has written a strategic update of "America's assumption of the imperial role after World War II."[10] Brzezinski's forthright acknowledgment of that imperial role, which "was never popular either within America's intellectual class or more recently within its mass media,"[11] is the basis upon which he has restated a deterrent strategy seen as essential for maintaining United States imperial power. He provides a contemporary point of reference to the deterrent strategy of imperial Rome, which crucified Jesus.

Brzezinski urges United States strategists to recognize that nuclear weapons "are no longer just crude instruments for inflicting massive societal devastation but can be used with precision for more specific military missions, with relatively limited collateral societal damage."[12] This diplomatically crafted language distinguishes between the still necessary threat to exterminate entire populations ("just crude instruments for inflicting massive societal devastation"), analogous to Rome's annihilation of Jerusalem, and what Brzezinski goes on to call "discriminate deterrence," a more precise use of nuclear and/or conventional weapons that would single out targets while presumably sparing much of a society (that is, "with relatively limited collateral societal damage"). The government decision-makers who read *Foreign Affairs* are well-aware that in all of this, but especially in the following summary sentence, Brzezinski is using a strategic code to refer to the first use of nuclear weapons: "The result is that nuclear weapons are no longer primarily blunt instruments of deterrence but can also serve as potentially decisive instruments of discriminating violence."[13]

These words convey a perennially new truth for United States nuclear war planners—new to Defense Secretary Robert McNamara in the '60s; new to his successor, James Schlesinger, in the '70s; new to Brzezinski in the Carter Administration; always new to Henry Kissinger, who claims to have discovered it, and now resurrected again by Brzezinski in *Foreign Affairs* as part of a new, American geostrategy. This ever-new, strategically useful doctrine is that nuclear weapons have *now* been made precise enough for their effects to be controlled. We are *now* liberated to launch them first at specific targets "as potentially decisive instruments of discriminating violence." The Pentagon's success in achieving these "instruments of discriminating violence" (nuclear weapons that can presumably be used like a surgeon's scalpel) is also assumed to have disproved the negative thesis of scientists that nuclear war would bring about a nuclear winter and the end of the human species. By reaffirming their total faith in the discriminate use of nuclear weapons, strategists can continue to believe in the expedient of threatening nuclear war—to the point of initiating it with "potentially decisive instruments of discriminating violence."

Anticipating a new empire, Brzezinski devotes the last part of his article to the need for an "upgrading of the U.S.-Japanese relationship from a transpacific alliance into a global partnership"[14] because of the two nations' complementary strengths and needs, in particular, United States military and Japanese economic power. In other words, to retain its influence while declining economically, the United States should promote its military and a "discriminate deterrent" capability as mercenary forces at the service of other, increasingly powerful economies, such as Japan's. We have already seen the United States take on such a mercenary role in the Persian Gulf War.

"DISCRIMINATE DETERRENCE"

Brzezinski's projection of a post–Cold War deterrent strategy is drawn from his involvement with a 1988 government-sponsored study, its very title employing the key term *Discriminate Deterrence*. It was co-authored by a commission of the national security elite, including both Brzezinski and Henry Kissinger.[15] Given the fact that two former national security advisors to presidents served on this commission, while not one of its members dissented from its conclusions, *Discriminate Deterrence* presents us with a national security consensus at the highest level. The integrated, long-term strategy the commission recommends is meant to guide United States weapons policies, nuclear and conventional alike, for "many years into the future at least twenty."[16] Assuming we survive the commission's recommendations that long, we can expect to see future presidents, of whichever party, being guided in their military policies by *Discriminate Deterrence*.

Whereas the American public has been led to believe that deterrence is designed to prevent nuclear war, "discriminate deterrence" allows for a wider, more aggressive policy of enforcing our new world order, carried out by a Rapid Deployment Force backed up with nuclear forces. Discriminate deterrence means enforcing United States dominance over other countries by a variety of threats, from covert intervention to the use of accurate, long-range "smart" bombs, as were used with conventional warheads to destroy the infrastructure of Iraq during the Persian Gulf War. A flexible deterrent, with weapons appropriate to any and every conceivable challenge, is required for the maintenance of United States power.

Discriminate Deterrence states:

> In the past forty years all the wars in which the United States has been involved have occurred in the Third World. . . .
> To defend its interests properly in the Third World, the United States will have to take low intensity conflict much more seriously. It is a form of warfare in which "the enemy" is more or less omnipresent and unlikely ever to surrender. In the past we have sometimes seen these attacks as a succession of transient and isolated crises. We now have to think of them as a permanent addition to the menu of defense planning problems.[17]

The imperial purpose of discriminate deterrence, acknowledged here and in Brzezinski's article in *Foreign Affairs*, helps to answer this question:

What is being deterred by this many-layered policy? The intensified threat to use both conventional and nuclear weapons *first*, even while pursuing low-intensity conflict in the Third World, can only mean that what is being deterred, as in the Roman Empire's crucifixion of rebels, is in fact social revolution. Due to global, systemic injustice, the fact of ongoing social revolution is also global. We are, in short, deterring the Third World. Its massive suffering and mortality under a geopolitical system heavily influenced by the United States is not mentioned or considered by the authors of *Discriminate Deterrence*.

Suppressing omnipresent enemies, as the above quotation suggests, is the burden of an economic empire. Extending the "menu" of defense planning is necessary to remain on top of a hungry world. One is reminded of Luttwak's comparison between the Roman Empire's and our own problems of deterrence:

> We, like the Romans, face the prospect not of decisive conflict, but of a permanent state of war, albeit limited. We, like the Romans, must actively protect an advanced society against a variety of threats.[18]

It is precisely our "advanced society" that poses the need for a deterrent force over most of the world's peoples, people who must suffer and die on a much lower level of consumption than ours.

The United States government has already "taken low intensity conflict much more seriously," as the policy-making authors of *Discriminate Deterrence* know well. What they want further from the government is a "protracted war" on the Third World, as they go on to say.[19] The particular case history they cite as an argument for this continuous war on the oppressed reveals concretely what the national security elite means by "discriminate deterrence." To exemplify the past success of United States intervention by low intensity conflict, the report cites "the saving of democracy in El Salvador."[20]

MODERN DETERRENCE AS CRUCIFIXION

We need here to cut through propaganda and diplomatic code language to the reality of what is being said. In El Salvador discriminate deterrence through low-intensity conflict means the bombing and displacement of villagers. It means tons of white phosphorus bombs, which can burn through to the bones of fleeing people. It means the gunning down of Archbishop Oscar Romero as he offered Mass. It means the rape and murder of the four United States missionaries who identified with the Salvadoran poor, Ita Ford, Maura Clarke, Dorothy Kazel, and Jean Donovan, by the security forces of the El Salvador government. It means the brutal killing of the six Jesuit priests and two Salvadoran women on November 16, 1989, at the priests' house in San Salvador because of their struggle for a just society.

It means especially the "disappearing" of thousands of Salvadoran men, women, and children slaughtered by death squads, their bodies thrown into shallow graves or down ravines. This disappearing of the Salvadoran poor may be the closest modern parallel to Jesus' crucifixion. "Discriminate deterrence" in El Salvador means a Central American crucifixion, a mass execution of the poor by a criminal client state of the United States.

Client states were a critically important part of the Roman Empire's security system. Luttwak uses a familiar concept, "low-intensity threats," in describing the deterrent function of Rome's client states:

> Efficient client states could provide for their own internal security and for their own perimeter defense against low-intensity threats, absolving the empire from that responsibility. Thus, no legions had to be committed to Judea while Herod's regime lasted. By contrast, after Herod that turbulent province required the presence of at least one legion (*X Fretensis*) and sometimes more. . . .[21]

The lesson was clear for Rome in Judea, as it is now for the United States in El Salvador: A willing client state relieves the imperial power of the direct responsibility of policing that region with its own troops. Thus freed, the central authority can deploy its military forces more flexibly over a much wider sphere of influence. Rome used client states such as Herod's brilliantly to help it maintain control over huge areas, yet with a minimum number of legions garrisoned permanently in the occupied territories. Roman legions, much like a Rapid Deployment Force, were then free to move quickly to any scene of rebellion and concentrate the empire's killing power there, as Rome did at Jerusalem in the Jewish-Roman War. Deterrent power over an empire is thus maximized.

The authors of *Discriminate Deterrence* underline the need for Washington to have the same kind of military flexibility through client states ("Third World friends and allies"): "*U.S. forces will not in general be combatants. A combat role for U.S. armed forces in Third World conflicts has to be viewed as an exceptional event . . . our forces' principal role there will be to augment U.S. security assistance programs*" (emphasis in original).[22] Security assistance programs for allies such as El Salvador can then be used as a base to "help anti-Communist insurgencies, especially those against regimes threatening their neighbors"[23] (for example, the contras versus Nicaragua's claimed "threat" to Central America).

In using client states to control neighboring states, Washington, unlike Rome, must sidestep modern democratic institutions while carrying out this security function. "Special Activity" or "covert action" is a necessary part of discriminate deterrence by the United States:

> If the U.S. support for these insurgents is a large and continuing effort, it is bound to be referred to in the press. Nevertheless, neigh-

boring countries that provide access to or bases for the freedom fighters often prefer that the U.S. Government role not be officially acknowledged. By designating the U.S. support as a "Special Activity" (also known as a "covert action"), the U.S. Government can maintain official silence. The laws governing "Special Activities" provide for a great deal of flexibility.[24]

Just as Rome's deterrence of the oppressed in Judea and across the Mediterranean world included both the crucifixion of suspected rebels and the levelling, "if necessary," of whole cities, so too in modern form does our deterrent over the Third World. However, the purpose of the uppermost rung of our deterrent, the threat of nuclear omnicide, has been as little understood by United States citizens as has been the purpose for the low-intensity conflict waged by the "disappearing" of countless Salvadorans.

Daniel Ellsberg, drawing on his inside experience as a policy planner but with different lessons to share than the authors of *Discriminate Deterrence*, points out that even before the Cold War ended, the *primary* purpose of United States nuclear weapons was never to deter an attack on the United States. That could have been done with the number of nuclear weapons on only one Poseidon submarine. We have needed our tens of thousands of nuclear weapons for a credible first strike capability against the Soviet Union, as a context within which we could threaten and control smaller nations that the Soviet Union often supported. We needed an edge over the Soviet Union so as to make our escalating threats credible, which, in turn, was necessary to enforce our economic dominance at lower levels of power. Ellsberg identifies this long-standing nuclear policy as one of *extended* deterrence. (Discriminate deterrence serves as its basic framework, including conventional forces, with extended nuclear deterrence as the ultimate sanction.) The purpose of extended deterrence is to control vast portions of the world by threatening repeatedly to launch a nuclear first strike:

> It's one of the great myths of our era — a lie worthy of Goebbels — that we buy weapons primarily or exclusively to deter an attack on the United States. It's never been true. Virtually all of the weapons we have ever bought have consciously reflected the requirements of extended deterrence — that is, of threatening credibly to initiate nuclear war under various circumstances.[25]

Ellsberg continues by documenting the cases of those presidents who have threatened to initiate nuclear war in order to continue our control over specific areas of the globe: Truman's threat over the Chosin Reservoir in Korea, 1950; Eisenhower's secret nuclear threats against China in order to force and maintain a settlement in Korea, 1953; Eisenhower's secret directive to the Joint Chiefs during the "Lebanon Crisis," 1958; Nixon's secret threats to use nuclear weapons, conveyed to the North Vietnamese by Henry Kissinger, 1969-72. Ellsberg's documentation covers every administration since 1945, possibly excepting President Ford's, with numerous "shows of nuclear force" involving demonstrative deployments or alerts and intended as "nuclear signals."[26]

Our actual nuclear policy since the Second World War Daniel Ellsberg sums up as one of

> *threatening* and preparing to initiate tactical nuclear warfare in the region, and to escalate if necessary, risking Soviet preemption or counter-escalation. In plainer language, the tactic is to threaten regional annihilation, with a link to global holocaust. Within their persistent frame of reference, these policy-makers see simply no alternative (emphasis in original).[27]

The frame of reference for every nuclear threat, as for low-intensity conflict, has always been to deter our political and economic colonies from breaking free from control. The purpose of nuclear weapons, in terms of a threat to strike first, has always been for the sake of United States interests, for maintaining power and control in a world where starvation increases. We are prepared to threaten to destroy the world at any of its pressure points to maintain our present hold over its peoples. Our security system needs low-intensity conflict and the threatened annihilation of cities to deter Third World peoples from revolution, just as Rome needed crucifixion and the threatened annihilation of cities to deter its provincial rebels.

TRANSFORMING THE CROSS

What the original *Sitz im Leben* ("setting in life," or "life situation") was for the various sayings attributed to Jesus is debated intensely by modern scripture scholars. I am concerned here with a broader meaning of *Sitz im Leben*. What I am suggesting by the foregoing analysis of the Roman Empire's (and our own) violence is that we cannot understand Jesus' alternative vision of the kingdom of God, or the reign of a new humanity, apart from its life setting of an imperial power that oppressed and threatened to annihilate Jesus' people.

Two questions are pertinent here: Did Jesus understand the threatening nature of Roman power? If he did understand it, how did he relate it to the deepening fate of his people?

These questions are necessary because we often theorize about Jesus as if he were either unaware of oppression or too otherworldly to be concerned about it. Can we not safely surmise that oppression by an empire which threatened to annihilate them would be at the center of consciousness of most first-century Jews? We may ask to what extent Jesus shared in that consciousness. The question is similar to asking a native South African if he or she is aware of the oppression of apartheid. While such a person may live a life that prevails over apartheid, that victory over evil must presume an awareness of the problem.

It is reasonable to assume that Jesus was profoundly aware of the Roman Empire's power over his people. He knew what it meant to be a Palestinian Jew under Rome. He knew the ruthless power of the oppressor. Jesus' own cross was undoubtedly not the first he saw. It is not Jesus who was blind to the collective situation in which he lived, but we who think of him too narrowly, as if he could have been unaware that he was a member of an oppressed people.

Was Jesus then insensitive to what lay in store for his people from that imperial violence? Or worse, did Jesus see the destruction of Jerusalem by Rome as an inevitable and divinely-willed revenge upon the Jewish people for rejecting him?[28] Millions of believers and nonbelievers alike have been led to believe this.

The thesis of this book is that, far from announcing Jerusalem's destruction as inevitable, Jesus' whole public life was an effort to create a radically alternative Jewish society. The nonviolent coming of God in that society would, he hoped, transform the violence of Rome, Palestine, and the world. It can and must be asserted that Jesus understood Jewish oppression under Rome. His life, death, and resurrection were a transforming response to that *Sitz im Leben*, that life setting of total violence. In our own setting of total violence, we need to understand the nonviolent coming of God.

Rome's deterrent policy was understood by Jesus to risk the destruction of the current Jewish world, an event which was in fact to occur in 70 C.E. Rome, like the United States, used an escalating threat to deter colonized peoples. Its uppermost threat, beyond the crucifixion of thousands of rebels, was, like nuclear war today, the most complete destruction it could accomplish, the razing of a city and a country.

At the center of the gospel is Jesus' understanding of this moral logic of violence as being ultimate destruction, leading to the end of life itself. In a lightning insight whose implications are still far beyond us, Jesus sensed the connections between the violence done to the poor, the outcast, and the rebellious in a colonized first-century Judea and a violent end of the world — his world or any world in which the logic of violence is followed to the uttermost.

This is not to say that Jesus envisioned nuclear weapons or predicted their use. But he knew profoundly — and died by — the logic of nuclear weapons. The logic of an extended deterrent over the colonized and rebellious poor requires a threat of annihilation from the beginning as its ultimate means of enforcement. Deterrence begins with the "discriminate," "low-intensity" killing of the poor: Jesus and other victims of crucifixion in the Roman Empire; the murdered and disappeared in our empire. Deterrent logic then leads ultimately to the end of a world: the razing of Jerusalem in 70 C.E.; the end of the planet, if nuclear deterrence continues. As we know, Jesus questioned this logic: Anyone who wants to save his or her life will lose it. His paradox questions security at every level. Wanting to preserve our way of life, which enslaves millions, will destroy not only our lives but all life on earth.

To grasp the logic of total violence bound up in the use of crucifixion as a deterrent is to see it leading to the end of the world; it is to see that Jesus' death symbolizes the death of the planet.

But something else, inconceivable to the people of Jesus' time, has happened to the reality of crucifixion because of Jesus' nonviolence. Crucifixion in and of itself follows the logic of total violence. Yet the cross has become, for nonviolent prophets such as Gandhi and Martin Luther King, the symbol of nonviolence. Once we recognize the reality of the cross in its original context of total violence, its use as a symbol of nonviolence is astounding, especially since it has served so many violent causes for so long a time. It is as if, suddenly, the electric chair became our symbol for life.

Yet the meaning of the cross has undergone such a transformation. As the Hindu, Gandhi, put it in a Christmas sermon, "Living Christ means a living cross, without it life is a living death."[29] Martin Luther King understood his nonviolent witness as one of "bearing the cross," the actual title given to a biography of Dr. King.[30] How could the logic of ultimate violence and the reality of a transforming nonviolence ever become linked in one and the same symbolic reality, the cross of Jesus' crucifixion?

To take up the cross is, in Jesus' transforming vision, to assume the suffering of the oppressed. It was the oppressed who suffered and died on Roman crosses. Yet Jesus' vision of life is to take on the suffering of the oppressed not as a passive victim but as one acting in loving, nonviolent resistance, thus risking one's own crucifixion. In a world of oppression enforced by extended deterrent polices, the nonviolent prophet ends up on the oppressor's cross or in an assassin's line of fire, a target for the "discriminate" deterrent of a threatened empire.

The inconceivable change that occurred at Jesus' cross was that an empire's terrifying deterrent was transformed through the nonviolent resistance of love, truth, and forgiveness. When Jesus suffered and died on the cross he had taken up, the cross was transformed. The latent possibility of its nonviolent side, life through suffering, was to become visible. The violence of a crucifixion meant to keep total violence in power was revealed instead, to the eyes of the oppressed, as the transforming power of a suffering, nonviolent love. The cross as deterrent became the cross as life. Through the cross Jesus entered into the crucifixion of the world. In so doing, he revealed the other side of violence, which is suffering, as a way of resistance — a way of transforming violence into life itself.

TRANSFORMING THE TRACKS

Railroad tracks extend from the Trident base at Bangor across the United States to our new home by the tracks in Birmingham, as if in a series of crosses. These tracks for Trident missiles are making possible a crucifixion of the world. Other tracks for other weapons are also crucifying humanity. Yet through the faith and love of a growing resistance community, the tracks, like the cross, are being transformed.

On September 1, 1987, Vietnam War veteran Brian Willson was run over and his legs amputated by a U.S. Navy train at the Concord Naval Weapons Station, thirty-five miles northeast of San Francisco. The train was carrying weapons to a dock, where they were to be loaded on ships for Central America. When Brian was hit by the train, he was just beginning a forty-day fast on the tracks to appeal for an end to the trains, whose end of the line he had seen in El Salvador and Nicaragua while visiting more than four hundred amputees in hospitals, victims of United States weapons and mercenary forces in Central America. Brian was to say later: "I think I grieved over the loss of so many legs in Nicaragua that I had already grieved over the loss of mine."[31]

Michael Kroll, an old friend of Brian's, was standing beside the Concord tracks on September 1 holding a banner. He saw the expression on Brian's face in the final moment before the train struck him. He recognized the expression from a photograph he had seen, taken of Brian while he was a security officer in Vietnam. The picture had shown his eyes focused on something just outside the range of the photo: "He had a puzzled look on his face, as if he were trying to understand something, something beyond his ken, though it lay right before his eyes."[32]

Brian had explained what he had been looking at when the picture was taken:

"They were unloading the body bags," he said. "They would bring them in on a truck and unload them for the count. I couldn't see the corpses inside. Just the bags. Piles of them."[33]

Now, as the Navy locomotive bore down on Brian sitting on the tracks, his friend recognized the same expression on his face:

He rose, slightly, from his cross-legged position to a half-crouch. He was leaning to the right, as if preparing to lurch from the tracks. I saw the expression on his face: It was the same puzzled look I had seen in the photo of Brian, the young soldier, contemplating the stacks of body bags before him.[34]

In the next few moments the train cut off one of Brian's legs, fractured his skull, opened his brain, and mangled his other leg so badly that doctors would have to amputate it a few hours later on an operating table. But Brian was alive. He was even alive in a way he had anticipated in Nicaragua—without his legs. But he never thought he would lose his legs in the United States. He had prepared himself for losing them in Nicaragua, while walking two weeks with other members of the Veterans Peace Action Team through war zones heavily mined by contras. The U.S. veterans had role-played medical procedures on how to stop the blood flow if their legs were blown off by contra mines, as was happening to Nicaraguans both in front of and behind the peace walkers. Holley Rauen, a midwife from California, was the medic on the walk and in the role-plays. On August 23, 1987, she and Brian were married. Nine days later on the Concord tracks Holley saved Brian's life by using her skirt to stop the arterial bleeding, in fulfillment of their Nicaraguan role-plays.

The train that ran over Brian was a train that had once delivered weapons to ships at the Concord dock on their way to Vietnam; now the train's cargo was destined for Central America. It was a train whose end of the line was body bags and amputees, but whose evil was countered by a spirit which could not dismiss those images. On September 1, 1987, the Concord train carried out both the foreign and domestic meanings of "low-intensity conflict": its cargo, inside the "EXPLOSIVES A" boxcar, white phosphorus bombs destined for the peoples of El Salvador and Nicaragua[35]; its immediate effect, a Vietnam veteran peacemaker being dismembered on the tracks beneath it.

At a press conference on the tracks before the train came, Brian had shared two truths which he had repeated many times in the previous month in announcements of his forty-day fast, in letters to the Navy and public officials, and in other statements to the press:

"If the munitions train moves past our blockade, other human beings will be killed or maimed. We are not worth more. They are not worth less."

And:

"You can't move these munitions without moving my body or destroying my body."

The weapons trains at Concord were moved by a larger purpose: to impose the logic of violence upon people, a logic summed up by our national security planners as "discriminate deterrence." The deterrent system behind the trains wanted to impose the logic of violence upon the peoples of Nicaragua and El Salvador targeted by the bombs on the trains. It wanted to deter them, and all neighboring peoples, from further steps in an ongoing social revolution. The deterrent system wanted to impose that same logic of violence upon United States citizens, by deterring them from acts of conscience.

Brian expressed a different logic and a different spirit: The lives of the people killed or maimed by these bombs are worth no less than our own lives; what you are doing to them you will have to do first to me.

The deterrent system took Brian seriously.

Previously, on August 21, 1987, Brian had written a letter to the Concord Weapons Station commander, Captain Lonnie F. Cagle, announcing the forty-day fast he and others would begin on the Concord tracks September 1. He wrote:

So-called Low Intensity Conflict is terrorist warfare of the most barbaric form. Our intervention into sovereignty violates a number of domestic and international laws.

... We plan a sustained presence that will include persons placing their bodies on the tracks and roadway, asking you and those moving the munitions to stop their movement. In so doing, we will be upholding the law under the Nuremberg Principles agreed to by the United States, and Article VI of our Constitution which holds our treaties to be Supreme Law.

... Under Nuremberg, every citizen, including military personnel, is duty bound to uphold the law, even when ordered otherwise by superiors. I would like to discuss with you your views and response to our concerns.

Captain Cagle received Brian's letter August 26 according to a Navy investigative report.[36] The next day Weapons Station Transportation General Foreman, Eugene S. Piazza, held a meeting of base department heads in which he informed them that, "starting 1 September, demonstrators would be on the tracks at the Port Chicago Highway crossing *and may not move when the train approaches,*" the Navy report said (emphasis added).

The day before the train ran over Brian Willson, Captain Cagle sent a report up his chain of command to Washington, D.C., stating that "fasters *will not move* for approaching rail traffic" (emphasis added).

On September 1 the order not to stop the train for protesters on the tracks went down the chain of command at Concord: Railroad Operations Foreman Edward W. Hubbard received the order from Jimmie L. Martin, a heavy-mobile-equipment foreman. Hubbard then gave the order not to stop to the train crew at 5:30 A.M. when they came on duty. The source of the order higher than Jimmie L. Martin has never been revealed.

According to a report by a detective at the local sheriff's office, the same order — not to stop the train for protesters on the tracks — was repeated down the same chain of command, Martin to Hubbard, Hubbard to the train crew, approximately one hour before Brian was struck by a train going seventeen miles per hour, *more than three times the posted five miles per hour limit.*

A further order to proceed in moving the train — with protesters visibly on the tracks, no deputy sheriffs present to arrest them, and the don't stop order in effect — was given at 11:50 A.M. to Operations Foreman Hubbard by John M. Banta. Banta was the security manager for the base commander, Captain Lonnie Cagle.

Is it likely that this systematically repeated, life-threatening series of orders would have been given without the at least tacit approval of Captain Cagle and his superiors at higher command levels?

At the November 18, 1987, congressional hearing about the incident, the Navy investigator, Captain S. J. Pryzby, said he had not received several key documents. As a result, none of the above evidence was presented. Perhaps Captain Pryzby's most revealing statement at the hearing (but only in the unavailable context of the chain of command order not to stop the train) was: "Oh, yes, *we knew all about Mr. Willson*, about his fasts, his trips to Nicaragua, and his being on the tracks since June 10 [in earlier protests], *and that he was a man of his word*" (emphasis added).[37]

That the government "knew all about Mr. Willson" was confirmed by another source in November 1987. FBI agent John C. Ryan revealed that he had been fired in August 1987 for refusing to take part in a "terrorist" investigation of Brian Willson, Duncan Murphy, Charles Liteky, and George Mizo, participants in the Veterans Fast for Life. The four veterans had fasted forty-seven days in Washington on the Capitol steps beginning September 1, 1986, as an appeal for a change in Central American policies. The FBI began its "terrorist" investigation of Willson, Murphy, Liteky, and Mizo after a protest in Chicago resulting in a broken window and jammed door locks. Leaflets were left saying the action was inspired by the fast. Ryan said he refused to take part in the investigation because he knew the veterans were not terrorists. After twenty-one years in the FBI, Ryan was fired in August 1987, one week before Brian Willson was run over by the Navy train.[38]

In light of the FBI investigation, we can ask if it was only coincidental from the government's standpoint that on September 1, 1987, the anniversary of the Veterans Fast for Life: 1) three of the four veterans were again beginning a forty-day water-only fast appealing for deeper nonviolent resistance to United States policies in Central America, with Willson and Murphy on the Concord tracks and Liteky again on the Capitol steps; 2) Duncan Murphy was publicly known to be one of the other "fasters [who] will not move for approaching rail traffic," as Concord Commander Cagle put it in his report, on the day before the train's assault, to his command in Washington, D.C.; 3) Duncan Murphy was in fact hit and almost killed by the same Concord train that ran over Brian Willson. In the moment before the train struck, Duncan sprang in the air hurling himself onto the cowcatcher and, as one observer described it, "seemed to capture the train in his arms" while also tearing a gash in his left leg. Duncan's survival is just as miraculous as Brian's—one veteran mangled under the Navy train, the other hit and carried through the air by it—and raises the same questions concerning the reasoning behind the government's chain of command order not to stop the train.

Navy investigator Pryzby's admission that the government "knew all about Mr. Willson . . . and that he was a man of his word" summarizes the background for the order not to stop the train: The Navy command knew that Brian Willson would *not* get off the tracks. Should we be surprised if a policy of "discriminate deterrence" abroad is, at least occasionally, backed up by a similar willingness to kill those at home who are most determined to resist it?

THE LOGIC OF VIOLENCE

The logic of the use of violence to deter others from acts of conscience—and from the social revolution such acts add up to—comes from the assumption that systematic violence can dictate its own terms to anyone on the face of the earth. The systemic evils based on this assumption cover the globe. A systemic evil is a social organization of killing and injustice into which we become locked by coercion, propaganda, and our own passivity. Hiding death and lying about death head the agenda of any systemic evil. The first lie systemic evil forces us to accept is our obligation to believe its official lies about killing.

For example, hiding and lying about death was central to the systemic evil of the Persian Gulf War. Generals told journalists in daily "pool" briefings what to report about the "necessary" killing of Iraqis and Americans, the latter by either the "friendly fire" of our own weapons or the reluctant fire of conscripted Iraqi soldiers, propagandized in turn by Saddam Hussein. As our air war slaughter of Iraqi troops and civilians ("collateral damage") continued, so, too, did the government's total control over media coverage: no pictures or information on the more than 100,000 Iraqi casualties, official film footage of U.S. "smart bombs" destroying isolated enemy buildings (without people visible), no on-the-spot reporting of the bombing massacre of the thirty-mile-long convoy of Iraqi troops attempting to flee Kuwait City, and the gradual introduction of new U.S. weapons into public consciousness, such as the "fuel-air explosive," first described as an Iraqi instrument of terror and "the poor man's nuclear weapon," then used instead by U.S. warplanes in bombing Iraqi troops trapped in desert bunkers. In the systemic evil of the Persian Gulf War, killing and dying were massively organized and propagandized on both sides so as to carry out ever more killing and dying.

One of the first Americans killed in the Persian Gulf War from "friendly fire" was Marine Lance Corporal Michael Linderman, Jr., 19 years old, a friend and former classmate of our son, Tom, at Central Kitsap High School in Silverdale, Washington. Michael, whose hopes were to get a college education and open a bookstore, had joined the Marines to help pay for that education. He is the victim of a systemic violence which extends from the front lines in the desert back to a system of higher education open to many poor and average-income citizens only if they enter into a contract to kill and be killed for their government's questionable policies. However, the words *killing* and *dying*, unlike *education* and *opportunity*, are little used in the military recruitment of high school seniors such as Michael.

The logic of violence which our government applied in the Persian Gulf War was the presumed ability of sheer power to impose its will on the physically, socially, or militarily less powerful. This logic of violence is the assumed prerogative of empires. It was once the logic of the Roman Empire and its client rulers, such as the Herodian kings in Palestine, a logic which in the gospel story massacred the innocents of Herod's kingdom in a step to maintain power. In that story, violence and power are asserting the same absolute claims as they will at Jesus' crucifixion.

The logic of violence, which rules empires yet survives their passing, asserts that death is supreme. Death and the fear of suffering unto death have been drafted from the human soul to serve as the deterrent system of every empire in history. Systematically organized, threatened, and inflicted, death functions as the defense ministry of every imperial regime, every client state, every petty kingdom. Death is the final argument, the bottom line of empire. Threatened death in the form of swords, guns, smart bombs, or nuclear missiles is the supreme argument of power. The logic is painfully simple: Submit to death's regime or die. The law of violence is that death is supreme.

But if death so rules the world, what about those whose kingdom is not of this world of death? What about those who through interior struggle have been given the grace to overcome the fear of death? What about those who refuse to submit to the law of violence, who refuse to pledge allegiance to the empire of death?

LIBERATION FROM THE LAW OF VIOLENCE

For those liberated from the fear of death, the law of violence is powerless. Violence can impose its will only to the extent that its companion, death, is feared. The law of violence can continue to rule only if it is met by another form of itself—by a counter threat of death or by a surrender to the fear of suffering and death. Nonviolence is neither of these. Nonviolence is the overcoming of death by a fearless love.

Against the nonviolence it met at Concord, the logic of violence and death was powerless. The train ran over Brian, but Brian stopped the train by not submitting to its law of death. He stopped the train's logic in its tracks. The most the train could get out of Brian was a puzzled look, the same puzzled look he had given the body bags in Vietnam. But the train could not get him to submit to the logic of fearing death. Brian did not move. He just looked puzzled.

The train ran over Brian, but Brian stopped the train by that inquisitive look: What were the body bags saying? What was the train saying? Whatever it was, it was not coercing the spirit in front of it, a spirit more concerned with understanding than with fear. How does one understand pile after pile of body bags or a train carrying death which runs down the humans in front of it? There was something extraordinary to be learned here, something deeper than the fear of death. But it could be learned only by looking straight at the body bags or at the train thundering down on one's body.

Nor could the impact of the train force Brian to retaliate against those at its controls, those who drove the wheels over his legs and the steel into his brain. Brian stopped the train again in his first meeting with reporters after he had lost both his legs. He told them:

> I'd like to say that I have compassion for the train crew. I know they have a soul and they have a heart and I can't believe that they would have wanted to run over me or anyone else. I feel no ill will toward the people who were on that train.[39]

In those words lies the transforming power of nonviolence.

The logic of violence, which sent a weapons train over Brian Willson's body, has fundamental limits: It has no power of truth. The Navy train which amputated his legs could not force Brian into *believing* that the train's cargo of weapons should, after all, be used against Salvadorans or Nicaraguans. On the contrary, the train's body-severing violence simply brought home the unifying power of the nonviolence facing it on the tracks—a realization that the lost limbs of Brian Willson, and of the Salvadorans and Nicaraguans at the end of the line, were all one. "I believed," said Brian, "that at some metaphysical level, their legs and my legs became the same, and that their legs were no less valuable than mine."[40]

Nonviolent action, as exemplified by Brian Willson on the Concord tracks, is love in action. It waits in faith for a transforming Reality to enter the world, waits in faith for the realization of a Great Spirit. Carried through in love of the enemy and forgiveness of injury, nonviolent action is itself the coming of that Spirit. That is because nonviolent action embodies in a beginning way what and who the Spirit of God is: at one with the poor and the suffering, resisting injustice, loving enemies, and forgiving unforgivable actions. So when we act in that way, as Brian Willson did, we begin to give God an opening into the world. God uses those openings in ways at which we can only marvel.

When we deepen in nonviolent action, both evil and God take us seriously. We are given the faith and fate of the prophets. We are given the cross. We are given a train whose tracks of death can become a way of life. We are given a community of hope. It is truly a gift—a terrible, beautiful coming of God through which our lives and the world are transformed.

MAKING THE CONNECTION

The trains running past our home in Birmingham continue to bring the end of the world—Department of Defense boxcars with their bright orange "EXPLOSIVES A" placards bearing Trident-2 missile propellants on their way to Kings Bay, Georgia. And beside the Birmingham tracks we see the end of the world now—decaying houses and hospitals, schools without resources, children pushing drugs, the growth of gang violence . . . evils whose remedies are being carried down the tracks, their funds having been absorbed by the missiles in the boxcars.

Will we make the connection?

That is the overwhelming question in our lives beside the tracks in Birmingham: Will we make the connection between what is on the trains and what is happening beside the tracks? Will we in Birmingham, and will we as a people, make the connection between the billion-dollar, world-ending weapons on these trains and the end of the world now for the people beside the tracks?

Will we make the connection?

The question arises all along the tracks. Besides Birmingham, the Trident missile trains roll through Topeka, Kansas City, St. Louis, East St. Louis, Evansville, Nashville, Chattanooga, Atlanta, Jacksonville—all cities where the end of the world is experienced now by forgotten people. East St. Louis, Illinois, is a symbol of them all.

In September 1988 I went to East St. Louis to join Rev. Buck Jones, civil rights leader and United Church of Christ minister, and his people in Project H.O.P.E. (Helping Other People Emerge) in a rally against the Trident missile. They taught me the fundamental realities of their city. East St. Louis is the largest all-black city in the United States. It has a population just over fifty-two thousand, ninety-eight percent African American. The people of East St. Louis are without jobs, resources, or services. East St. Louis has gone as long as ten months without a garbage pickup. In 1986, because the city could not afford a new floodgate, the Mississippi River backed up into the homes of East St. Louis. Twelve thousand mainly low-income people lost all their possessions. The Mississippi's assault on the city was a dramatic example of the kind of suffering that East St. Louis residents experience daily. As Buck Jones says, East St. Louis mothers put bread on the floor at night to keep the rats from biting their sleeping babies, and they stuff rags in their babies' ears to keep the roaches out. Because of economic racism, East St. Louis is a third-world country in the middle of the United States.

Through the center of this suffering city pass weekly missile shipments for the most expensive weapon in history, the $155 billion Trident system.[41] In their journey across the country Trident missile propellants stop longest, and threaten people the most, in East St. Louis, where their highly explosive boxcars are shunted among three railroads. The "EXPLOSIVES A" placards on the sides of the Trident boxcars signify that in the event of an accident the residents of East St. Louis should be at least one mile away for their own safety.[42] In fact, the people's substandard housing is backed up against the fences of that switching yard. If an accidental explosion occurs, the same people who are now being robbed by Trident will be blasted by it.

Will we make the connection?

This is what Trident and all our other billion-dollar weapons are doing now to many of the people they are said to defend. The world-ending weapons on our trains are ending the world by the tracks now economically — and will do so physically as well, should they explode. That immediate end of the world foreshadows the end of the line, Kings Bay, Georgia, where the deployment of Trident submarines threatens the end of life on our planet earth. To ignore the first end is to accept the second. The immediate end of the world, for poor people in the United States and across the world, reflects the basic reason why our corporate and government leaders threaten to destroy the whole world: a threat serving as the ultimate deterrent to a social revolution. It is because a few have what the rest of the world needs and wants. Thus those few also have a special need for bigger weapons abroad, and more police commanding bigger prisons at home, to protect their hold upon what others need desperately.

Will we make the connection?

Alabama has had one of the highest proportions of soldiers, especially African American soldiers, in the Persian Gulf of any state in the nation.[43] Alabama is also one of our poorest states. From the economically most devastated communites of Alabama, where do young black men end up? They end up dead before the age of 25, or in prison, or volunteering for the military to escape the first two possibilities. Many were sent to the Persian Gulf, the poor of this country forced to face off against the poor of Iraq. African Americans, Hispanics, Native Americans, and poor whites made up the majority of our service people ordered to do battle against poor Arabs so as to maintain Western dominance over the richest oil deposits on earth.

Will we make the connection?

Buck Jones has.

In 1988 Buck Jones and I went on a pilgrimage into the other world of Trident, that forgotten world alongside the Trident tracks. For thirty days, we did a joint speaking tour, following the Trident tracks through ten states and twenty cities. Our theme was "Together We Can Stop This Train" — the Trident missile train of militarism, racism, and poverty. At each stop we made, Buck identified the suffering of the communities beside the tracks with the train going through their midst. But in spite of the enormity of that suffering, as experienced especially in his own community of East St. Louis, Buck remained hopeful. He offered examples of what people could do through nonviolent action in cities such as East St. Louis. One of his examples, like Brian Willson facing the Concord train, particularly showed the unifying power of nonviolence:

> Edlow International stored uranium hexolfloride in a warehouse in the middle of an East St. Louis residential area. The storage was continued in spite of pleas from the community and information from a Washington University physicist that uranium hexolfloride if inhaled or ingested can cause cancer, leukemia, and birth defects. It is also

worth mentioning that this uranium was being stored in East St. Louis on its way to France and ultimately South Africa.

However, as a result of two years of nonviolent protest, Project H.O.P.E. succeeded in getting the Nuclear Regulatory Commission to close the Edlow warehouse.[44]

The active hope of a nonviolent community in East St. Louis is at one with the hope for transformation in South Africa. To go to East St. Louis, Illinois, is to discover an American apartheid. But to go to the heart of East St. Louis is also to discover, in the vision of Buck Jones and Project H.O.P.E., a transforming alternative.

In our monthlong journey along the tracks Buck Jones also told a parable that reflected the enduring hope of his two decades following a way of nonviolence through the streets of East St. Louis:

My challenge to you who are involved in the struggle for peace, justice, and liberation is to be patient and persistent.

As a boy, I sometimes enjoyed destroying anthills in South Florida. I became an observer of ants and noticed that after I destroyed their homes, the ants would simply rebuild.

I didn't see any ants throw up their hands in disgust and complain, "We'd just as well give up because every time we build our home, Buck Jones will come along and destroy it."

No, the ants didn't call a meeting. They didn't set up a study group. They didn't engage in long investigation. Instead they went to work. Each ant grabbed a piece of dirt and began the job of rebuilding their common home. The ants did not stop until their home had been completed.

My challenge to you is: If we are to stop this train and end the nuclear madness in America, we must learn to be patient and persistent.[45]

HOPE ALONG THE TRACKS

The patience and persistence of Buck Jones and others along the tracks will transform the tracks from death to life, as these rails become the links of an extended nonviolent community.

An image that returns to me is one of children waiting for the train.

When our Ground Zero community has prepared to block a train coming to Bangor, our children have waited with us at the tracks. I remember their holding their hands on the rails. From our house and vigil site by the base gate, it is not possible to see the train coming until it rounds a bend a quarter of a mile away. But the children know that through the steel rails they may be able to feel the train approaching before it actually comes into sight. So one occasionally sees children among the vigilers holding their hands on the rails, listening with their whole bodies for the throb of the coming train. The image is one of faith: children waiting for the weapons train, knowing the train can be stopped by a community such as the one around them.

Now, having moved to a new trackside home in Birmingham, on a day when these tracks are deserted I think of the children and put my own hands on the rails. What I feel is not a train coming. I feel life in these rails. I feel the life of the community through the tracks.

I feel the lives of Buck Jones and Project H.O.P.E. in East St. Louis, who helped inspire Shelley's and my decision to move to Birmingham. I think of their patience and persistence in a devastated city, stopping a daily train of injustice and rallying against the constant coming of Trident trains. I feel their lives through these rails.

I feel the lives in the community at the Peace Farm in Amarillo, Texas, alongside the railroad tracks leading from the Pantex Plant, final assembly point for all U.S. nuclear warheads. I think of their years watching the White Train so as to alert Ground Zero, always in the darkest hours, when the train with its hundreds of hydrogen bombs switches from the spur of the Pantex Plant onto the Santa Fe main line and begins its journey across the country. I feel their lives through these rails.

I feel the lives of Diana, Milton, and the Salt Lake City Agape Community, who have been vigiling for years outside the Hercules Corporation, final plant for the Trident missile propellant. I think of them checking the railroad spur from Hercules until they see the Department of Defense boxcars ready to depart so that they can alert us of their coming.

I feel the lives of Martina, John, Judy, and Joe at Metanoia Community, the other end of the line, alongside the tracks leading into the Kings Bay, Georgia, Trident base. Their community by the Kings Bay tracks has created a continuous nonviolent presence at the East Coast Trident base which corresponds to Ground Zero's on the West Coast.

I feel the lives of Ann Sorenson and the Make Tracks for Peace Community beside the tracks in Evansville, Indiana. I feel the faith of Ann, who after moving to Evansville to watch for the Trident trains, goes out at all hours of the night and day to identify these boxcars and pass the word along; she has faith that God's Spirit moving along the tracks will stop them.

I feel the lives of people in Birmingham who vigil beside the tracks, seeing that vigil as one with the struggle for justice in our city. I feel the lives of Sister Mary McGehee and Scott Douglas, founders of Citizens Against Trident, who made possible our move to Birmingham. I feel the life of Colonel Stone Johnson, Jr., vice-president of Birmingham's Southern Christian Leadership Conference and retired railroad worker, whose vigiling against the Trident trains is another side of his lifelong work for human rights. I feel the lives of Rev. Fred Shuttlesworth and Rev. Abraham Woods, two of Birmingham's greatest civil rights leaders, who have inspired us with their prophetic speeches identifying resistance to Trident with economic justice.

I feel the lives of thousands of people along the tracks who, over the last ten years, have received relayed phone calls in the middle of the night — or in the middle of work schedules, home obligations, school or church commitments — and who have nevertheless found a way to be present at the tracks, so as to break the silence around these trains of death and bear witness to life.

I feel the lives of this community through these steel rails that join us, an extended community linking hundreds of towns and cities, brought together by a hope that the life and love and witness of people by the tracks, and on the tracks, will prove more powerful than the world-ending cargoes on the trains.

Holding my hands on the rails in a time of silence makes me realize more deeply than ever that the tracks are being transformed. It is true that the tracks still carry death. The end of the world keeps coming. But there is a greater life coming through these tracks, the beginning of a new world. I can feel its presence.

2

THE NEW HUMANITY

The present era will be associated by the future historian with two world-shaking events, viz. the discovery and release of atomic energy and the demonstration of the power of the atman *to resist the power of armaments successfully. . . .*

With a certitude characteristic of him Gandhiji affirmed: "We are constantly being astonished these days at the amazing discoveries in the field of violence. But I maintain that far more undreamt of and seemingly impossible discoveries will be made in the field of non-violence."

Pyarelal, Gandhi's secretary, in his conclusion to
Mahatma Gandhi: The Last Phase[1]

Is humankind now on the edge, as Gandhi believed, of making transforming discoveries in the field of nonviolence?

A 19-year-old student in a white shirt, Wang Weilin, stands at attention before an advancing column of tanks near Tiananmen Square in June 1989. The lead tank stops within a few feet of the solitary figure. Wang climbs onto the turret of the tank and pleads with the soldiers in it to turn back and stop killing people. Returning to the pavement, he continues to stand at attention before the tanks. Millions of people from around the world, simultaneously watching this encounter via satellite television, hold their breath. Seconds seem like hours. The tanks remain motionless. Eventually, bystanders lead Wang Weilin away into the crowd. The column of tanks resumes its march to Tiananmen Square to carry out its appointed task of slaughter. Wang Weilin, like thousands of other pro-democracy students, disappears. His friends fear he has been put to death.

But who, in this encounter between the unarmed student and the column of tanks, has really won the victory? Which of these two parties has tapped the more powerful force in the future of China and the world?

Again, in the early morning hours of January 13, 1991, in Vilnius, Lithuania, a photograph is taken of a group of Lithuanians pushing against an advancing Soviet tank. The picture, printed the next day in newspapers around the world, reveals under the tank the legs of a woman wearing black leather boots—all that can be seen of 24-year-old Loreta Asanaviciute, who died some hours later in the Vilnius Red Cross Hospital. Loreta Asanaviciute was one of at least fourteen people killed and more than six hundred wounded, as a remarkably disciplined crowd of forty thousand Lithuanians engaged in a nonviolent defense of their newly independent republic's television buildings against Soviet troops. The photograph of Loreta Asanaviciute's legs being crushed by the tank treads on that "Bloody Sunday" became a transforming symbol of nonviolent resistance for the Lithuanian people, as they continued to stand without guns before Soviet tanks.

Can we see in Wang Weilin and Loreta Asanaviciute, and in the Chinese and Lithuanian freedom movements they represent, the beginning signs of a spiritual transformation, the nonviolent coming of God in a new humanity?

TERMS OF TRANSFORMATION

The historically conditioned term *revolution* is inadequate to describe the events of 1989 in Eastern Europe. In only one country, Romania, did the fall of a Communist regime occur with the violence we associate with a revolution. Timothy Garton Ash, the premier historian of these events, notes:

> Nobody hesitated to call what happened in Romania a revolution. After all, it really looked like one: angry crowds on the streets, tanks, government buildings in flames, the dictator put up against a wall and shot. It is, however, a serious question whether what happened in Poland, Hungary, Bulgaria, or even Czechoslovakia and East Germany, actually qualified for anything but a very loose usage of the term "revolution." This doubt was expressed by several intellectuals in the countries concerned. Should popular movements which, however spontaneous, massive and effective, were almost entirely nonviolent, really be described by a word so closely associated with violence? Yet the change of government, no, the change of life, in all these other countries was scarcely less profound than in Romania. By a mixture of popular protest and élite negotiation, prisoners became prime ministers and prime ministers became prisoners.[2]

Gandhi reached as deeply as he could into human language to come up with a term that could describe the kind of power that he experienced in South Africa and India and which we have seen sweep through Eastern Europe toppling Communist dictatorships in 1989. He settled finally on his own creation, *satyagraha*, "truth-force" (a compound of two Sanskrit nouns, *satya*, "truth," and *agraha*, "firmness," a synonym for force), as the best word for a spiritually explosive power that he saw transforming the world. As a devout practitioner of the Sermon on the Mount and the way of the cross, Gandhi knew that his term, *satyagraha,* was a re-creation of Jesus' "kingdom of God." He had derived his own initial understanding of non-violence from Leo Tolstoy's interpretation of Jesus' saying, "The kingdom of God is within your power" (Luke 17:21).

Jesus also used another, more mysterious symbol to speak of the transforming power of nonviolence, one expressed by the Aramaic phrase *Bar Enasha.* This intriguing symbol of Jesus will be the focus of this chapter. It is usually translated into English via the Greek of the gospels as "the Son of Man." The idiomatic meaning of this Aramaic phrase, which has so puzzled Christian scholars over the years, is more simply "the human being." As we follow "the Human Being's" unique development by Jesus, the only person in the gospels who uses it, we will be confronted by a radical vision of nonviolent transformation, which the early church developed in its own context into the doctrine of Jesus' Second Coming.

At the heart of Gandhi's *satyagraha,* and of Jesus' "kingdom of God" and "the Human Being," is an infinite force of transformation: the nonviolent power to change violence and oppression into community, the soul-based power to realize unity progressively in a person, a society, and a world. That transformation and realization is occurring in the remarkable time in which we live.

TRANSFORMATIONS OF 1989–91

We have seen it happen in East Germany, as described in Timothy Garton Ash's chronicle of 1989's popular explosion in Leipzig:

> To say the growth of popular protest was exponential would be an understatement. It was a non-violent explosion. Those extraordinary, peaceful, determined Monday evening demonstrations in Leipzig — always starting with "peace prayers" in the churches — grew week-by-week, from 70,000 to double that, to 300,000, to perhaps half a million. The whole of East Germany suddenly went into labour, an old world — to recall Marx's image — pregnant with the new. From that time forward the people acted and the Party reacted. "Freedom!" demanded the Leipzig demonstrators, and Krenz announced a new travel law. "Free travel!" said the crowds, and Krenz reopened the frontier to Hungary. "A suggestion for May Day: let the leadership parade past the people," said a banner, quoted by the writer Christa Wold in the massive, peaceful demonstration in East Berlin on 4 November. And more leaders stepped down. "Free elections!" demanded the people, and the Council of Ministers resigned *en masse.* "We are the people!" they chanted, and the party leadership opened the Wall.[3]

We have seen it happen also in 1989 in the streets of Poland, Hungary, Bulgaria, and Czechoslovakia — and in 1990–91, in the fifteen republics of the Soviet Union. We have seen the power of nonviolence sweep through one country after another, transforming them from police states into struggling democracies.

We have seen it happen during the "Second Russian Revolution," August 19–20, 1991, in response to the attempted Soviet coup. The coup was overcome by hundreds of thousands of unarmed citizens. Some, as in China and Lithuania earlier, stood before columns of tanks. Three Russian resisters were martyred by the tanks. Hundreds, then thousands of other citizens encircled the Russian Parliament Building in Moscow as a civilian defense force shielding Boris Yeltsin and other elected leaders from an imminent military assault. All afternoon and evening on the second day of the coup, loudspeakers blared warnings to the people that tanks were rolling toward the building and planes filled with paratroopers were preparing for an airborne assault. Yet the people kept coming. In fact a further three-pronged assault was secretly being mounted against them. It was to include K.G.B. agents who had infiltrated the crowd within the building, helicopters bearing shock troops, and elite units prepared to rush into the building from twenty-four subterranean entry points whose existence was unknown to Yeltsin supporters. A Tiananmen Square in Moscow was averted only by the moral force of the resistance and the noncooperation of soldiers who refused to murder their Russian brothers and sisters.

One exemplar of the moral force which prevailed over the coup was Father Aleksandr Borisov, an Orthodox priest and member of the Moscow City Council. Father Borisov prayed with the civilian defenders, baptized them for their nonviolent mission, then confronted their opponents in an equally prayerful way. He went from tank to tank, distributing 2,000 Bibles to the soldiers who were expected to assault the Parliament. Only one soldier refused a Bible. Father Borisov then gave another 2,000 Bibles to the people on the barricades. Finally he took part in a key meeting with Patriarch Alexis of the Russian Orthodox Church who then made a proclamation that any soldiers who fired on civilians would be excommunicated.

It was this moral force, embodied in the lives of thousands of willing martyrs ("witnessess") to the truth, which rendered the Soviet coup impotent.

The changes in Eastern Europe and the Soviet Union are chapters in the greatest story of our time, and of all time: the nonviolent coming of God in a new humanity. Evidence of this profound change is surfacing throughout the world. As nonviolent theorist and trainer George Lakey has put it, " 'People power' is being discovered as a resource for justice and transformation in Burma, Nepal, Eastern Europe, China, the Middle East, Latin America—more places and on a larger scale than I know of at any time in history."[4] We live in both the time of the end—the time of nuclear weapons, mass starvation, global warming, and the hole in the ozone layer— and the time of the beginning, the time of God's coming in violence-transcending ways we could not have imagined only a short time before. Massive United States intervention in the Middle East and Soviet repression in the Baltics can both be seen as desperate, last-ditch attempts to reassert a reign of violence that has been losing ground in the world to its alternative, a nonviolent transformation of humanity.

"THE GLORY OF THE COMING OF THE LORD"

In the last hours of his life, Martin Luther King expressed his belief that there was already such a nonviolent coming of God. On April 3, 1968, King had returned to Memphis, Tennessee, to march with striking sanitation workers. That night before his death in Memphis has become a source of contention concerning King's own moral code, due especially to the description of it by Ralph David Abernathy in his autobiography.[5] Before the publication of Abernathy's book, however, it was well-known from other studies of King's life that Martin King died before overcoming sexual weaknesses in himself that he was deeply aware contradicted his fundamental beliefs.[6] Dr. Martin Luther King was a great prophet as well as a man killed before his own transformation was complete. We need to hear the prophet, while acknowledging his flaws.

On April 3, 1968, King's assassin was stalking him and would fire a bullet into his head the following day. In his last words to the striking sanitation workers, and the world, King envisioned being asked by God, "Martin Luther King, which age would you like to live in?" He said he then took mental flight through the most eventful periods of history until he arrived at our time, and he continued:

Strangely enough, I would turn to the Almighty, and say, "If you allow me to live just a few years in the second half of the twentieth century, I will be happy." Now that's a strange statement to make, because the world is all messed up. The nation is sick. Trouble is in the land. Confusion all around. That's a strange statement. But I know, somehow, that only when it is dark enough, can you see the stars. And I see God working in this period of the twentieth century in a way that [people] in some strange way, are responding—something is happening in our world. The masses of people are rising up. And wherever they are assembled today, whether they are in Johannesburg, South Africa; Nairobi, Kenya; Accra, Ghana; New York City; Atlanta, Georgia; Jackson, Mississippi; or Memphis, Tennessee—the cry is always the same—"We want to be free."

And another reason that I'm happy to live in this period is that we have been forced to a point where we're going to have to grapple with the problems that [people] have been trying to grapple with through history, but the demands didn't force them to do it. Survival demands that we grapple with them. [People], for years now, have been talking about war and peace. But now, no longer can they just talk about it. It is no longer a choice between violence and nonviolence in this world; it's nonviolence or nonexistence.

That is where we are today. And also in the human rights revolution, if something isn't done, and in a hurry, to bring the colored peoples of the world out of their long years of poverty, their long years of hurt and neglect, the whole world is doomed. Now, I'm just happy that God has allowed me to live in this period, to see what is unfolding. And I'm happy that [God's] allowed me to be in Memphis. . . .

Well, I don't know what will happen now. We've got some difficult days ahead. But it doesn't matter with me now. Because I've been to the mountaintop. And I don't mind. Like anybody, I would like to live a long life. Longevity has its place. But I'm not concerned about that now. I just want to do God's will. And [God's] allowed me to go up to the mountain. And I've looked over. And I've seen the promised land. I may not get there with you. But I want you to know tonight, that we, as a people will get to the promised land. And I'm happy, tonight. I'm not worried about anything. I'm not fearing any man. Mine eyes have seen the glory of the coming of the Lord.[7]

What Martin Luther King said about the signs of our time is a way into the nonviolent coming of God. What King saw, while speaking to the black sanitation workers of Memphis, is what Moses saw from the mountaintop for his people struggling through the desert, and what Jesus saw among poor Palestinian Jews: each saw the coming of God in and through an oppressed, suffering, and freedom-loving people; each saw the glory of the coming of the Lord. They saw that transformation is possible, that it is happening right now, that the kingdom of God is at hand. Our eyes can see the glory of the coming of the Lord, if only our hearts will let us.

NONVIOLENCE OR NONEXISTENCE?

But vision of God's coming has a counter-vision. Just as Jesus knew that the kingdom of God was at hand, he also knew that the destruction of the Jewish nation by the Roman Empire was at hand. These alternative sides of Jesus' vision correspond to Martin Luther King's alternative of God's nonviolent coming in the beloved community as against the deepening threat of the world's destruction by nuclear war: nonviolence or nonexistence. Either possibility, the kingdom or annihilation, was just as much at hand in the Israel of Jesus' time as it is globally today. Because of nuclear weapons, the consequences of our choices have increased astronomically. But the stark choice was the same for Jesus and his people as it is for us: Choose the nonviolent kingdom or the razing of Jerusalem. Today Jerusalem has become the world.

I have tried to understand by analogy, in my own experience, what Jesus and his people had to face as poor, colonized Jews in an outpost of the Roman Empire. My analogous experience came from twice being a prisoner in the Los Angeles County Jail for civil disobedience actions. What I witnessed in the Los Angeles County Jail serves as a model for the oppressions of colonial power: ten thousand prisoners, mainly African American and Hispanic, controlled by a few hundred guards, with the less visible, white bureaucracy, above them: the means of control, systematic brutality. The question drilled instantly and reiteratively, day and night, into every prisoner, was the question of survival: How can I get through this experience? The sense of violence and oppression in the L.A. County Jail was thicker than its concrete walls. The question of survival deepened for some into questions of conscience: How can I live through this experience in a human way? in a nonviolent way? in a faithful, compassionate way? How am I liberated from the oppression of fear?

The point is that the prisoner in the L.A. County Jail cannot avoid such questions of survival any more than the third-world peasant can—or the poor Palestinian Jew living under the oppression of the Roman Empire and a collaborating aristocracy in the first century C.E.

We can see the systemic violence of the Palestine in which Jesus lived through an archaeological discovery. In 1968 a team of archaeologists discovered four cave-tombs just north of Jerusalem, the burial site of several families of Jesus' time. The discovery has become famous because it includes the only extant bones of a crucified man, whose name was Jehohanan. His bones have made it possible to reconstruct the terrible ordeal of an execution by crucifixion under the Roman Empire. Perhaps as significant, the site reveals the over-all systemic violence in the time of Jesus. The four caves contain the bones of thirty-six individuals, at least ten of whom were killed by oppression or violence. Specialists have determined that three of the children died from starvation; a child of 4 died from an arrow wound in his skull; a boy about 16 years old was burned to death bound on a rack; a slightly older girl was also burned to death; an old woman was killed by the crushing blow of a mace-like weapon; a woman in her 30s died in childbirth, with her unborn child in her pelvis, because of the lack of a simple intervention by a midwife; and the man Jehohanan was crucified.[8] This was the oppression and violence suffered by Palestinian Jews in Jesus' time.

Christians have paid slight if any heed to this systemic violence as the real situation out of which Jesus proclaimed the kingdom of God. As with so many of the world's peoples, then and now, Jesus had to decide how to respond to the overwhelming oppression surrounding and bearing down upon him. His response was a deepening vision of a nonviolent transformation of his people, in which the kingdom of God, and "the Human Being," became his principal terms for expressing a new reality.

THE COMING OF THE HUMAN BEING

This chapter will deal with that mysterious dimension of Jesus' vision which he called, remarkably enough, "the Human Being," *Bar Enasha* (or *Bar Nasha*) in Aramaic, usually translated through an intermediate Greek phrase *ho huios tou anthropou* as "the Son of Man." It is a commonplace of biblical scholars that *Bar Enasha* is the most authentic layer of Jesus' self-identification in the gospels. As John McKenzie puts it, "The very fact that the phrase is attributed to Jesus [82 times] and to no one else in the Gospels is a persuasive consideration that the phrase goes back to Jesus. It then becomes a question of what he meant by the phrase."[9]

The question of the meaning of *Bar Enasha* has mired scholars in endless debate, even as they have (perhaps not coincidentally) accepted "Son of Man" as the term for that debate. Two thorough scholarly studies which uncover the root meaning of Jesus' term without, however, ceasing to use "the Son of Man" in their own titles and texts are *Son of Man* by Maurice Casey and *Jesus Son of Man* by Barnabas Lindars, SSF.[10] But as McKenzie points out concerning "Son of Man" and its Greek derivation, "the phrase was as meaningless in Greek as it is in English."[11] The Aramaic idiom, with the nuances given it by Jesus, transcends what McKenzie calls the "excessively literal 'Son of Man.'"[12]

To begin to understand *Bar Enasha,* we may need to see it through a more nuanced translation, as well as through those dimensions of our own experience which parallel most closely the human reality Jesus was probing. Walter Wink has suggested a linguistic approach to *Bar Enasha* emphasizing its collective meaning. Concerning "Son of Man," Wink says, "'son of' is merely a semitic idiom meaning 'of or pertaining to the following genus or species.'" He adds, in a comment upon this chapter: To translate *Bar Enasha* as "the 'True Humanity,' or 'the Human Being,' or your own 'divinely revolutionized humanity,' or M. L. King's 'Beloved Community' would all be better [than 'Son of Man']."[13]

Thus, perhaps it is in terms of the Human Being—understood personally, collectively, and interchangeably with the synonyms suggested by Wink— that we can begin to understand this self-designation of Jesus, fraught with overtones of something about to happen:

"But that you may know that the Human Being has authority on earth to forgive sins"—he said to the paralytic—"I say to you, rise, take up your pallet and go home" (Mark 2:10-11).

Bar Enasha stands at a theological junction. Besides having been Jesus' way to refer to himself, *Bar Enasha* was to become the basis for the Christian church's doctrine of Jesus' Second Coming. In almost every passage of the gospels that has been interpreted to mean Jesus' Second Coming, Jesus refers specifically to himself as the Human Being. A vivid instance is Jesus' *parousia* saying, "The coming (*parousia*) of the Human Being will be like lightning striking in the east and flashing far into the west" (Matt. 24:27).

As we shall see, that *Bar Enasha* or "Human Being" by which Jesus identified himself and his vision has, in its original context in the Hebrew Scriptures, a collective meaning as well. *Bar Enasha* bridges two powerful concepts. What was to become for the church a statement of Jesus' return in glory was, for Jesus himself, a vision of Israel's and the world's nonviolent transformation. The Palestinian Jew, Jesus of Israel, envisioned for his people, and strove to create, a nonviolent society based on faith, a reality which for us remains all but unthinkable. A recovery of his vision, within the visions of the synoptic gospels, can mean our seeing for the first time the nonviolent coming of God, both then and now.

I believe that the Second Coming of *Bar Enasha,* the Human Being, Jesus Christ, is happening right now. Christ, the Human Being, is coming into the world today, as Martin Luther King realized when he said, "I see God working in this period of the twentieth century in a way that [people], in some strange way, are responding—something is happening in our world. The masses of people are rising up. And wherever they are assembled today . . . the cry is always the same—'We want to be free.' "[14] But this Second Coming of *Bar Enasha,* as identified prophetically by Martin Luther King, has been repressed in our consciousness and has gone unrecognized.

The reality of the Second Coming of *Bar Enasha* is seldom recognized as it was by King, when it happens in nonviolent revolutionary movements all across the world. The point here is similar to one that was made by William Stringfellow, when he was pressed by a friend to declare whether he really believed in the Resurrection. Stringfellow paused and said, "Phil Berrigan going to jail."[15] The transforming point for our consciousness concerning the related doctrine of the Second Coming is, as Stringfellow himself put it in *An Ethic for Christians and Other Aliens in a Strange Land,* that "for all its mystery, the Second Advent is faithful to the mission of the First Advent, and is no disjuncture or disruption."[16] Thus we can recognize a Second Coming, "faithful to the First," whose humble yet transforming power can be seen today in *Bar Enasha,* the Human Being, all the way from Phil Berrigan going to jail, to Chinese students being machine-gunned in Tiananmen Square, to the crumbling of the Berlin Wall (remember those who died earlier in its shadows), to the devastating impact of international sanctions upon the economy of South Africa's apartheid regime (remember Nelson Mandela's twenty-seven years in prison). It is this Second Coming of *Bar Enasha,* rolling across the world in the creation of a nonviolent humanity, that can be identified with the radically hopeful vision Jesus of Nazareth had for the Human Being, a collective Human Being, almost two thousand years ago. Jesus' vision of a nonviolent coming of God in *Bar Enasha,* which in the early church's understanding became Jesus' Second Coming in himself, is happening today.

SEEING JESUS' SECOND COMING WITH NEW EYES

One reason why it is so difficult for us now to reconnect the church's vision of the Second Coming, with that of Jesus behind it, is that the doctrine of Christ's Second Coming has been twisted out of recognition by evangelists of oppression. There is a kind of preaching in the nuclear age that seems almost driven by demons to nullify the radical power to change the world inherent in the Second Coming of Jesus Christ in a resurrected *Bar Enasha*. This transforming coming of a new humanity, initiated by God in the Human Being, Jesus, has in its gospel roots the power to free the world from every kind of violence and injustice. But it is the preachers of Jesus' return in judgment on a nuclear cloud who, through their media evangelism, have defined for the public the doctrine of the Second Coming. Neither Jesus' own humanity, nor the new humanity he proclaimed, has any role in that Second Coming. The nuclear evangelists' Second Coming has in fact become so distorted and militarized a doctrine as to become indistinguishable from a Pentagon war scenario.

Thus we see popular Armageddon theologians such as Hal Lindsey in his *Late Great Planet Earth* trying to ease the pain of a violent fatalism in our culture by identifying God's will with nuclear war. It is said by Lindsey and by Jerry Falwell, along with many other writers and preachers, that the final war we United States citizens are now paying for with our taxes, has been foretold by prophets. They say this ultimate evil with which we are cooperating was known already thousands of years ago by the Hebrew prophets (who were in fact talking about their own wars). Moreover, they claim such a war was prophesied especially in connection with the Second Coming of Jesus and must therefore be necessary for his coming in glory.

In *The 1980's: Countdown to Armageddon,* Hal Lindsey illustrates these claims by an account of his speaking at the Pentagon some time after his having already spoken at the American Air War College:

> One year later I was invited to speak at the Pentagon. It seems that a number of officers and non-military personnel alike had read *Late Great* and wanted to hear more.
>
> A meeting was set and when I arrived I was amazed to find hundreds of people jamming the room. Outside, others were trying to crowd in. All of these people wanted to hear what the prophets had to say about our destiny. When I finished, the response was overwhelming.
>
> After my talk, one officer told me that various Pentagon officials had independently come to the same conclusions I had reached regarding the future of the Middle East. They had reached those same conclusions with virtually no knowledge of what the Hebrew prophets had predicted 2,000 to 3,000 years earlier.[17]

Confirmed in the nuclear fatalism of his interpretation of the prophets by "various Pentagon officials," Lindsey asks us to believe in a returning Jesus who would "rapture" us from the earth before the war we are preparing for is waged on others. He asks us to believe in a Jesus who would thereby save us from the consequences of our own deliberate choices.

Because of such nuclear evangelism, the promise of Jesus' return and the threat of nuclear war have become closely linked in American religious culture, especially where it supports the nuclear weapons industry. In Amarillo, Texas, where nuclear weapons are assembled at the Pantex plant, the image of Jesus coming on a nuclear cloud is at the heart of religious culture. In her portrait of that culture, *Blessèd Assurance: At Home with the Bomb in Amarillo, Texas*, A. G. Mojtabai has described how Amarillo churches affirm a Second Coming that repudiates the peacemaking message of the first:

> Going from church to church in Amarillo, the impression is unavoidable: some of the most ardent born and born-again Christians are writing Christianity off as something that did not, could not work — at least, not in the First Coming. The conviction that mankind is bent on its own destruction, that goodness cannot succeed in a world so evil, the constant recourse to the Old Testament (to the most bellicose sections), the turning for betterment to the dire remedies offered by the book of Revelation, the only light left to the Second Coming — all this strangely negates the "good news" of the Gospels and the First Coming.[18]

Catholic Bishop Leroy Matthiesen, however, brought the good news of Jesus back to Amarillo in August 1981 with a single sentence that electrified the local community and the national media: "We urge individuals involved in the production and stockpiling of nuclear bombs to consider what they are doing, to resign from such activities, and to seek employment in peaceful pursuits."[19] The furor caused by this beautifully simple application of the gospel indicates the life-and-death struggle between our own violence and the new humanity of a truly returning Jesus.

To see Jesus' Second Coming with new eyes is to see, first of all, the term which helped give birth to the idea: *Bar Enasha*, "the Human Being." "The Son of Man" as a translation of *Bar Enasha* is misleading because it narrows to a single male individual the scope of the Aramaic idiom which has both personal and collective implications. "The Human Being" or "the New Humanity" is the fuller meaning of this frequent expression of Jesus, a meaning which gained depth as he continued to use it. Like his kingdom of God parables, the term was Jesus' strikingly simple way of cracking open a new world. Perhaps it is because Jesus transformed *Bar Enasha* through his experiments in a new reality that the meaning of the term has been mystifying scholars ever since. It may be that we can understand that New Humanity of his only as we experience it.

Bar Enasha is a transforming concept for Jesus in three kinds of sayings: 1) present sayings, in which *Bar Enasha*, the Human Being, often breaks through the recognized limits of the present; 2) passion sayings, in which

Bar Enasha is to be transformed through suffering and death; 3) future sayings, in which the coming Human Being transforms the world.

My purpose here will be to see the nonviolent transformation expressed in all three dimensions of *Bar Enasha,* as background to an understanding of Jesus' Second Coming. In what follows, I can only suggest what may have been the original meaning of Jesus' Second Coming, underlying the already interpreted sayings of Jesus in the gospels that were set down decades later. In other words, Jesus himself understood *Bar Enasha* in ways that are not necessarily the same as the meanings of Matthew, Mark, and Luke when they later cite Jesus using *Bar Enasha.* I offer this reflection less as a reconstruction than a testimony. I hope it can serve as a testimony to good news in Jesus' time that is also good news in our time.

Behind this approach is the hypothesis that Jesus is probing the world's limits of thought and action. As those limits are broken by him or by the human being following him today, humanity experiences the nonviolent coming of God.

LIBERATING THE PARALYTIC IN US

" 'But that you may know that *Bar Enasha* has authority on earth to forgive sins' — he said to the paralytic — 'I say to you, rise, take up your pallet and go home' " (Mark 2:10-11; par. Matt. 9:6, Luke 5:24).

The setting in Mark's gospel for this transforming saying is a house at Capernaum where Jesus is living, probably Peter's house. Jesus is preaching to his people, poor and oppressed Galilean Jews, who are packed into the room. "And they came, bringing to him a paralytic carried by four men" (Mark 2:3). "They" are perhaps the paralytic's parents. Blocked by the overflowing crowd around the doorway, the parents and friends take the paralytic up on the roof. They dig through the earth over the beams and rafters, make an opening, and let down the stretcher on which the paralytic is lying. When Jesus sees their faith, he says to the paralytic, "My son, your sins are forgiven."

We know that illness and sinfulness were linked in Jesus' culture. The disciples reflect the conventional prejudice of their day when, in John's gospel, they ask Jesus about a blind man, "Rabbi, who sinned, this man or his parents, that he was born blind?" Jesus, rejecting the premise, says that neither he nor his parents sinned and restores the man's sight (John 9:2-7).

In Mark's scene at Capernaum the paralytic-sinner was probably destitute. Unable to work, immobilized on a pallet, the man was totally dependent on others, who as Galileans would have been poor themselves.

But the stretcher-bearers and the paralytic had faith that Jesus would heal him. For Jesus to do so, he first had to address the cause of paralysis: sin. Because the paralytic's illness was seen as a punishment for sin, his sins had to be forgiven before he could be healed. Jesus says that they are in fact forgiven, using the passive tense to indicate the forgiveness of God.

The idea that sin caused the oppression of the paralytic was not unwelcome to those in the room who are higher in the social order, such as the scribes. These scribes are a more modest version of church and state functionaries who control modern sins. It is not surprising that those with a greater stake in God's order say to themselves, "Why does this man speak thus? It is blasphemy! Who can forgive sins but God alone?"

Then Jesus responds to the question in their hearts: " 'But that you may know that *Bar Enasha* has authority on earth to forgive sins' — he said to the paralytic — 'I say to you, rise, take up your pallet and go home.' " The man had already been released by *Bar Enasha* from his sins. Now he is released as well from the culturally imposed consequences of his sins: paralysis and oppression. He rises and leaves the room.

Most of the people on earth today are paralyzed by what are said to be the consequences of their sins. The destitute of the world have it hammered into their consciousness — by those who, like the scribes, have the power in our day to define sins — that they are poor because they are lazy; or that they are poor because they have mismanaged their resources; or because they have squandered opportunities; or because, in the most blatantly evil definitions of guilt, they are black or female or homosexual or members of whatever part of humanity the powerful choose to define as subhuman and sinful. Paralysis, hunger, homelessness, and early death are, according to the rich and powerful, the direct consequences of the poor and powerless having sinned in one way or another.

In Mark's story Jesus as *Bar Enasha,* the Human Being, frees the paralytic from both sin and the consequences of sin. Jesus, then, is himself a transforming *Bar Enasha.* But it is Matthew's account that confirms that *Bar Enasha* bridges the senses of a single human being and humanity. In his version (Matt. 9:1-8), after Jesus cures the paralytic, Matthew 9:8 then reads: "When the crowds saw it, they were afraid, and they glorified God, who had given such authority to . . ." As Walter Wink points out in correspondence concerning the meaning of *Bar Enasha,* precisely here is where we would expect Matthew of all people to write "Jesus": "and they glorified God, who had given such authority to *Jesus.*" But, in fact, the sentence concludes "and they glorified God, who had given such authority to *humanity.*" This is, as Wink says, a "powerful confirmation of the corporate interpretation; at least *Matthew* clearly understands it thus."[20]

Moreover, Jesus' way of using *Bar Enasha* suggests that the liberating interaction between himself and the paralytic has the authority of a new humanity in the making. The paralytic walks away because he has become a new human being. Transformed within and without, he is freed from paralysis. The source of his freedom to walk again is *Bar Enasha,* a new humanity with a forgiving, transforming power of God within it that Jesus extends to him and that he simultaneously discovers in himself.

The paralytic is like all the wretched of the earth who are viewed as guilty by the dominant orders of society for the inferior status those same orders have imposed on them by racism, sexism, poverty, oppression in all its forms. But all have been forgiven both their real sins and the paralyzing sense of sin imposed from within and without. All are forgiven in *Bar Enasha,* the presence of God in a new humanity. That *Bar Enasha,* in which God's abolition of every sin is realized, is telling all of us to take up our pallets and walk. There is no reason on earth for paralysis, because the God in us all is calling us to stand up. Yet that new humanity's liberation can sometimes begin by sitting.

LESSONS IN LIBERATION

On December 1, 1955, seamstress Rosa Parks refused to stand up in a Montgomery, Alabama, bus when ordered to surrender her seat to a white passenger. Her example was the spark that ignited the new humanity of black Americans in the civil rights movement. In his later formulation of a transforming nonviolence, Martin Luther King would speak of the need to create a crisis in the conscience of the nation whereby its people could then undergo conversion. In his own case, it was Rosa Parks's refusal to obey a racist law which created the crisis of conscience that resulted in King's conversion. Rosa Parks had to sit down before Martin Luther King would stand up.

When word of Rosa Parks's jailing leaped from house to house in Montgomery's black community, Jo Ann Gibson Robinson, an English professor at Alabama State College, put into execution a plan formulated by black women to organize a city-wide bus boycott. As president of the black Women's Political Council (WPC), Robinson had initiated the boycott plan months earlier. In a letter written on behalf of the WPC to Montgomery Mayor W. A. Gayle on May 21, 1954, more than one and a half years before Rosa Parks's arrest, Robinson insisted upon improved conditions for black riders of city buses and threatened a boycott if city and bus officials did not offer significant improvements.[21] As black passengers continued to be abused on city buses in 1954-55, the Montgomery women drew up plans for the distribution of "fifty thousand notices calling people to boycott the buses; only the specifics of time and place had to be added."[22]

Once she learned of Rosa Parks' arrest, Jo Ann Robinson, with the assistance of two of her students, worked through the early morning of December 2, 1955, mimeographing tens of thousands of leaflets announcing the bus boycott. Thanks to the distribution system already set up by the women, practically every black man, woman, and child in Montgomery knew of the bus boycott within a few hours. Robinson wrote later, in a memoir on this turning point in American history:

No one knew where the notices had come from or who had arranged for their circulation, and no one cared. Those who passed them on did so efficiently, quietly, and without comment. But deep within the heart of every black person was a joy he or she dared not reveal.[23]

The first day of the boycott was overwhelmingly successful. That night a nervous, 26-year-old minister, Martin Luther King, about to be drafted from his first pastorate in Montgomery to lead this movement, addressed a church overflowing with thousands of boycotters. These were people who, like the paralytic and others at Capernaum, knew the lifelong paralysis of a sin as defined by their society. In Montgomery the sin was being black, a sin defined by whites, paralyzing the masses whom it segregated and dominated.

Martin King, like the master he followed, spoke with the authority of the Human Being, who can awaken the Godly humanity of the paralyzed:

"And you know, my friends, there comes a time," he cried, "when people get tired of being trampled over by the iron feet of oppression." A flock of "Yeses" was coming back at him when suddenly the individual responses dissolved into a rising cheer and applause exploded beneath the cheer—all within the space of a second. The startling noise rolled on and on, like a wave that refused to break, and just when it seemed that the roar must finally weaken, a wall of sound came in from the enormous crowd outdoors to push the volume still higher. Thunder seemed to be added to the lower register—the sound of feet stomping on the wooden floor—until the loudness became something that was not so much heard as it was sensed by vibrations in the lungs. The giant cloud of noise shook the building and refused to go away. One sentence had set it loose somehow, pushing the call-and-response of the Negro church service past the din of a political rally and on to something that King had never known before.[24]

The Human Being Jesus spoke of and embodied has the authority on earth to act as Rosa Parks and Jo Ann Robinson did, to speak as Martin King did, and thus to raise a new humanity from the paralysis of oppression.

In this first political address of his life, Martin Luther King, like Jesus at Capernaum, becomes an apparent blasphemer. As he articulates more and more the rising humanity of the thousands of his people around him, King cries out to them, "If we are wrong—God Almighty is wrong! If we are wrong—Jesus of Nazareth was merely a utopian dreamer and never came down to earth! If we are wrong, justice is a lie!"[25]

The blasphemy is obvious: "If we are wrong—God Almighty is wrong!" It is just as obvious as the blasphemy of Jeremiah and Isaiah when the prophets became one with their suffering people and God spoke in the first person singular through the mouths of suffering prophets.

The blasphemy of prophets is obvious when God's presence in a suffering people goes unrecognized. In his passionate outburst to his people, King fused as one their own cause in Montgomery, a transforming justice, Jesus of Nazareth, and God Almighty. Such electrifying words to the oppressed can be nothing but blasphemy, if a human being has no authority on earth to transform paralysis into freedom. If God can't be seen in their humanity, the people are paralyzed. The charge of blasphemy comes from privilege. In condemning the prophets, it condemns the people to paralysis.

How does one distinguish the true prophet from the blasphemer? Jesus tells us: *"But that you may know* [he was speaking here to the blasphemy critics] that *Bar Enasha* has authority on earth to forgive sins, I say to you [here to the paralytic], rise, take up your pallet and go home."

Are the people rising? Is their paralysis gone? Are they walking? If they are, it is not blasphemy but the presence of God in the Human Being. God is walking with that suffering people in their new humanity.

TRANSFORMATION THROUGH SUFFERING AND DEATH

As seen in his interaction and words to the paralytic, a present *Bar Enasha* saying, Jesus was proclaiming a new humanity for his people. Rosa Parks, Martin Luther King, and the movement they helped initiate have seen a new humanity begin to break into view in our time. The *Bar Enasha* Jesus spoke of is the Human Being he lived, whom we have only begun to live in our time. God is profoundly present in *Bar Enasha,* in the Human Being we are all invited to become. Yet our sense of our God is still too remote and unforgiving, our sense of our humanity still too sinful and paralyzed, for us to live through fully with Jesus the divinely human miracle of *Bar Enasha.* Nevertheless, *Bar Enasha* is emerging. As Martin Luther King said, God is working in some strange way so that people are responding. Something is happening in our world, beneath the surface of people and events, to take humanity from oppression to freedom, to invite us all into inconceivable possibilities. That emerging nonviolent humanity, in whom a forgiving, transforming God is more present than we think possible, is *Bar Enasha.*

A further step taken by Jesus into this new humanity is represented by his passion sayings, in which *Bar Enasha* is transformed through suffering and death.

"And he began to teach them that *Bar Enasha* must suffer many things, and be rejected by the elders and the chief priests and the scribes, and be killed, and after three days rise again" (Mark 8:31; par. Matt. 16:21, Luke 9:22).

"For he was teaching his disciples, saying to them, '*Bar Enasha* will be delivered into the hands of men, and they will kill him; and when he is killed, after three days he will rise' " (Mark 9:31; par. Matt. 17:22-23, Luke 9:44).

"And taking the twelve again, he began to tell them what was to happen to him, saying, 'Behold, we are going up to Jerusalem; and *Bar Enasha* will be delivered to the chief priests and the scribes, and they will condemn him to death, and deliver him to the Gentiles; and they will mock him, and spit upon him, and scourge him, and kill him; and after three days he will rise' " (Mark 10:32-34; par. Matt. 20:17-19, Luke 18:31-33).

The specific details of these sayings have likely been heightened after Jesus' death to correspond to his passion, as in the third saying. The less detailed first and second sayings indicate the original direction of Jesus' thought: The Human Being (who according to the idiomatic *Bar Enasha* is Jesus but not only Jesus) must suffer, be rejected by the ruling powers, be killed, and rise again. Resurrection was thought of by Jews at the time as the resurrection of a great community as a whole.[26] To rise again was to be part of a great corporate resurrection.

The Human Being that Jesus shows us by the example of his life must suffer and die so that a new humanity will rise. This idea of a corporate passion is a recurring theme in the gospels: "Once the idea that Passion predictions were concerned with a corporate body, to which they themselves belonged, had established itself as a working theory in the minds of the disciples, there were a good many sayings of Jesus that would tend to confirm it."[27] The disciples fear to follow Jesus to Jerusalem, because he tells them exactly what is demanded of their humanity. It is no different than the demands placed upon himself. The only specific mention Jesus makes anywhere of the executioner's cross is just as relevant to those following him as it is to himself: "He called the people and his disciples to him and said, 'If anyone wants to be a follower of mine, let that person renounce self, take up the cross, and follow me' " (Mark 8:34).

As Mark makes abundantly clear, the disciples were careful to follow the Human Being only at a distance, and at the critical moments, not at all. The clear implication of the gospel story is that Jesus wanted the disciples with him all the way, as a new humanity. Instead, he was crucified between two believers in violence; no one else in his own community would then walk a nonviolent way as far as the cross and enter with him into the new humanity.

Whatever Jesus says in the gospels about *Bar Enasha's* suffering and death, he then says specifically about the disciples in a barrage of statements that terrify them. Again and again they are told that to follow him into a new humanity will mean hatred, contempt, torture, and finally death by the Roman Empire's means of executing revolutionaries, the cross.[28] Whatever Jesus says about the startling mission of *Bar Enasha,* he applies directly to those in his own community. Not surprisingly, they resist it at every turn. They repeatedly misunderstand or reject this teaching about the life-giving route into a new humanity, just as readers and hearers of the gospels have been doing ever since. The point of it all, according to Jesus' sayings, is that through the human necessity of suffering and execution *Bar Enasha* is transformed. A new humanity will rise on both sides of death. A new people will be born. The cross in-forms life and re-creates life anew in the resurrection of humanity. Saving one's life is losing it; losing one's life is saving it. To see all this in the transforming depths of a new humanity, as Jesus explores it and shares it step by step, is to see the overwhelming implications in one's own life. For *Bar Enasha* to rise, for the new humanity to increase, you and I must die.

WHY MUST THE HUMAN BEING BE KILLED?

On March 24, 1980, Archbishop Oscar Romero was shot to death while once again preaching the gospel of nonviolence to the Salvadoran people. The rifle bullet that smashed into his chest that morning was the almost inevitable conclusion to the relentless words of nonviolence pouring out of him week after week, as violence to his people and death threats to himself mounted.

Why must the Human Being be rejected by the powers and killed?

In his February 17 homily at the Basilica of the Sacred Heart in San Salvador, Archbishop Romero had spoken of the poor and of institutional sin. Through the poor the church was learning to understand better the nature of sin, whose fruit is death, "the death of Salvadorans, the rapid death of repression or the slow death of structural oppression."[29]

In a pointed commentary on such sin, the archbishop read for the people's approval his draft of a letter to United States President Jimmy Carter. He asked the president — "if you really wish to defend human rights" — not to send more military aid to El Salvador and "to guarantee that your government will not intervene directly or indirectly, by military, economic, diplomatic, or other pressures, in determining the destiny of the Salvadoran people."[30]

The letter, approved by the people's applause, was sent to the president. The next day a bomb placed by the far right destroyed the Salvadoran Catholic Church's radio station, on which the archbishop's homily had been broadcast.

Why must the Human Being be killed?

On Sunday, February 24, a Costa Rican short-wave radio station began broadcasting Archbishop Romero's homilies to all of Central America. That morning Romero made an appeal to the oligarchy and revealed a threat to himself:

> I hope that this call of the church [to social justice] will not further harden the hearts of the oligarchs but will move them to conversion. Let them share what they are and have. Let them not keep silencing with violence the voice of those of us who offer this invitation. Let them not keep killing those of us who are trying to achieve a more just sharing of the power and wealth of our country. I speak in the first person, because this week I received notice that I am on the list

of those who are to be eliminated next week. But let it be known that no one can any longer kill the voice of justice.[31]

On succeeding Sundays Archbishop Romero addressed ever more urgently a series of government and rightist killings. On Sunday, March 9, he said a Mass in the basilica for a Christian Democratic leader who had been murdered. Many Christian Democratic leaders were present. The next day a workman discovered a suitcase with seventy-two sticks of dynamite in it, enough to destroy the basilica and the whole block.

Why must the Human Being be killed?

On Sunday, March 16, Archbishop Romero preached a long sermon on reconciliation, addressing every sector of the society, making specific appeals to the oligarchy, the government, and guerrilla groups. The next day, in response to a general strike, government military forces killed at least sixty people throughout the country.

On Sunday, March 23, the day before Romero's death, the church radio station was back on the air. Once again his homily was broadcast to the nation. The Costa Rican station had been bombed but continued to carry the archbishop's words. The Vatican was urging him to tone down his preaching. Death threats had intensified.

In this final Sunday homily, Archbishop Romero recounted the violence of the previous week. Then, with the people interrupting him frequently with applause, he made the appeal to conscience that likely sealed his own death sentence, but will never be forgotten by suffering Salvadorans:

> I would like to make an appeal in a special way to the men of the army, and in particular to the ranks of the Guardia Nacional, of the police, to those in the barracks. Brothers, you are part of our own people. You kill your own campesino brothers and sisters. And before an order to kill that a man may give, the law of God must prevail that says: Thou shalt not kill! No soldier is obliged to obey an order against the law of God. No one has to fulfill an immoral law. It is time to recover your consciences and to obey your consciences rather than the orders of sin. The church, defender of the rights of God, of the law of God, of human dignity, the dignity of the person, cannot remain silent before such abomination. We want the government to take seriously that reforms are worth nothing when they come about stained with so much blood. In the name of God, and in the name of this suffering people whose laments rise to heaven each day more tumultuous, I beg you, I ask you, I order you in the name of God: Stop the repression![32]

Why must the Human Being be killed?

There is a response to this question in the gospel text on which Archbishop Romero was preaching when he was shot the following day. In the text, Jesus responds to this question in terms of the transformed Human Being: "The hour has come for the Human Being to be glorified. Truly, truly, I say to you, unless a grain of wheat falls into the earth and dies, it remains alone; but if it dies, it bears much fruit" (John 12:23-24).

Speaking with a reporter two weeks before his death Archbishop Romero also responded to the question. He, too, spoke in terms of humanity, the rising humanity of his people:

> I have often been threatened with death. Nevertheless, as a Christian, I do not believe in death without resurrection. If they kill me, I shall arise in the Salvadoran people. I say so without meaning to boast, with the greatest humility.
>
> As pastor, I am obliged by divine mandate to give my life for those I love—for all Salvadorans, even for those who may be going to kill me. If the threats come to be fulfilled, from this moment I offer my blood to God for the redemption and for the resurrection of El Salvador.[33]

The paradox of Jesus restated by Oscar Romero is that by the Human Being's nonviolent gift of life in death, the people will rise. They are rising now.

THE SYMBOLISM OF THE SECOND COMING

Jesus of Nazareth was familiar with *Bar Enasha* in another way suggesting human transformation. Variations on this phrase occurred in the Hebrew Scriptures that Jesus would have known by heart from his childhood. The most significant of these was a well-known passage from the Book of Daniel (7:13), which referred to the one "like a human being," *kebar enash*. Traces of this Danielic human being are found in Jesus' sayings. This passage from Daniel provided Jesus with the perspective on the transforming Human Being that was to become, in turn, a vision of the Second Coming.

The primary source in the gospels for the belief in the Second Coming of Jesus is a courtroom scene (Mark 14:53-72; Matt. 26:57-75; Luke 22:54-71). When thinking of this scene, we should be very conscious of how courtrooms function to legitimate violence. From Jesus' day to our own, courtrooms have legitimized the imprisonment and execution of rebels, identified by those courts as criminals, so that the violence of privilege and power can carry out its legally sanctioned will.

In the synoptic gospels' account, Jesus' guards have led him to an arraignment before the high priest (identified by name as Caiaphas in Matthew) appointed by the Romans. The high priest was a key collaborator in Rome's imperial rule over Palestine, able to remain head of the Temple's priestly aristocracy only through the good graces of the governor of Judea,

Pilate. In the courtroom, witnesses accuse Jesus of being in revolt against the Temple establishment, which the judge himself heads. Some of the witnesses claim Jesus said he would destroy the Temple, but their testimony does not agree. The high priest is therefore frustrated in getting charges that can be brought before Pilate. The logic of the narrative, as Walter Wink has pointed out to me, is that "none of the charges can be corroborated, so the high priest tries to make Jesus incriminate himself."[34]

The high priest therefore asks Jesus a political question, in a politically explosive context. The priests, scribes, and elders present at this arraignment, who also act as judges with the high priest, are intensely aware of their own equivocal position and the threats to it. They know that while they hold a power over the Jewish people which mediates the final power of Rome, the hope of an oppressed peasantry is said by various popular movements to lie in a messiah ("anointed one" or "christos"). Peasant leaders periodically identified themselves as a messiah, a popularly based king of Israel, whom God would give the power to liberate the people from foreign and domestic oppressors.[35] For a suffering peasantry doubly taxed by Rome and the high priesthood, the recurring hope raised by such messiahs was that of liberation from foreign rule and from the oppressive power structure of the Temple aristocracy. The head of that power structure, the high priest, asks the Jew accused of revolution, Jesus, point blank if he is the revolutionary messiah whom the people are awaiting.

Concerning Jesus' response to this dramatic question, Walter Wink writes: "Both Matthew and Luke in their parallel accounts show Jesus *not* answering affirmatively. They both have an ambiguous answer whose meaning can be either 'That's what *you* say' (= no) or 'You said it' (yes)."[36] Mark has him answer unequivocally, "I am," but some manuscripts read the more ambiguous, "You say that." Jesus' refusal, in Matthew and Luke, to give a direct answer to the high priest's question is borne out by all three synoptic accounts of the trial before Pilate. There Jesus says, "su legeis" ("you say"), which Pilate interprets as no in all three gospels. As Wink emphasizes, we therefore have six and possibly seven (if we follow Mark's variant reading) synoptic versions where Jesus refuses to answer over against one Marcan, "I am": all three synoptic descriptions of the dialogue with Pilate; Matthew's and Luke's parallel account of the response to the high priest; Luke's special source where he has another version of an ambiguous, noncommital answer (Luke 22:67); even some Greek manuscripts' renditions of the otherwise exceptional Mark 14:62, which instead of "I am" read "You said that," meaning "I didn't." Wink suspects that "a later scribe changed Mark to 'I am' after Matthew and Luke had already used a version that said 'You said that.' "[37]

After his ambiguous, noncommittal "You said that," Jesus continues responding to his judge's question of revolution with those words which are today the primary source for the belief in his Second Coming: "And you will see *Bar Enasha* sitting at the right hand of Power, and coming with the clouds of heaven" (Mark 14:62; par. Matt. 26:64).

This statement by Jesus, as given in Mark and Matthew,[38] is considerably more complex than the popular visions of the Second Coming it has spawned in the church. In the first place, it combines two distinct symbols, which in a literal interpretation pose a problem for the imagination: You will see *Bar Enasha sitting* at the right hand of Power, and *coming* with the clouds of heaven. "The only way one can take this [literally] is to visualize Jesus sitting on the right hand of God, and both of them (God and Jesus) approaching the earth."[39]

If we try to draw from Jesus' reply to the high priest a literal picture of Jesus' Second Coming, then we in fact have Jesus and God sitting side by side and descending from the sky in a vision that looks uncomfortably like a divine roller coaster. We can doubt if that is the intended meaning.

Exegetes are agreed that the statement is not to be taken literally.[40] They point out that what Jesus is doing is drawing upon the different symbols of two well-known scriptures, Psalm 110:1 and Daniel 7:13, to tell the high priest that the judge in this case stands under a higher judgment. In Psalm 110:1, a triumphant king of Judah is enthroned at the right hand of God. Jesus, in citing the psalm, has replaced the king by "the Human Being" (now given the further dimension of Daniel 7:13) to avoid any sense of the glory of a military victory. In Daniel 7:13, which is the controlling text, the one "like a human being" (in the Aramaic of Daniel) is portrayed as coming with the clouds of heaven to the courtroom of God, where this symbolic figure is given the kingdom of God. When Jesus says to the high priest that he "will see the Human Being sitting at the right hand of Power, and coming with the clouds of heaven," he is suggesting to the priest-judge, for whom those scriptures have a divine authority, that the defendant standing before him will somehow lead a successful revolution, to be vindicated in God's courtroom. Matthew (26:64) and Luke (22:69) make this assertion even more explosive, prefacing it with the words, "From now on," thus making the revolution and the divine counter-judgment simultaneous and immediate. The high priest reacts by the formal, judicial gesture of tearing his robes, saying that Jesus is guilty of blasphemy. To this, the other judges agree.

This classic Second Coming scene from Jesus' trial is held by C. H. Dodd to have provided (specifically in Mark 14:62) the only explicit prediction of Jesus' Second Coming in the earlier gospel tradition.[41] Yet the interpretation given it thus far suggests a Second Coming far different from the one to which we are accustomed. Perhaps this text can tell us more about the meaning of the Second Coming, if we follow it to its source in the Book of Daniel.

A COLLECTIVE HUMAN BEING IN DANIEL

Another reason for returning to Daniel is that Jesus' other sayings in the synoptic gospels from which the doctrine of the Second Coming has been developed (Mark 8:38, 13:26; Matt. 10:23, 24:44, 25:31; Luke 12:40,

17:24, 26, 30, 18:8)[42] are made up entirely of *Bar Enasha* statements, all of them heavily influenced by Daniel.[43] For example, Mark 13:26, "And then they will see *Bar Enasha* coming in clouds with great power and glory," is, like Jesus' trial statement, nearly a direct quote from Daniel. In the synoptic gospels Jesus' Second Coming is identical with "the coming Human Being," a vision drawn from Daniel. To determine the original meaning of this vision, we need to look at its prior frame of reference in the Book of Daniel.

The Book of Daniel was written as a primer of Jewish resistance during the religious oppression of the Jewish people by the Hellenistic King, Antiochus IV Epiphanes, in the 160s B.C.E. A century later, when Palestine was occupied by another foreign power, Rome, the Book of Daniel again became the people's resistance manifesto. Oppressed Jews were inspired and strengthened by Daniel's stories of Jewish youths, Shadrach, Meshach, and Abednego in the fiery furnace, Daniel in the lions' pit, each upheld by their God as they refused to obey the blasphemous laws of a foreign ruler. Daniel's stories and his apocalyptic imagery would have been for oppressed Jews the equivalent of anti-establishment political cartoons in modern newspapers. And Jesus would have known much of the Book of Daniel by heart.

The Human Being to whom Jesus referred in his arraignment when confronting the high priest was the *Bar Enasha* of his own transforming experiences in Galilee. But this was also, in a growing vision of transformation, *ke-bar enash,* the one "like a human being," whom Jesus knew from the seventh chapter of Daniel.

There, in a dream which begins with a vision of four terrible beasts, Daniel sees "the Ancient of Days," God, take his seat on a courtroom throne of fiery flames. The last of the beasts, which represents the persecuting kingdom of Antiochus IV, is condemned by the court and executed. The dream continues with the coming of one like a human being:

> I saw in the night visions,
> and behold, with the clouds of heaven
>   there came one like a human being,
> who came to the Ancient of Days
>   and was presented before him.
> And to the human being was given dominion
>   and glory and kingdom ... (Dan. 7:13-14).

An angel interprets this dream for Daniel, explaining that the human being who has been given the kingdom of God is "the saints of the Most High" (Dan. 7:18), and later, "the people of the saints of the Most High" (Dan. 7:27), those who had been persecuted by the fourth beast.

T. W. Manson, the late British scholar, pointed the way to an understanding of Daniel's human being:

What the symbol stands for is made crystal clear in verses 18 and 27 of this same chapter, where we are told that "the saints of the Most High shall receive the kingdom, and possess the kingdom for ever, even for ever and ever"; and again, "The kingdom and the dominion, and the greatness of the kingdoms under the whole heaven, shall be given to the people of the saints of the Most High: his kingdom is an everlasting kingdom, and all dominions shall serve and obey him." Just as the beasts stood for the pagan empires, so the Son of Man stands for Israel or for the godly Remnant within Israel.[44]

The human being of Daniel's dream, then, "who came to the Ancient of Days," Manson identifies as the symbol for a people, not an individual. The one "like a human being," *ke-bar enash,* is a people of enduring faith, the Israelite people persecuted by Antiochus Epiphanes, or more narrowly, "the godly remnant within Israel" who maintain their faithful noncooperation with the king's laws. Living in the midst of the persecutions whose end he presents, the author of the Book of Daniel has, in effect, set down a promise by God to a faithful, suffering people: The kingdom of God will be theirs.

This is the meaning in the Book of Daniel, a collective meaning, of the human being. When combined with its original Danielic imagery of clouds, the coming human being became the basis for the belief in Jesus' Second Coming. In its original context in the resistance manifesto of Daniel, the human being is a collective humanity, "the people of the saints of the Most High," whose faith under persecution results in their being given the kingdom of God.

Being given the kingdom of God does not mean, however, that either the Book of Daniel or the vision of Jesus is beyond history. In Daniel's vision the coming of the human being is not the end of the world. It is the symbolic representation of a new world or a new time, beyond the overwhelming persecution of Antiochus Epiphanes. The power of God will respond to the patience of the saints by giving them such a new world, the kingdom of God.

In the same way, in Jesus' teaching and practice, for *Bar Enasha,* the Human Being to come, means that a people is given the power of God to break out of oppression and violence into a new age of history. As one exegete has put it, Jesus' references to the coming of *Bar Enasha* on the clouds of heaven were "never conceived as a primitive form of space travel, but as a symbol for a mighty reversal of fortunes within history and at the national level."[45] For Jesus, the coming *Bar Enasha* was a symbolic representation of a continuous nonviolent revolution empowered by God.

There is no question that "the Human Being, as understood by the writers of the synoptic gospels, applied, first of all, to the person of Jesus. Their application of the vision to the visionary was right. It was Jesus who had initiated the new revolution of the kingdom of God, and who, in the early church's eyes, became that revolution. Thus, as Lloyd Gaston puts it, "when the evangelists use the phrase Son of Man they use it nearly consistently as a designation of Jesus, but when Jesus used the phrase he used it just as consistently as a designation of the community he came to found."[46] What is being suggested here is that Jesus himself, in his awareness of the collective meaning of *Bar Enasha,* applied it to his own people, and through a transformed and transforming people of God, saw a transformed humanity.

In Mark's story of the paralytic at Capernaum, noted earlier, Jesus used *Bar Enasha* to describe a new humanity. Matthew's version of the same story provided us with a striking confirmation of the corporate interpretation of *Bar Enasha* — Matthew's use of "humanity" where we would have expected him to say "Jesus" (Matt. 9:8). Thus we see Jesus suggesting, in the interaction between himself and the paralytic, a new *Bar Enasha,* a new Human Being: personal, collective, and transforming, bearing the presence of a revolutionary God within it. In the passion sayings that new Human Being is transformed through suffering and death.

The Book of Daniel's use of *ke-bar enash,* the one "like a human being," as a symbol for the faithful of Israel, gave Jesus a further basis on which to explore a new humanity. Jesus' sayings on the coming Human Being carry a deeper Reality. Taken both in themselves and in relation to Jesus' proclamation of the kingdom of God, the Second Coming statements envision the nonviolent coming of God in a widening historical movement. In that sense they make sense of Jesus' own history. They also cast a new light on our history.

"ALL FLESH SHALL SEE IT TOGETHER"

In a sermon that he gave early in his public life, Martin Luther King envisioned this nonviolent coming of God, a vision that would return to him in a transforming way the night before his death. In his early sermon King in effect combined the different dimensions of Jesus' new humanity that have been outlined here: a new humanity that is present, suffering, and coming in transformation.

In March 1957, King returned to his church in Montgomery, Alabama, from a trip to Africa. There he had attended the independence ceremonies marking the transition from the Gold Coast to Ghana, the first free nation of sub-Saharan Africa, led into independence by Kwame Nkrumah.

"The thing that impressed me more than anything else that night," King told the members of his church, "was the fact that when Nkrumah walked in with his other ministers who had been in prison with him, they didn't come in with the crowns and all of the garnish of kings, but they walked in with prison caps and the coats that they had lived with for all of the months that they had been in prison."[47]

From the inspiration of having seen the people of Ghana transformed through suffering to freedom, King turned to the words of Isaiah and the transformation of humanity:

> Then I can hear Isaiah again, because it has a profound meaning to me. That somehow "every valley shall be exalted, every hill shall be made low, the crooked places shall be revealed, and all flesh shall see it together." And that's the beauty of this thing. *All* flesh shall see it together. Not some from the heights of Park Street [in Montgomery] and others from the dungeons of slum areas. Not some from the pinnacles of the British Empire and some from the dark deserts of Africa. Not some from inordinate, superfluous wealth and others from abject, deadening poverty. Not some white and some black, not some yellow and some brown, but all flesh shall see it together. They shall see it from Montgomery! They shall see it from New York! They shall see it from Ghana! They shall see it from China! For I can look out and see a great number, as John saw, marching into the great eternity, because God is working in this world and at this hour and at this moment.[48]

Jesus saw God working in this world and at this hour and at this moment, in the already dawning horizons of a new Human Being. He saw that new humanity rising in his people in response to a terrible crisis of violence.

"When they persecute you in one town, flee to the next; for truly, I say to you, you will not have gone through all the towns of Israel, before *Bar Enasha* comes" (Matt. 10:23).

Sometime during his ministry (the gospels cannot be relied on for chronology), Jesus sent his disciples on a missionary journey of the utmost urgency. Traveling light and fast, greeting nobody on the road, wasting no time in towns that would give them no hearing, the disciples were to keep moving across Israel. They could expect trials and persecution from sanhedrins, governors, and kings (Matt. 10:17-18). They would experience hatred and torture (Matt. 10:22, 17). Jesus' words to his disciples on the eve of this journey sound rather like those of a leader exhorting his troops before a terrible battle. But in their battle the disciples' only weapon would be that they become as "wise as serpents and innocent as doves" (Matt. 10:16), always reliant on the Spirit.

G. B. Caird has proposed that Jesus' sense of urgency with his disciples came from his awareness that he was "working against time to prevent the end of Israel's world, that the haste of the mission was directly connected with the many sayings which predict the fall of Jerusalem and the destruction of the Temple."[49] Jesus was profoundly sensitive to the sufferings of his people beneath the violence and threats of a several-tiered power structure. The purpose of this missionary journey was to initiate a divine/human revolution in Israel and avoid a national disaster.

In the instructions for that critical mission, Matthew's gospel cites Jesus saying, "When they persecute you in one town, flee to the next; for truly, I say to you, you will not have gone through all the towns of Israel, before *Bar Enasha* comes" (Matt. 10:23).

The meaning is that the Human Being comes within history. There is to be a revolution, but a revolution with divine roots. Jesus envisions the revolutionary coming in his time of a faithful, nonviolent people, who like the faithful Israelites in Daniel can expect to experience not only persecution but also a realization of the kingdom of God. In response to a mounting crisis, Jesus is engaged in a radical experiment with his disciples, sending them out through all the towns of Israel to realize a revolutionary divine hope before it is too late. In terms of both his faith and a nonviolent social program, Jesus has gone beyond the Book of Daniel. But the new humanity Jesus hopes for, in response to a collective crisis, is also a fulfillment of Daniel's vision.

Jesus' response to the high priest, however, comes at a time of abandonment by his followers. The suffering and death that he had said must come for transformation is imminent. Nevertheless, combining the vision of Daniel and his own experience of *Bar Enasha,* he still professes faith in a new humanity: "And you will see *Bar Enasha* seated at the right hand of Power, and coming with the clouds of heaven" (Mark 14:62).

In response to the high priest's question of revolution, as we have seen, Jesus refuses to give a direct answer. But with his *Bar Enasha* response, he shifts the focus of revolution from a leader ordinarily associated with war, the messiah, to a nonviolent people, "the saints of the Most High," with whom he identifies in his mission and in its divine vindication. Although Jesus stands alone and abandoned before the high priest, he still says in faith that a collective nonviolent transformation is already taking place through God's action in his life and work. (When Martin Luther King kept saying in the darkest moments of his life and history, "I *still* have a dream," he was echoing this act of faith by Jesus.) According to an added phrase in Matthew and Luke, this divine/human revolution is happening "from now on": "But I tell you, from now on you will see *Bar Enasha* seated at the right hand of Power, and coming on the clouds of heaven" (Matt. 26:64).[50] In Jesus' faith, that revolutionary new humanity — "the people of the saints of the Most High" — is already coming with the clouds of heaven into God's presence: "From now on . . . ."

A DIVINELY REVOLUTIONIZED HUMANITY

The point of this exegesis is that beneath the symbolic language which has been developed into the Second Coming of Jesus Christ we can begin to discern the possibilities of a new humanity based on the humanity of Jesus. These coming *Bar Enasha* sayings are identified by Rudolf Bultmann as containing very old tradition. He believes they are "probably original words of Jesus."[51] These words convey Jesus' vision of a faithful community, which will be vindicated through the power of God to experience a transformed world.

What Bultmann and many of the writers on this question have ignored is that the "Human Being," like the "kingdom of God," was Jesus' inspired response to his people's oppression. The life situation I am suggesting for these symbols is a first-century imperialism and a nonviolent revolution initiated by God in Jesus. Its closest analogy in history is Gandhi's "constructive program" in India, with its focus on a *swaraj* or freedom that began with the Self-liberating steps of the poorest Indian villager. The key for both Jesus and Gandhi was not the action or reaction of the imperial power over them, but the independent freedom possible to the most oppressed villager each encountered.[52]

At this point in our discussion, the "Human Being," while a literal rendering of the Aramaic *Bar Enasha,* has become an unnecessarily long translation of Jesus' real intent. The Human Being in Jesus' vision of transformation simply means Humanity, a divinely revolutionized Humanity. It is Humanity, a New Humanity transformed by God, which Jesus envisions as seated at the right hand of Power and coming with the clouds of heaven. This nonviolent coming of God in Jesus, in Israel, and in all of Humanity was Jesus' experience of God, an experience which spilled over from the symbol of the kingdom of God to the symbol of the Human Being, Humanity.

In the very depths of his heart and soul Jesus experienced both the suffering of his people and the Spirit of God overcoming the powers of evil that bore down on them: "I saw Satan fall like lightning from heaven" (Luke 10:18). He especially experienced that overcoming Spirit of God in his healing: "If it is by the Spirit of God that I cast out demons, then the kingdom of God has come upon you" (Matt. 12:28; Luke 11:20). Satan's fall corresponded to the coming of the kingdom, God's rising revolution in Humanity, overturning the world's powers of evil. Jesus experienced a revolution from within which he saw transforming the very life of Humanity.

Before his death, Jesus' final way of saying that "the kingdom of God is at hand" comes in his words, "from now on you will see Humanity seated at the right hand of Power and coming on the clouds of heaven." This is the vision of a divine/human revolution that will explode through Israel and the Roman Empire. The Second Coming envisioned by the accused revolutionary standing alone before the high priest was to be the communal coming, "from now on," of a suffering, faithful people, empowered by God in their history to break through to a nonviolent Humanity, the kingdom of God. Abandoned by his followers, alone before his judge, anticipating execution, Jesus still saw that total divine revolution coming from within Humanity. He knew that God would somehow make it happen, and he was determined to embody it by his own death. He did, and the nonviolent coming of God took over.

Remember that lone 19-year-old student in the white shirt, Wang Weilin, standing at attention before the column of tanks rolling toward Tiananmen Square. Remember him finally being led away, to disappear like thousands of his brothers and sisters since June 1989, passing down corridors of death into the heart of a new China and a new Humanity. And recall the legs and black leather boots of Loreta Asanaviciute beneath the Soviet tank treads advancing through Vilnius, Lithuania, on "Bloody Sunday," January 13, 1991 — an empowering symbol of nonviolent resistance for her people and all people. Wang Weilin and Loreta Asanaviciute were saying to the masters of the tanks, just as Jesus was saying to his judge, "From now on you will see Humanity seated at the right hand of Power and coming on the clouds of heaven."

Remember Jo Ann Robinson and the other black women who used the spark of Rosa Parks's arrest to light the fire of the Montgomery Bus Boycott and the civil rights movement. Reflecting three decades later on how slow black Montgomery ministers had been, prior to Parks's arrest, to pick up on their congregations' grievances, Jo Ann Robinson wrote:

> At first the ministers would soothe the anger of their congregations with recommendations of prayer, with promises that God would "make the rough ways smooth" and with exhortations to "have patience and wait upon the Lord."
> The members had been patient and had waited upon the Lord, but the rough ways had gotten rougher rather than smoother. As months stretched into years, the encounters with some of the bus drivers grew more numerous and more intolerable.[53]

In those days of desperation, it had been the Women's Political Council who had said, in effect, in their prophetic boycott letter to the Montgomery mayor, "From now on you will see Humanity seated at the right hand of Power [on Montgomery's buses!] and coming on the clouds of heaven."

Once Rosa Parks had gone to jail and the women had flooded Montgomery with boycott leaflets, as Robinson says, "the time had come for the black people to stop 'waiting on the Lord,' and to help God to 'make rough ways smooth.' The Lord was opening the way; everything had pointed to it."[54] The time had come in Montgomery for a New Humanity to emerge. The nonviolent coming of God took over.

Again, remember the four cave-tombs north of Jerusalem. Remember their revelation of the violence of Jesus' time. The bones of thirty-six individuals were found by archaeologists, of whom at least ten were killed by violence and oppression — starved, shot by arrows, burned to death, smashed by crushing blows, abandoned in childbirth, and crucified. Remember, too, that of those ten victims of violence, eight were women and children — corresponding roughly to the proportion of women and children in the enormous toll which systemic violence continues to take daily among the oppressed of the world. It was to this depth of suffering, in forgotten victims such as these, that Jesus addressed his revolutionary kingdom.

Whereas the male disciples despaired and fled in terror from Jesus' execution, many of the women disciples stayed to witness Jesus' death: Mary of Magdala, Mary who was the mother of James and Joset, Salome, and "many other women who had come up to Jerusalem with him" (Mark 15:40-41). In a striking demonstration of the New Humanity, a group of these women had been disciples of Jesus ever since Galilee (Luke 8:1-3). Contrary to every dictate of their society concerning women, they had remained with Jesus all the way to Jerusalem. In the final events that shattered and dispersed the male disciples, this core group of women continued, in spite of their fear, to "look on from afar" (Mark 15:40). Perhaps because of their experience as women, the people most devastated by violence as revealed in the cave-tombs, they could understand more deeply the price and the hope of the kingdom. They become the foundation of the New Humanity, the decisive community for the continuation of the Jesus movement after Jesus' arrest and execution.[55] When three of them go to anoint his body in the tomb, they are the first disciples to be overwhelmed by his resurrection (Mark 16:1-8).

Here, among the most radically powerless and oppressed of the world, is where the nonviolent coming of God begins, at that moment when faith catches fire in their hearts. Jesus himself experienced such a beginning. The little-noticed basis of the entire Christian faith is that moment when faith moved the poor Jew, Jesus, living under the heel of an empire, to believe in the transforming power of the kingdom of God. Once that fire was ignited in Jesus, nothing on earth could extinguish his faith in the nonviolent coming of God, nor God's actual coming through that faith. No empire has ever had the power to stand against such faith. The British Empire had as little success with Jesus' Hindu successor, Gandhi, as the Roman Empire had with Jesus and the early Christians. The nonviolent coming of God is a growing force in Humanity that will not be denied its full flowering in the world.

When Martin Luther King on the night before his death expressed his faith in God's unfolding will in this century, he was deeply aware of the nuclear violence threatening to burn up all humankind. But a more powerful fire was burning in Martin King's heart. When he said we no longer have a choice between violence and nonviolence in this world, that now it's a choice between nonviolence or nonexistence, he was recognizing the infinite darkness on all sides of us. But that same faith in God's nonviolent coming, that Jesus expressed on the eve of his cross, had caught fire in Martin Luther King's heart on the eve of his bullet. Just as Jesus had seen the Roman Empire's cross coming and had told his disciples to expect it, King as one of those disciples said yes to his own death, because with that yes to the death of self went a yes to the nonviolent coming of God in the world's oppressed.

Jesus told his judge that he would see a nonviolent Humanity coming with the clouds of heaven, transforming the earth through God's power. In his last public words Martin Luther King told not only his people but also his waiting assassin, and all those whose hatred had loaded the assassin's gun, the same truth Jesus had spoken:

"I want you to know tonight, that we as a people will get to the promised land. And I'm happy tonight. I'm not worried about anything. I'm not fearing any man. Mine eyes have seen the glory of the coming of the Lord."

3

TRANSFORMATION OR ANNIHILATION

We all share the responsibility today for choosing either the end dictated by our age, annihilation, or a nonviolent beginning (already begun) whose end is the world's transformation. The strange calling we have experienced at Ground Zero is that seeing the means of our annihilation has compelled us to seek transformation.

When did we first see the White Train? Some of us feel we saw it first in Franz Jagerstatter's dream.

Jagerstatter was an Austrian peasant who refused to fight in Hitler's wars because he believed that the Nazi movement was anti-Christian. He was beheaded by the Nazis in 1943. The story of his solitary witness[1] has been told and retold as a way of life in an age of death.

REFUSING THE TRAIN TO HELL

The train Jagerstatter saw in a dream five years before his martyrdom (and which he wrote about shortly before his death) corresponded to the White Train we saw passing our homes and exploding in our dreams:

At first I lay awake in my bed until almost midnight, unable to sleep, although I was not sick; I must have fallen asleep anyway. All of a sudden I saw a beautiful shining railroad train that circled around a mountain. Streams of children—and adults as well—rushed toward the train and could not be held back. . . . Then I heard a voice say to me: "This train is going to hell."[2]

The train to hell in Jagerstatter's dream was a symbol of cooperation in the Nazi movement. Our White Train to hell was both symbol and reality. It contained the annihilation it symbolized.

For the sake of his soul Jagerstatter had to refuse to board his train to hell. For the sake of our souls and of life itself, we felt we had to stop the White Train.

We began tracking the White Train, although we did not know it existed then, when we moved into our house alongside the railroad tracks entering the Trident submarine base at Bangor, Washington.

We saw the house by the tracks for the first time in 1977, while seeking a piece of land that could become Ground Zero Center for Nonviolent Action. The house we discovered by the tracks was too remote to serve as such a center, but it brought another possibility to mind. It stood on a hill overlooking the gate where railroad shipments enter the Trident base. By living in such a house one could, simply by being there, begin to break through the invisibility and silence of one critical means toward nuclear holocaust: the missile shipments that travel the United States by rail, analogous to the boxcars that moved unchallenged through Europe in the '40s on the way to an earlier holocaust.

Through a series of miracles, Shelley, our son, Tom, and I moved into the house by the tracks four years later. The intervening time had been marked by my knocking on the door of the house every six months or so to ask if the couple living there ever planned to sell it; a friendly no was always the answer. Then one day I knocked on the door to no answer at all, and saw through its window a house empty of both people and furniture. From that moment on, the miracles took over. Through the grace of God and the gifts of many wonderful friends, we were able to buy the house by the tracks and move into it in July 1981. At the same time the Agape Community was born.

We held a workshop at Ground Zero that month entitled "Christian Roots of Nonviolence" and included a pilgrimage around the fence of the base. It ended at the railroad tracks with a meditation on the trains entering Bangor and on their parallel meaning to the trains entering Auschwitz and Buchenwald. As a part of the meditation we named some of the cities and towns along the tracks, as they wound their way up from Salt Lake City, near the Hercules Corporation, source of Trident's missile propellant shipments. (At the time we knew nothing of the White Train's journeys to Bangor from the Texas Panhandle.) When we finished our litany of the tracks, we realized that most of the workshop participants lived along those same tracks.

We all recognized that this was a workshop whose community could truly be deepened in meaning by our going home and becoming an extended nonviolent community in our various towns along the Trident tracks. We decided to become the Agape Community and adopted a community statement which said in part: "We believe the spiritual force capable of both changing us and stopping the arms race is that of *agape*: the love of God operating in the human heart." By this definition, we were basing our community especially on Martin Luther King's understanding of *agape*.

As we tracked and opposed Trident missile propellant shipments through Utah, Idaho, Oregon, and Washington in 1981-82, two truths found a special life in the Agape Community. The first is that systemic evil shuns the light. The government and the railroads did their best to keep us from seeing the missile shipments. The second truth we experienced is that once evil is brought into the light, it can be overcome by God's love operating in our lives.

Evil's power lies in darkness, our own darkness. Evil's power to destroy life comes from our denial of its presence and our refusal to accept responsibility for it. The essence of our life-destroying evil lies in our unseen, unacknowledged cooperation with it. As we began to claim personal responsibility for the missile propellant shipments and sought to express our love for the train employees, we experienced the faith to overcome the evil which was in us and on the trains: faith in the redeeming power of nonviolent love, faith in the cross. Our growing community of faith and nonviolent action made the tracks linking us a double symbol—of not only holocaust, but hope.

But we were about to experience a deeper sense of these realities along the tracks.

THE WHITE TRAIN

On December 8, 1982, I received a phone call from a reporter asking if we knew anything about a special train carrying nuclear warheads that was on its way to the Trident base. It had been spotted in Everett, Washington, two days before: an all-white, armored train, escorted by a security car traveling along highways.

I said we knew nothing of such a train. It bore no resemblance to the missile-propellant shipments that we witnessed going into the base every week. After the phone call I walked down our front steps to the tracks. I could see signs of unusual activity across the tracks at the base gate. More security cars than I had ever seen for an arriving train were parked by the gate, waiting for something. I went back in the house, loaded film in our camera, and came down the steps just in time to see the train approaching.

Perched outside the first Burlington Northern engine was a man, like a film director scanning his set. After the second engine came a string of all-white, heavily armored cars. Each of the two rail security cars had a high turret, like a tank's. Sandwiched between the security cars were eight middle cars, lower in height, white, and armored. When the final security car came opposite me, the armored flaps on the side of the turret clanked open, and an object was extended in my direction.

The White Train passed by, a train to holocaust, and I remembered the train of Jagerstatter's dream and the words: "This train is going to hell."

In response to the news of the White Train, the Agape Community grew rapidly. We surmised the source of the train must be the Department of Energy's Pantex plant in Amarillo, Texas, final assembly point for all United States nuclear warheads. A friend and railroad buff, Tom Rawson, drew up a likely rail route between Pantex and the Bangor base. We then sought old and new friends along this hypothetical White Train route, sharing with them the Agape Community's vision of love toward the people on the trains and nonviolent resistance to their cargo. As we contacted more train-watchers, we waited for the White Train to come out of its Bangor lair—and, we hoped, follow our route.

It did so on January 5, 1983, rolling past our house in the opposite direction. As friends along the tracks monitored the train, we confirmed that it was traveling the route Tom Rawson had drawn up. The train returned to Amarillo via Spokane, Denver, and Pueblo; it was seen entering the Pantex plant the night of January 12 by Les Breeding of Northwest Texas Clergy and Laity Concerned.

"It was a haunting sight," said Les, "this white train moving slowly into the distance where amber lights were glowing with a light fog all around. It brought to mind a phantom train bound for Hades."

The White Train may be the most concentrated symbol we have of the hell of nuclear war. It carries a world-destructive power within it, guarded by Department of Energy "couriers" who, according to a DOE spokesperson, are armed with machine guns, rifles, and hand grenades, and are trained to shoot anyone who threatens the train. Yet there is another side to all this, as indicated by an experience Les Breeding had with the "phantom train bound for Hades."

On the night of January 12 Les had a unique, forty-five-minute conversation in the middle of the Amarillo switchyards with the head security guard of the White Train, prior to the train's final movement to Pantex. The White Train watcher and White Train defender discussed issues of interest to them both: peace, the nuclear freeze movement, and the Soviet threat. After this conversation Les lost the White Train when it moved out of the switchyards into the darkness. He pursued it by car, discovering it again just outside Pantex. There was a tense moment when he drove up to the train and a searchlight suddenly glared at his car. He got out of the car and heard the security guard say, "Hey, Les, is that you?"

At the heart of perhaps the greatest outward symbol we have of nuclear war, this train bearing instruments of hell, there is a human voice asking if we are there. The question alters our sense of the train as absolute evil. There are people inside the train. We must stop this White Train to hell, but we can stop it only through a truthful, loving process which affirms the sacredness of that life within it. The security guard and his question to us are at the center of the tracks campaign.

For three years Ground Zero and the Agape Community tracked the White Train back and forth across the United States as it carried thousands of hydrogen bombs to their destinations. Half of these cargoes went to Bangor on the West Coast, the other half to the Charleston Naval Weapons Station in South Carolina, the East Coast base for Poseidon submarines. Hundreds of people were arrested for sitting in front of the White Train. Hundreds more vigiled by the tracks at all hours of the day and night, as

Ground Zero notified people in each town along the various routes when the White Train would be coming.

Karol Schulkin of Ground Zero describes one such "coming of the train" and the deepening and widening of the community by the tracks:

On Wednesday, February 22, 1984 a call came from a reporter in Emporia, Kansas: a local man there had just reported seeing the White Train traveling north through town on the Santa Fe/Wichita rail line. It was a little after noon in Washington when the call came. By 10 p.m. on Friday, February 24, the White Train was locked behind the fences of the Trident submarine base at Bangor. It was not to pass there unnoticed. What followed that message from Emporia is a story of vigilance and waiting, of prayer and protest.

From Emporia, Kansas to Bangor, Washington throughout Nebraska, Wyoming, Idaho and Oregon this all white heavily guarded train was sighted and tracked by a network of peace-loving people. Shortly after the first call, a second sighting was made. Looking out the window of the Acapulco restaurant just south of Topeka, a customer saw a train pass by. Having seen the previous White Train, this man knew what was passing before his eyes. He notified his local peace group which notified Ground Zero. Phone trees throughout Kansas and Nebraska were immediately activated and people closest to the train headed to their stretch of tracks. Soon more eyewitness accounts gave the details: 17 white cars—10 weapons cargo cars, four buffer cars, and three turreted security cars—plus two engines and a caboose. The train was traveling fast. Throughout Nebraska, people driving alongside the train would clock it at speeds between 50-60 mph. A handful of residents in Frankfort, Kansas, because of their rapid response, managed to witness the train's passage before it headed on to Nebraska. The chain of vigils had begun.

By 7 p.m. as the train sped toward Hastings, Nebraska a group of 18 vigilers with signs, candles, and Bibles were waiting in the snow by the tracks. Singing hymns beneath a street light, these people in the heartland of America stood in witness to this train. A few days later Ken Gonsior, OSC, a brother at Crosier Monastery, wrote of how the train had moved within his life:

"At this point, I'm still coming to grips with the fact that the train actually passed through our town. Initially, when I first saw the articles in *Sojourners* and saw Hastings listed on the train map, I figured it would be rare for it to actually hit here. . . . I never dreamed that the interest that I expressed to your group in my first note to you would be called upon to act. I was plain afraid after you telephoned that one evening—what could I do? What did I want to do? What would the ramifications be for me personally, for us as a religious community in this conservative diocese in this conservative state? These questions and others haunted me for days. I discussed it with friends here; I prayed about it; I delayed acting upon it. Fortunately, I finally contacted the Marshes here in town and we shared similar apprehensions about involvement—we were all afraid, but yet we were all concerned about the reality of what the train was carrying and the arms race in general. I am thankful for finally having the courage to reach out to the Marshes. I am thankful to you for having prodded me along in describing the needs your organization had for common folk to work together in witnessing opposition to the train. I am thankful that our apprehensions and fears were re-created into a prayerful witness broadcast to the public. People were touched, I know, and at least the public's consciousness was raised. . . ."

An hour later, when the train barreled through Kearney, Nebraska the number of vigilers had doubled to 35. At North Platte, Ogallala, Sidney and Kimball people kept watch.

It was morning now of the second day. In the pre-dawn darkness of Cheyenne, 100 people stood waiting for the train. Unknown to them, the train stood outside town for an hour; the crew was changed. At 2 a.m. the vigilers moved to a viaduct overlooking the railroad yard. From this windy vantage point they watched for another hour singing "This Land Is Your Land," "I've Been Workin' on the Railroad," and "America the Beautiful." It was 3:30 a.m. when the train finally passed and the vigilers tossed their flowers onto the top of the train. There were tears and prayers and the linking of arms as the train rolled on to Laramie where 50 more vigilers waited. In Rawlins, Rock Springs, and Granger the train was met again and again with protest and prayer. It was noon of the second day. The train was entering Idaho.

It was on the second day of the train's trip, February 23, 1984, that the *New York Times* released a story headlined, "Bishops Protest Train Carrying Atom Weapons." The story told of a statement signed by 12 Roman Catholic bishops in the West, ones through whose states the White Train is likely to pass. They urged direct action to impede the deployment of nuclear weapons and urged their parishioners to join in prayer vigils along the route of the train. In an interview given during these days, Bishop Lawrence Welsh of Spokane, Washington said:

"Protesting the train may be a small step, but it is an important one. It questions the good of nuclear weapons. To say nothing is to fall prey to moral apathy. To let these weapons pass through our towns without any response is to welcome them as friends. That is wrong. Our salvation comes not from weapons, but in God alone. I speak out against the preparation of nuclear weapons. I stand in union with those who vigil and pray."

In Spokane, a city through which the train did not travel this time, but might have, a vigil was held nonetheless. Near a railroad trestle on the edge of town, 18 people stood beneath an Air Force recruiting billboard and joined hands in a circle of prayer, songs, and readings. From Thursday evening through Friday evening they kept vigil, taking turns throughout the snowy night.

In other towns where the train did not go vigils were also held. In Pueblo, Colorado and Billings, Montana people of faith and good will stood together in opposition to the momentum of the arms race. There was a vigil of solidarity and concern in Sheridan, Wyoming with the group holding a large banner which asked, "Why 480 Hiroshimas?" [This was the vigilers' estimate of the nuclear firepower on the current White Train as compared to the Hiroshima bomb. They probably underestimated the train's cargo by as much as fifty percent. A more likely equivalent for the train's destructive power was 960 Hiroshima bombs.[3]] Throughout the South a chain of prayer was activated in support of those facing the train on the western route. The people in the South knew that when next the train leaves Pantex it is likely to head their way en route to the Charleston Naval Weapons Station in South Carolina.

On through Pocatello the train traveled, heading west to Shoshone, where 40 people waited with a candlelight vigil. At Gooding, a family stood together on the soil of their own farm holding up signs to the passing train. It was nearly 11 p.m. when the train went through Mountain Home, Idaho, a military town in which 40 people stood to publicly speak their "NO" to the weapons-carrying train.

It was in Orchard, Idaho that this train first encountered people on the tracks. In sub-freezing temperatures a vigil of 70 people had gathered here, a number driving in from nearby Boise. When four elderly women walked onto the tracks several minutes before the train's arrival the state police and sheriff's deputies moved in quickly to remove them. One deputy confided to one of the women as he led her away that if it weren't for their positions, many of the officers would be in the vigil line. No charges were brought against the women. Due to the openness of the demonstration planners in Orchard, the location and plans of the group were announced on the six o'clock news. Eight women in a bridge club heard this announcement, put down their cards, and went to the vigil. Two of the women had never been to a public protest before.

Although a police roadblock prevented the people at Orchard from driving on to Nampa to again meet the train, there were, nonetheless, about 80 people waiting in Nampa when the train reached there at midnight. Living out an action they had planned for over eight months, eight people crossed a police barricade in an attempt to reach the tracks. Seven were arrested and charged with trespass. As they were taken to a police van the others sang "We Shall Overcome." The train barreled through town at 50 mph. Cathy Posey, one of those arrested, explained the reasons for her action:

"I'm a simple homemaker, not a public figure. I choose to make my public statement by standing on the tracks. I have two children, seven and eight years old. I am convinced that if they are to have a chance to grow up ... our government will have to take the initiative in leading the world toward peace. Building nuclear weapons doesn't make the world more secure. It leads the world to war."

As the train crossed into Oregon about 1:00 a.m., 15 members of the Interfaith Peace Fellowship held a prayer vigil in the Ontario depot. In Baker, a dozen people waited for two hours until the train passed at 2:20 a.m. Two feet of snow covered the ground. Two hours later in LaGrande 28 people ranging in age from three to fifty met the train with large signs and banners reading "Give Peace a Chance — Stop the Arms Race" and "We Believe in Peace." In the Amtrak station in The Dalles 50 people held hands in prayer; the train passed at 10:22 a.m. Half an hour later 40 people vigiled in Hood River as the train passed headed toward Portland.

Then the unexpected happened. The train was stopped. It was two-and-a-half hours before it would move again. In northeast Portland 200 people stood together on the tracks. Some 80 police and security officers worked to remove the protesters, only to find that once removed, they would return again and again to the tracks. In the end, 35 people were arrested and charged with trespass. Despite rain and a chilling wind, spirits remained high. At 3:30 p.m. the train made its way out of Portland and into Washington.

At Kelso, Castle Rock, Chehalis, and Centralia the train was again met as the people of the state of Washington added their signs and prayers to the litany of protest which preceded the train. It was now 6:30 p.m. In Elma a group of 80 people lined both sides of the tracks. Carrying candles, they joined together in a liturgy of resistance and hope. As eight people attempted to make their way onto the tracks they were dragged off by officers. They were not charged.

The train was reaching the end of the line — Bangor. Just outside the fence of the Trident submarine base several hundred people had waited for hours into the night. They lined the final stretch of tracks, holding candles and lanterns, listening to readings, joining in songs and prayer. This vigil had actually begun the day before in Seattle, where members of the Seattle Agape Community maintained a vigil outside the corporate offices of Burlington Northern Railroad. Rebecca Johnson, an Agape member, explained, "We're asking people to just go see it. It will change their lives to see the White Train. It did mine."

Now everyone had gathered at Bangor. The train, expected at 3 p.m., was long overdue. About an hour before the train appeared a group of nine persons walked onto the tracks. Holding a large wooden cross in their midst, they stood facing the vigil line beside the tracks. Together, the vigilers on the tracks and those beside them sang songs of hope and prayed for a faith deep enough to end the violence which sends the trains. Then the nine knelt facing the on-coming train. The vigil line stood in silence. The nine were removed from the tracks and driven away by the sheriff's deputies as the train, with its spotlights now dimmed, passed into the darkened base. It was 10 p.m. on the third day. The crowd encircled the tracks, proclaiming together an affirmation of faith and breaking bread. There were songs. There were tears. There was a deep sense of connectedness along the tracks. Another train had passed through our lives. It had not passed unnoticed. One person standing with a candle was enough to pierce the darkness, one voice enough to break the silence. There had been many such gestures in the preceding three days.

It's hard to determine which is the greater danger, the moral or the physical one. These trains, with their deadly cargo of nuclear warheads, make visible the reality of an arms race propelling us toward destruction. These trains travel through our midst bringing the bombs close to us — right through our towns, right into our lives. They are no longer figures on a budget sheet or lines inching their way up a weapons production chart. They are here: in Topeka and Sheridan, Pocatello and Baker, in Jonesboro and Memphis, Birmingham and Jesup. The arms race has come home.

All across this country people are deciding they will not ignore this passage of destruction. These White Trains are not a matter for indifference or apathy. People of faith have roused themselves. They are bearing witness. There is a place for prayer and for resistance. One place they meet is by the tracks where the White Train travels.[4]

GOVERNMENT RESPONSES: REROUTE IT, REPAINT IT, STOP IT

The Department of Energy responded to the tracks campaign, first of all, by rerouting the White Train. The DOE command center for the White Train, located at Kirtland Air Force Base in Albuquerque, New Mexico, changed the train's route periodically onto whatever was perceived to be the track of least resistance. The result was an ever-widening and deepening nonviolent campaign, as hundreds of people on new routes became vigilers to the train. Because of people's willingness to stand in testimony to a power greater than this awesome train, lives were being transformed.

The DOE's next step was to repaint the train to make it less noticeable and less notorious. A secret July 30, 1984, DOE memorandum headed "Color Change of Safe-Secure Railcars" (obtained through the Freedom of Information Act) reads: "We recognize that the painting of these railcars will not stop dedicated protesters from identifying our special trains. However, it will make tracking our trains more difficult and this, we believe, enhances the safety and security of our special trains."[5] The cars of the "White Train" were therefore painted red, green, gray, and blue. (They remained white on top for safety reasons, to reduce heat inside the cars.) As the DOE memorandum recognized, this was not a very effective camouflage. The train's armor and turrets remained conspicuous. Its Pantex source and nuclear cargo were too widely known by this time for the train to return to obscurity. Moreover, it was being watched vigilantly at Pantex by Hedy Sawadsky, a Mennonite woman of deep faith, who had moved to Amarillo at Ground Zero's invitation to be a light to unmask the darkness (Eph. 5).

Resistance to the multicolored Nuclear Train continued to grow. Reporters kept calling it the White Train, explaining that the government had painted it to try to evade protesters. In February 1985, 146 people were arrested in the course of the train's journey to Bangor. In June, a jury from our conservative Kitsap County returned a "not guilty" verdict for the twenty who had sat on the tracks at the Bangor gate in front of the February train. The county government then decided to stop charging people who were arrested for resisting the federal government's unpopular weapons trains. It was a waste of local taxpayers' money.

In the face of such developments, the Department of Energy stopped sending the White Train. Its nuclear weapons were put on trucks instead. The H-Bomb trucks have in turn been followed and vigiled in an effective campaign coordinated by Nukewatch of Madison, Wisconsin.[6]

We learned from a Department of Energy statement that the White Train had been on the rails for more than twenty years before the nonviolent campaign arose that drew public attention to it. A question immediately presents itself: How did a heavily armored, all-white train carrying holocaust weapons across the United States remain virtually invisible for more than twenty years?

The question brings others to mind: How did boxcars carrying millions of Jewish people across Europe in the 1940s remain invisible until after the victims had gone to their deaths? How did radiation victims of our nuclear testing remain unnoticed by us until recent years? Have we always known instinctively that if we choose to see systemic evil, it will open an abyss that can only be bridged by faith?

A white light of annihilation is carried in the cars of the White Train. It is an evil so inconceivable in its effect that it calls forth an opposite kind of power.

We remember again Franz Jagerstatter's train to hell, and most important, his refusal to board that train. His resistance to it was a choice of the kingdom of God. It is said that Jagerstatter's eyes shone with such joy and confidence in the hour before his death that the chaplain who visited him in prison was never able to forget that look.

We remember the kingdom of God in Jagerstatter's eyes when he chose life. Out of the nightmare of a White Train to the end of the world can come an awakening to our Nonviolent God.

THE END OF JESUS' WORLD

The end of Jesus' world occurred four decades after his death. The Roman Empire, which had in 30 C.E. executed Jesus as a revolutionary on a hill outside Jerusalem, in 70 C.E. burned Jerusalem, destroyed the Temple, slaughtered up to a million Jews, and made slaves of tens of thousands more.[7] Remnant Palestinian Jews were decimated in a final unsuccessful war against Rome in 132-35 C.E., after which for centuries Jews were forbidden under penalty of death to enter the pagan city Rome built on the site of Jerusalem.[8] This end of Jesus' world, the end of his people's world, was the terrible conclusion of a gathering storm of violence under whose clouds Jesus had lived from his childhood.

In response to the forces behind that coming storm of total destruction, Jesus proclaimed a nonviolent revolution whose purpose was to liberate the Jewish poor and, in the process, free also their oppressors—a divinely empowered transformation to free the world of violence. Jesus knew the looming alternative to such a nonviolent coming of God in humanity was the end of the world through violence: his people's world, and in some undisclosed sense, the world itself. "Put your sword back into its place; for all who take the sword will perish by the sword" (Matt. 26:52). He saw that end-time crisis of violence happening in his own world, and in his language and imagery revealed the same eventual alternatives to all of humankind, what his later disciple, Martin Luther King, was to call "nonviolence or nonexistence." In responding to the threatened end of his world, Jesus experienced a transforming power of God whose only limit is human choice: "The kingdom of God is within your power" (Luke 17:21).

DETERRENCE AT SEPPHORIS

As we saw in Chapter 1, the Roman Empire, like the modern empire of the United States, had a deadly deterrent and threatened massive retaliation. The Jewish people experienced Rome's deterrent of violent death in the burning of whole cities and the mass crucifixion of rebels, both carried out as examples to the Jews of the consequences of defying the empire. The threat of Rome's deterrent was immediately visible to Jesus growing up in Nazareth whenever he raised his eyes to the nearby city of Sepphoris.

By walking to Sepphoris, Jesus could see the disastrous effects of the Roman deterrent to Jewish revolt. When we look at a map of Jesus' Palestine, we discover that the village he lived in, Nazareth, was about four miles southeast of the city of Sepphoris.[9] As a youth, Jesus probably walked to Sepphoris many times. When Herod Antipas rebuilt the city, Jesus and Joseph may have worked there as carpenters. Jesus probably had no fondness for the nearby Sepphoris, however. Its name goes unmentioned in the gospels.[10]

Sepphoris had a history of blood and tears, a history Nazareth knew well. Nazareth's collective memory of Sepphoris, at the time when Jesus was a young man, has been depicted by modern Jewish novelist A. A. Kabak:

> The older inhabitants of Nazareth had stark memories of the burning of Sepphoris after the great revolt against the kingdom. The city had blazed for three days and three nights. By day a column of smoke, like a black shroud, rolled incessantly into the sky and by night a column of fire crackled from the gutted pyre of the city, throwing fear and panic over a wide area. From the hilltops the flames could be seen dancing in the macabre gloom of night, and through the stillness resounded the piercing cries and wailing of the people being stabbed and massacred; and the smell of roasting flesh of man and animal drifted to the nostrils.[11]

In 4 B.C.E. after the death of Rome's client-king Herod the Great, uprisings against Roman authority occurred all over Palestine. Josephus reports that in one such rebellion the revolutionary leader, Judas, with a "multitude of men" assembled from the area of Sepphoris (probably including men of Nazareth), captured the Herodian palace and arsenal at Sepphoris.[12] Judas became a terror to Sepphoris' population, and by his capture of the city brought down on its people the even worse terror of Rome. The Roman governor of Syria, Quintilius Varus, retaliated against the entire city, sending an auxiliary force that burned Sepphoris down and made slaves of its survivors. In his parable of the Royal Marriage Feast, Matthew applied the following verse of his gospel to the destruction of Jerusalem: "The king was angry, and he sent his troops and destroyed those murderers and burned their city" (Matt. 22:7). The same description could have been known, however, by the boy Jesus as a graphic folk-memory in Nazareth of the nearby burning of Sepphoris by Roman troops.[13]

By living in Nazareth, Jesus knew another pattern of violence from Sepphoris. From rabbinic sources we know that Sepphoris was the home of wealthy landowners, allied by kinship with the Temple priesthood, who possessed property in the Galilean countryside.[14] As absentee landlords, this aristocracy lived off the labor of peasants tending their rural estates. The Jewish aristocracy owned land "at the good pleasure of the Romans, paying for it in terms of heavy taxes which, as always, the weakest in the community must carry."[15] The Jewish peasantry in villages such as Nazareth suffered the consequences of this system. In raising his people's army, Judas may have been drawing on a mixture of anti-Roman and anti-Sepphoris resentments. This conflict between city and country is also reflected in the Jewish-Roman War. The civil war within the war against Rome not only set peasants against landowners but also country against city in terms of the participants' backgrounds. It was a civil war by the rural poor against the landed aristocracy in Jerusalem, within the larger context of a Jewish war of independence against Rome. The native aristocracy served and benefitted as Rome's client-rulers. But the violence of the Roman system rebounded on them.

Jesus, like everyone else in Nazareth, would have known that after Varus' forces razed Sepphoris in 4 B.C.E., they marched on, burning villages. The climax of the Roman policy of retaliation was the crucifixion of two thousand presumed agitators across Palestine as an example and deterrent to the Jews.[16] Thus imperial Rome set the historical pattern for the "discriminate deterrence" we see today in a United States client-state such as El Salvador, where peasants who speak out for human rights are regularly murdered by government death squads to deter others.

At Nazareth Jesus grew in age and wisdom (Luke 2:52), in the shadow of exploitation, burnt cities, and mass crucifixions. Although nuclear weapons lay nineteen centuries ahead, as a Galilean peasant under Roman rule Jesus was already firmly acquainted with the policy of deterrence, carried out in acts of massive retaliation to revolutionary violence.

Whenever the boy Jesus walked to Sepphoris, he would have seen there the ruins left by Roman imperialism and revolutionary counter-violence. Jesus would also have known peasant families—possibly his own among them—which had lost members in that struggle against Rome. The suffering legacy of that violence is present in the gospels. John Pairman Brown suggests that "some at least of the maimed and lame [Jesus encountered] were so as a result of the sack of Sepphoris; some of the mourning (Matt. 5:5) was for those lost there."[17]

As Jesus grew up in a time of continuing Roman-Jewish conflict, he may have stood beneath the dying bodies of other men of Nazareth crucified for their resistance to Rome. Rome's logic of deterrence for oppressed Jews, the cross and the razed city, was no abstraction to a child of Nazareth. The very term "Jesus of Nazareth" tells us more than has been recognized about Jesus' growing consciousness. Like a modern child of Soweto or the Gaza Strip, Jesus had a history of violence at his doorstep.

Jesus' consciousness of Sepphoris would have deepened into fears for Jerusalem. The synoptic gospels present us with the prophetic result of that deepening consciousness, his repeated warnings of Jerusalem's destruction by Rome. Jesus was to apply the lessons he learned as a youth in Nazareth from the ruins of Sepphoris to a tragedy he feared in the future for the Temple and Jerusalem.

A CONTINGENT PROPHECY

While Jesus gained a tragic insight into the violence of power from living at Nazareth, that insight was intensified by his teachers, the prophets.

The issue that frightens the prophets, according to Abraham Heschel, is that "a people may be dying without being aware of it; a people may be able to survive, yet refuse to make use of their ability."[18]

Jesus knew this had been true in the time of Jeremiah. Prior to the first destruction of Jerusalem, in 586 B.C.E. at the hands of the Babylonians, the prophet Jeremiah recognized that his people were walking into a volcano. Jeremiah was filled with what Heschel has described as "the divine pathos,"[19] God's passionate care for Israel and the world which issued in terrible words designed to shake the people from their moral blindness before it was too late. Jeremiah appealed to the entire nation to change, but focused his indictment, as did all the prophets, on the ruling elites who exploited the poor and drove their nation toward destruction:

> Yes, there are wicked men among my people
> who spread their nets;
> like fowlers they set snares,
> but it is people they catch.
> Like a cage full of birds
> so are their houses full of loot;
> they have grown rich and powerful because of it,
> fat and sleek.
> Yes, in wickedness they go to any lengths,
> they have no respect for rights,
> for orphans' rights, to support them;
> they do not uphold the cause of the poor.
> And must I not punish them for such things
> —it is Yahweh who speaks—
> or from such a nation
> exact my vengeance? (Jer. 5:26-29, *JB*)

Jeremiah was moved by God's love and anger toward Israel to speak time after time of a coming disaster. The disaster was not inevitable. It was contingent on whether the people would change in time. The people could change, and God would then change the movement of history. Contingency, the possibility of change, was at the heart of God's prophetic word.

In the eighteenth chapter of Jeremiah, Yahweh tells Jeremiah what contingent prophecy is. The text repudiates any deterministic understanding of prophecy. The future is totally open, for both God and humanity.

"On occasion, I decree for some nation, for some kingdom, that I will tear up, knock down, destroy; but if this nation, against which I have pronounced sentence, abandons its wickedness, I then change my mind about the evil which I had intended to inflict on it. On another occasion, I decree for some nation, for some kingdom, that I will build up and plant; but if that nation does what displeases me, refusing to listen to my voice, I then change my mind about the good which I had intended to confer on it" (Jer. 18:7-10).

Jesus knew that in the case of Jeremiah the nation did not listen to a contingent prophecy. The event Jeremiah had feared, which he had threatened as an expression of God's anger, struck the people. In 586 B.C.E., Babylonian soldiers burned Jerusalem and deported most of its people.

We know from the gospels that the prophet whose teaching Jesus took most deeply to heart was the prophet who baptized him, John the Baptist. The contingent prophecy Jesus learned from John is expressed in the image of the ax: "Yes, even now the ax is laid to the roots of the trees, so that any tree which fails to produce good fruit will be cut down and thrown on the fire" (Luke 3:9, *JB*).

The symbolic meaning of the ax in Jesus' time was specific. It meant Roman authority. An ax with a projecting blade stood among a bundle of rods to make up the *fasces*, an official symbol of Roman authority used in courts. "We have at least to allow for some imposition of Roman symbolism on John and Jesus when their poetry gives prominent place to the *ax* laid at the foot of the tree, the *sword* which will destroy all those who take the sword."[20] When the prophet John the Baptist spoke of an ax being laid at the root of a tree, his listeners would have thought of the Roman Empire poised to strike. Rome in John's and Jesus' time, like Babylon in Jeremiah's time, was the contemporary form of God's judgment in history.

The tree against which the ax was laid was equally familiar. Israel was traditionally symbolized as a vine or fig tree. C. H. Kraeling in his seminal work *John the Baptist* has analyzed prophetic language to clarify John's intended meaning:

> Prophetic usage makes the trees of the forest the symbol of the nations, and those of the orchard a symbol of the People of Israel. ... In John's saying, it is the trees of the orchard that are to be hewn down if they do not bring forth good fruit. It is God's own planting, it is Israel itself upon which the judgment impends . . .[21]

By proclaiming that the Roman ax was laid at the root of the trees of Israel, John the Baptist was warning the people that Yahweh's judgment would fall on Israel through the instrument of pagan armies. John addressed his prophecy especially to the "unrepentant powerful of the nation,"[22] the ruling priestly aristocracy in Jerusalem. John's strongest words were directed to these rich and powerful exploiters of the poor: "Brood of vipers, who warned you to fly from the retribution that is coming? But if you are repentant, produce the appropriate fruit, and do not presume to tell yourselves, 'We have Abraham for our father,' because, I tell you, God can raise children for Abraham from these stones" (Matt. 3:8-9, *JB*).

John called on the huge crowds who came to hear him, described in

Mark 1:5 as "all Judaea and all the people of Jerusalem," to repent, to turn their lives around. In the moment before God's judgment, they were to repent by choosing new lives of compassion and justice, sharing their food and clothing with those who had none: "When all the people asked him, 'What must we do then?' he answered, 'If anyone has two tunics that person must share with the one who has none, and the one with something to eat must do the same' " (Luke 3:11, *JB*).

John made radical ethical demands of tax collectors and soldiers that would lighten the burdens of the poor. Under a tax-farming system, tax collectors were a class accustomed to exploiting those subject to them. "Exact no more than your rate," said John (Luke 3:13, *JB*), a demand which undercut the very rationale of the system.

Soldiers (who were more like police or militia, under Herod Antipas) probably worked closely with tax collectors to extort excessive toll payments and pocket the surplus.[23] To these soldiers he said, "No intimidation! No extortion! Be content with your pay!" (Luke 3:14, *JB*), which if followed would not only tend to impoverish the soldiers but also place them in direct conflict with their superiors and the power structure over them. Intimidation and extortion were prime reasons for a military presence.[24]

John the Baptist was calling on the Jewish nation, and especially the exploiters of the poor, to repent by choosing a just, compassionate way of life. They also had to undergo a symbolic immersion in the waters of the River Jordan in the presence of the prophet.

The meaning of John's rite of baptism has been uncovered by the meticulous historical research of Carl Kraeling.[25] Kraeling distinguishes John's baptism from proselyte ablution for converts to Judaism in three particulars: John's baptism is performed in running water; it has an eschatological setting, the wilderness; it applies to those who are themselves already Jews. A satisfactory explanation for all three distinguishing factors is necessary in determining the meaning of John's baptism.

Kraeling discovers the origin of that meaning in the symbol of the river of fire, which appears in Daniel 7:10. There a fiery stream flows from the Ancient of Days as he sits upon his throne in judgment. The river of fire is God's instrument of judgment. In Jesus' day the river of fire was embodied in Roman legions. The symbolism of the river of fire had antecedents in Persian eschatology, in the vision of a final act of judgment whereby mountains made of metal "melt at the end of the world, and the molten metal pours over the earth like a river."[26] All people then pass into this river of fire and are either purified or destroyed. Today, this awesome symbol of a river of fire has been enclosed within the multiform presence among us of thermonuclear missiles.

Through the discovery of the Dead Sea Scrolls, Kraeling's hypothesis has been given an additional witness. Numerous scholars have suggested that John the Baptist was a dissident Essene, perhaps once a member of the same wilderness community that produced the Dead Sea Scrolls. He may then have known by heart the Thanksgiving Psalm discovered among the scrolls; it describes a river of fire consuming the foundations of the mountains and all the sentient beings of the earth in a final judgment of God.[27]

Kraeling points to John's saying, "I baptize you with water, but he will baptize you with a holy spirit and fire" (as drawn from Mark 1:8, Matt. 3:11, and Luke 3:16). In John's baptism the running water symbolizes the coming fiery torrent of judgment – Roman legions then, nuclear missiles in our time. Those who immerse themselves in the water enact in advance before God their willing submission to the divine judgment the river of fire will perform. In John's eyes the mightier one who was to come after him would baptize humanity in a river of fire. John's baptism was, then, a rite symbolic not of initiation into Judaism but a repentant people's acceptance of God's coming judgment.

Jesus was one of those who submitted themselves to God's judgment through the medium of John's baptism. By his baptism Jesus accepted John's vision of a coming judgment on the nation and his call for national repentance and a new society. As Jeremiah and Isaiah had in similar situations, John made prophetic sense out of the ruins and suffering of Sepphoris, which Jesus had seen. A continuing exploitation of the poor would lead to a judgment on the nation. Jesus would differ from John, however, in his ultimate vision of God and humanity.

Besides the ax laid at the root of the tree, John had spoken also of "one who is to come, someone mightier than I, and I am not fit to undo the strap of his sandals" (Luke 3:16). The imagery of the sandal strap is important because it indicates that John is anticipating a human being as the mightier one.[28] John continues: "He will baptize you with a holy spirit and fire. His winnowing-fan is in his hand to clear his threshing-floor and to gather the wheat into his barn; but the chaff he will burn in a fire that will never go out" (Luke 3:16-17).

The mightier one is John's warrior image of the prophet or messiah who will purge Israel and inaugurate a reign of freedom for the people. In John's preaching judgment had always been dominant, whether the judgment was to come through the Roman ax or the fire of the mightier one. The mightier one would also bear a judgment, one reason why commentators have not distinguished his coming from the symbol of the ax. When the mightier one comes, "the chaff" of the nation, those who exploit the poor, will be burned up in the river of fire. Only "the wheat," those who repent in time, can hope to survive the mightier one's terrible messianic war. For the chaff, the fire of the mightier one will be unquenchable, a violent judgment no better than what they will receive alternately (and perhaps simultaneously) from the Roman ax.

The Roman ax was to be more decisive in John's life and death than his envisioned river of fire. Josephus tells us that Rome's client-king, Herod Antipas, finally imprisoned and killed this revolutionary of the wilderness "lest the great influence John had over the people might put it into his power and inclination to raise a rebellion (for they seemed ready to do anything he should advise)."[29] In terms of systemic Roman violence, which extended to Galilee and Peraea through Herod's rule, John was a victim of Rome. John the Baptist, who proclaimed God's judgment through the Roman ax, was one of the trees of Israel cut down by it. Jesus was to be another.

We can see why John would have been puzzled, after his imprisonment by Herod, to hear that his former disciple, Jesus, was attracting great crowds and was teaching them: "Love your enemies, do good to those who hate you, bless those who curse you, pray for those who treat you badly" (Luke 6:27-28).

This was not John's understanding of the mightier one to come. Jesus, who had immersed himself before John in a rite symbolic of judgment, was proclaiming a different kind of prophetic vision. The imprisoned prophet of judgment, wondering at this turn of events, sent two of his disciples with a question to the prophet of nonviolence: "Are you the one who is to come, or must we wait for someone else?" (Luke 7:19-20; Matt. 11:3).[30]

Jesus responds with his testimony to a nonviolent coming of God: "Then he gave the messengers their answer, 'Go back and tell John what you have seen and heard: the blind see again, the lame walk, lepers are cleansed, and the deaf hear, the dead are raised to life, the Good News is proclaimed to the poor' " (Luke 7:22).

"And blessed is that person," Jesus adds, "who does not lose faith in me" (Luke 7:23) — encouraging John to accept a radically new way of understanding his "mightier one."

In short, John the Baptist seems to have anticipated the First Coming in a way similar to that with which some Christians in the nuclear age await the Second Coming: by envisioning a destructive, triumphant coming with fire and judgment. All Jesus can offer in response to such high hopes is a more humble, yet ultimately more transforming coming of God. His final words to John apply to anyone who yearns for deliverance by a mightier one: "And blessed is that person who does not lose faith in me."

What Jesus had learned from John was a prophetic response to the destruction and suffering he had seen first in Sepphoris and now saw looming ahead as a threat to the entire nation. John had faced the evils of injustice and violence in his own nation, as had the classic prophets, by proclaiming a divine judgment, one that would come from both the Roman ax and the mightier one. Jesus adopted John's penetrating truth of judgment as the contingent prophecy it was and posed a total alternative to that judgment: the nonviolent coming of God, the nonviolent transformation of Israel and the world. John was bewildered by Jesus' alternative. And so, it seems, are we.

BY WATER AND SPIRIT

In a Navy artist's sketch included in the Congressional Record in 1975, a Trident submarine was shown cutting through the shadowy depths of the sea. A plume of bubbles rose from the hull behind the conning tower, tracing the path of a missile which had just been launched. Was that the end of Moscow? Of Leningrad? The image carried an aura of absolute silence. That was my first, unforgettable image of a Trident submarine, of its possible destruction of the world as we know it, firing its missiles from the depths of the ocean.

I think of that evil Trident image (much nearer realization today, now that 12 Trident submarines have been deployed) as an anti-baptism. Trident is an immersion, but a reversal of conversion. The immersion of a Trident is an anti-baptism on behalf of us whose lifestyle and refusal to change it represents. The crew members immerse themselves with the missiles they sleep beside to become agents of our ultimate refusal of life. Their and our immersion in the ocean depths is an anti-baptism of annihilation. When they return to the surface, mission accomplished, completing the anti-baptism, they will find the silence of those depths matched by a silence across the world.

The anti-baptism of Trident is countered by the baptism of Jesus. Instead of an anti-baptism of annihilation, we can choose a transforming baptism of nonviolence, as it is represented in Jesus' immersion by the prophet John in the River Jordan. By recovering these biblical symbols whose transforming Nonviolent God has sunk beneath our consciousness, we can awaken today to a new creation.

The key with which we can unlock the meaning of Jesus' public life is the event with which it began, the experience he was given through his teacher, John the Baptist. That experience, Jesus' historic immersion in the waters of the River Jordan, has been persistently misunderstood because of its association with a Christian liturgical ceremony usually performed while holding an infant in arms over a font. Yet Jesus' immersion in the Jordan, among masses of people accepting the prophet John's call to take a new direction, has less in common with infant baptism than it does, for example, with the solidarity of those who accepted Martin Luther King's call to march on Washington.

If we want to understand Jesus at the Jordan, we can begin by picturing the mass movement that was occurring there. Both the gospels and Josephus testify to such a movement. For Mark, John's movement coincided with the entire Jewish nation: "And there went out to him all the country of Judea, and all the people of Jerusalem" (Mark 1:5). For Matthew also, the crowds baptized by John were all-encompassing, including "Jerusalem and all Judea and all the region about the Jordan" (Matt. 3:5). For Luke, those who came out to be baptized by the wilderness prophet are identified as "the multitudes" (Luke 3:7). As we saw already, according to Josephus, it was "the great influence John had over the people," and the possibility that influence raised for rebellion, which moved Herod to imprison and execute John. Even allowing for the hyperbole in Mark and Matthew, it remains clear from our sources that a great many people did go out to immerse themselves in the Jordan and to listen to John's fiery words—a popular movement which Rome's client-ruler Herod feared and treated with deadly seriousness.

Jesus' immersion in the Jordan occurred, according to Luke, in the midst of a mass baptism: "Now when all the people were baptized and when Jesus also had been baptized . . ." (Luke 3:21). When Jesus lowered his body beneath the surface of the River Jordan, he did so in the midst of dozens, perhaps even hundreds of other Jews, in an act of solidarity in response to their nation's crisis and looming judgment, as proclaimed by the prophet John. The gospels, in their accounts of this event, describe what is in essence the experience of a new creation, which Jesus would identify later as the coming of a new humanity or the kingdom of God.

The picture we are given by the evangelists combines the realism of Jesus coming up from the water with a dramatic symbolism we can hardly understand: "And when he came up out of the water, immediately he saw the heavens opened and the spirit descending upon him like a dove; and a voice came from heaven, 'Thou art my beloved son; with thee I am well pleased' " (Mark 1:10-11).

Martin Buber, with the eyes of a prophet and a scholar, has discovered a way into this symbolism in his *Two Types of Faith*. Buber begins by assuming with critics of the text that the baptism tradition is genuine, and that a saying of Jesus lies behind the symbolic picture of the spirit descending like a dove. The synoptic gospels have not preserved such a saying. But Buber discovers the trace of such a saying in an unlikely place, in one of "the enclaves of genuine tradition in St. John's Gospel,"[31] in the dialogue between Jesus and the Pharisee town-councillor Nicodemus: "I tell you must solemnly, unless one has been created anew by water and spirit, one cannot enter the kingdom of God" (John 3:5).

Buber explains Jesus' meaning, seen in the light of the Hebrew Bible. "Water and spirit," he points out, refer in the Jewish circle of ideas to the creation of the world; this Jesus evokes.

Ruach (the feminine Hebrew word for "breath," "wind," or "spirit") is said to hover above the waters in the creation story. The symbol of the Spirit of Creation is "that of a bird which, with outspread wings, hovers above its nestlings, the tips of its wings vibrating powerfully."[32] It is this Spirit, "the *ruach*, the *pneuma*, the *spiritus*, the divine breath, which experienced from the beginning in religious sensuality, blows towards the cosmos," like a stirring and enlivening wind.[33] *Ruach* has created, and according to Jesus, is creating anew, the mind of humanity with the breath of God.

Ruach becomes then the transforming power of Jesus and of all who enter the kingdom of God: "Unless one has been created anew by water and spirit, one cannot enter the kingdom of God."

The *ruach*, which in the creation story hovers above the water, is the *pneuma* which in the baptismal story descends like a dove on Jesus as he comes up from the water:

> The *pneuma*, according to the account of the baptism, flew down "like a dove" (Mark i. 10 par.), as the Babylonian Talmud (Chagiga 15a) made it hover at the beginning of the creation of the world "like a dove" above the waters.[34]

Martin Buber has brought into focus the Spirit of Jesus' baptism. What Jesus experienced then, in response to the national crisis he recognized with John, was the power of a new creation. In response to our anti-baptismal symbol of annihilation, Trident, it can be experienced again today.

THE SUFFERING SERVANT

The specific nature of Jesus' new creation emerges from its immediate identification in the baptismal tradition with the *ebed Yahweh*, the servant of God whose vocation is redemptive suffering. The voice from heaven, which accompanies the Spirit hovering over Jesus, proclaims the opening words of the first song of the servant of Yahweh:

> "Here is my servant (or son)[35] whom I uphold,
> my chosen one in whom my soul delights" (Isa. 42:1).

Whether or not Jesus actually heard such a voice, the Second Isaiah text in the baptismal tradition suggests that his fuller understanding of the new creation which he then experienced was as the suffering servant of Yahweh.

The song of Isaiah then describes the servant as one endowed with the spirit of Yahweh to bring true justice to the nations (Isa. 42:2). The way in which the servant brings true justice is, however, a sharp departure from an older messianic tradition of the king. Justice comes to the nations through this servant of Yahweh not by triumphant violence but by undeserved suffering. The songs of Second Isaiah take the theme of redemptive suffering to great depths:

> As the crowds were appalled on seeing him
> —so disfigured did he look
> that he seemed no longer human—
> so will the crowds be astonished at him,
> and kings stand speechless before him;
> for they shall see something never told
> and witness something never heard before:
> "Who could believe what we have heard,
> and to whom has the power of Yahweh been
> revealed?"

Like a sapling he grew up in front of us,
like a root in arid ground.
Without beauty, without majesty (we saw him),
no looks to attract our eyes;
a thing despised and rejected by people,
a man of sorrows and familiar with suffering,
a man to make people screen their faces;
he was despised and we took no account of him.

And yet ours were the sufferings he bore,
ours the sorrows he carried.
But we, we thought of him as someone punished,
struck by God, and brought low.
Yet he was pierced through for our faults,
crushed for our sins.
On him lies a punishment that brings us peace,
and through his wounds we are healed

(Isa. 52:14-53:5, *JB*).

When I tried two decades ago to fathom the profound meaning of these words in writing *The Nonviolent Cross*, I recognized a critical problem but missed its deeper implications. What I did understand then was:

The problem of the Servant's identity in the poems of Isaiah has centered on the question whether an individual personality or a collective one was intended by the unknown author. The problem is resolved by the interpretation of modern scholars based on the corporate personality of Israelite thought, according to which the prophet is thought to have intended the individual in whom the people are recapitulated. So far as the more divisive question goes, of the fulfillment of the Servant figure in history, Christians should be prepared to acknowledge at this point that its corporate meaning has been revealed profoundly in the continuing pilgrimage of the people who gave it birth. ... A Christian interpretation of Jesus in the light of the *ebed Yahweh* must begin by acknowledging the figure's corporate realization in the suffering history of Israel. The Judaism from which Jesus drew his developing consciousness of the *ebed Yahweh* is the Judaism which has lived out the role of the *ebed Yahweh* through the millennia of tears since then.[36]

My way of dealing in *The Nonviolent Cross* with Israel's identification with the suffering servant was simply to acknowledge it in the above statement and then go on to speak about Jesus' personal identification with the servant. But I seem to have missed the point. Jesus was a Jew, not a Christian or an individualist. He would have thought of the servant, first of all, in collective terms, as representing his people, and would only then have drawn from that collective meaning the servant's particular application to his own life. If we reflect more deeply upon that collective Jewish perspective as basic to Jesus' thinking, it adds another dimension not only to Jesus' baptism, but to the entire gospel story.

The burning issue Jesus had brought to the prophet John was the question of a systemic violence which threatened his people's survival. John's preaching and rite of baptism were the beginning of an answer. It was the stark, prophetic answer of a judgment on the nation, with hope lying in repentance, the prior acceptance of God's judgment, and a mightier one to come who would carry out the judgment and spare the repentant. In obedience to John's prophecy, Jesus immersed himself in the Jordan to pre-enact his acceptance of God's judgment.

GOD LOVES ENEMIES

To understand fully the meaning of that moment, we should reflect upon the people who provided the human context for Jesus' baptismal experience. Jesus' immersion was in a mass baptism with other Jews. Who could they have been?

We are told in Luke's gospel that the huge crowds who came to John included tax collectors (Luke 3:12). The people hated tax collectors, who exploited them ruthlessly. But John told the tax collectors, "Exact no more than your rate," and accepted them, because of their willingness to accept judgment in the rite of immersion.

We are also told by Luke that the crowds who came to John included soldiers (Luke 3:14). These were probably Jewish soldiers in Herod's service — in terms of their function, police agents who accompanied the tax collectors. They were known for intimidation and extortion, all of which John demands that they cease. Again, the soldiers were a group hated by the people, enemies of the people. But John accepted them in baptism, because they chose to repent.

Matthew adds a despised class of women to John's followers: prostitutes. These women who were exploited and shunned by their patriarchal society believed John's message, and were in turn accepted by him (Matt. 21:32).

The careful research of Charles Scobie in his book, *John the Baptist*, suggests the remarkable presence of a fourth group of people at John's baptisms, a group even more thoroughly despised and hated by the people than tax collectors, soldiers, and prostitutes: Samaritans.[37]

The mutual hatred between Samaritans and Jews had gone on for centuries. Samaritans were religious rivals to Jews. They had their own version of the Pentateuch and believed the true site of the Temple was on Mount Gerizim — claims which caused constant hostility between them and Jews. Samaria had been under the control of the Jewish nation until 63 B.C.E., when it became part of the Roman province of Syria. Samaritans regarded the change from Jewish to Roman rulers as a liberation. Samaritans were the longest-standing enemies of the Jewish people in the time of Jesus. John's gospel puts it bluntly: "Jews have no dealings with Samaritans" (John 4:9). The social reality of Samaritans and Jews as enemies lies behind the shocking revelation in Jesus' Parable of the Good Samaritan.

Charles Scobie has linked John the Baptist with Samaritans by drawing out the implications of a passage in the fourth gospel which says, "John was baptizing at Aenon near Salim, where there was plenty of water, and people were going there to be baptized" (John 3:22). Scobie locates Aenon at a village now called 'Ainun, at a site that was seven miles from the first-century town of Salim, in Samaria. Between the two is the great Wady Far'ah, where there is "a succession of springs, yielding a copious perennial stream, with flat meadows on either side, where great crowds might gather,"[38] an ideal site for John's baptizing of Samaritans.

Scobie shows strong similarities between Samaritan sects and Jewish sects (especially the Essenes, from whom John himself may have emerged) which, in spite of the conflicts between more orthodox Samaritans and Jews, would help to explain John's having had a particular mission to Samaritans. Scobie presents a convincing case that John did in fact baptize in Samaria, and that members of Samaritan sects may have already come south to be baptized by him in the Jordan.

When we add Samaritans to tax collectors, prostitutes, and soldiers in the crowds of the baptized, a striking characteristic of John's ministry begins to emerge. While John proclaimed a message of God's coming judgment and baptized the crowds in a river symbolic of fire, bitter enemies were immersing themselves side by side in the River Jordan.

To Jesus, who sought a way out of his people's total destruction, immersion in John's "river of fire" would have seemed more like immersion in a river of reconciliation.

In his baptism in the River Jordan, Jesus experienced the nonviolent coming of God in the creation of a new people. When he came up from the water, surrounded by mutual enemies who in the prophet John's presence had put aside their hatred of one another, Jesus experienced the breath of God creating a new people in the form of the suffering servant of Isaiah.

In response to Rome's power of annihilation, Jesus discovered at the heart of his people, in the deepening wisdom of the prophets, a way out which was in reality a way in. It was the way of nonviolent transformation, as first conceived by the nameless prophet of Second Isaiah in the collective Jewish experience of exile and suffering. The way of suffering, seen by Jesus in a different way in relation to God, was a way of hope. It was a new way of active suffering, which even Second Isaiah had not seen fully. Suffering the violence of Rome was to be turned around, to become a way of nonviolent change. It was to be seen not as God's punishment of the people, but as the people's being called by God for the redemption of all peoples: "I will make you the light of the nations so that my salvation may reach to the ends of the earth" (Isa. 49:6). For the people to become God's suffering servant was seen by Jesus not as passive but as active, initiated in resistance to evil as a way of overcoming evil through God's very being— Love of the Oppressor, Love of the Persecutor, Love of the Enemy as the hidden heart of Yahweh.

"Love your enemies and pray for those who persecute you; in this way you will be children of your loving God in heaven, who causes the sun to rise on bad people as well as good, and the rain to fall on honest and dishonest people alike" (Matt. 5:44-45).

One had to give way to the mystery of God and simply enter that mystery. One had to enter the new creation, the new humanity, the new reign of God.

The problem Jesus faced in the threatened destruction of his people was, above all, the problem of God. The Jewish people, Jesus recognized, were headed toward destruction in a confrontation with the Roman Empire. This was a people who understood themselves in terms of God. Jesus sought a deeper way of understanding God. To understand God more deeply was to see a new way of life for his people, a way out through a way into God. The two ways were one. To think in terms of changing the people was to think in terms of changing, by deepening, one's perception of God. It was possible to enter the mystery of God so as to see, and not simply see but experience the power of God in a new way, a way not only of liberation but of transformation.

That was the question Jesus had brought to John the Baptist. It was the question Jesus carried into his baptism in the Jordan. The question was the question of God: Could God do more than liberate the people from their enemies? Could God transform the people in a way that would transform their enemies? This was the dawning question Jesus brought to the great prophet of judgment and repentance.

Through that prophet Jesus discovered an answer, but it was only in part the prophet's answer. The answer was really God's answer, given through the prophet in ways he never knew, symbolized in the gospels by Jesus' baptism by John. It was the answer of a new creation, an active, suffering, transforming people, formed by the breath of a God who loved enemies.

I believe that people is being formed now. With each breath of God in humanity, in the nuclear age, we are being drawn into an active, compassionate response to those who may hate and exploit us, or threaten to destroy us, yet at the same time breathe with us in testimony to the creation of a new humanity. I believe God is breathing through us all in ways we have yet to discover.

The White Train carries in it the means to incinerate the world. Yet I remember White Train watcher Les Breeding's story of his encounter with the head security guard in that symbol of evil. At the moment when Les got out of his car alone at night and faced the glare of a searchlight pointed at him from the train, he heard the security guard say, "Hey, Les, is that you?" At the center of a train to hell, there is someone breathing with us all.

The guards in the White Train, the crews on Trident submarines, the thousands of missile technicians throughout the world who can plunge all of us into a river of fire, breathe with you and with me and with God. In that one breath of God is our hope of transformation.

4

THE TRANSFORMATION OF POWER

I tell you that the Third World War has already started—a silent war, not for that reason any less sinister. This war is tearing down Brazil, Latin America, and practically all of the Third World. Instead of soldiers dying there are children; instead of millions of wounded there are millions of unemployed; instead of the destruction of bridges there is the tearing down of factories, hospitals, and entire economies. It is a war by the U.S. against the Latin American continent and the Third World. It is a war over the foreign debt, one which has as its main weapon interest, a weapon more deadly than the atom bomb. . . .

Luis Ignacio da Silva,
Leader of the Brazilian Workers Party[1]

The weapon of third-world debt interest, which is squeezing life from millions of suffering people, and the weapon of nuclear annihilation suspended over the same people, are two aspects of one systemic evil. The global environmental crisis is a further dimension of the same evil.[2] It corresponds both to economic and to military casualties. The earth and its peoples are in the end both seen as expendable for the sake of immediate profits for the few.

Nuclear weapons stand as the ultimate enforcement of profit. The exploited of the world vastly outnumber the exploiters. In order to remain in power, the privileged must therefore rely on economic controls, torture and murder by police states, military intervention, and as a threatened last resort, weapons of annihilation. The Third World War, which is now being fought through interest, will some day be fought, if the exploiters find it "necessary," by nuclear explosions on the poor in the Third World—in the name of a defense against terrorism.

On January 19, 1990, at a change of command ceremony on the explosives handling wharf of the new Kings Bay, Georgia, Trident submarine base, Vice Admiral Roger F. Bacon, commander of the Navy's Atlantic Fleet Submarine Force, declared, "Trident submarines are essential as a strategic deterrent to enemy forces and *as a defense against terrorism, drug trading and other global conflicts"* (emphasis added).[3] "Strategic deterrent to enemy forces" is a Pentagon phrase that applies primarily to Soviet targets, even in a time when the U.S.S.R. has refused to act any longer as our enemy. But Vice Admiral Bacon's additional Trident targets, terrorism and drug trading, are first-world designations for a variety of third-world struggles. And "other global conflicts" widens the range of Trident missiles to the entire world, most of it in fact inhabited by the poor and suffering.

We have now witnessed the role of nuclear weapons in "other global conflicts" — as the ultimate threat against Iraq on United States warships in the Persian Gulf. In January 1991, United States military leaders felt confident in launching the Persian Gulf War partly because they held the trump card of massive nuclear forces, the final means of enforcing United States control over Middle Eastern oil fields. On the other side of the conflict, one of the economic reasons for Saddam Hussein's invasion of oil-rich Kuwait may have been to gain the resources necessary to pay off Iraq's outstanding debt of thirty to thirty-five billion dollars owed to the United States and other countries, much of it derived from Iraq's own reckless military expenditures.

If the United States should resort finally to nuclear weapons to insure the victory of "a new world order" governed by our economic interests and policed by our military forces, it would probably be against a poorer, non-nuclear country such as Iraq, presumed to be unable to retaliate against us. Thus our nuclear weapons target the world's poor, and ultimately the earth itself, for first-world economic interests. Nuclear war, like "low intensity conflict" and "police actions," would be an extension of the silent, economic war that is today devastating masses of people, especially through debt interest.

Is it possible to discover within this first-world/third-world volcano a deeper fire, one of nonviolent transformation? Can a transforming fire of hope, within the heart of humanity, be glimpsed even now through the vision and parables of a first-century prophet?

A CRY OF WARNING

> The message of Jesus is not only the proclamation of salvation, but also the announcement of judgement, a cry of warning, and a call to repentance in view of the terrible urgency of the crisis. The number of parables in this category is nothing less than awe-inspiring. Over and over again did Jesus raise his voice in warning, striving to open the eyes of a blinded people.[4]

I first read these words about the terrible urgency of the crisis in Jesus' parables while I was serving a prison sentence for responding to a modern crisis. I had been sent to the Lompoc federal prison camp in California for praying at nuclear weapons bunkers in the Bangor, Washington, Trident submarine base. The above words on the crisis Jesus responded to are from *The Parables of Jesus*, written by the great scripture scholar Joachim Jeremias—a book I studied daily as a prisoner, using it as a companion volume to the gospels. Today, when I thumb through my bible, I find beside Jesus' parables all the Jeremias notes I wrote in the margins while I was a prisoner at Lompoc. It was Joachim Jeremias especially who helped me to journey through Jesus' world while living in the world of Lompoc.

Yet I found Joachim Jeremias's words about Jesus' crisis deeply puzzling. Jeremias wrote powerfully but enigmatically about the urgent crisis running through Jesus' parables. The great scripture scholar fulfilled his promise in providing the fine details of the historical setting behind each individual parable. It is these details of interpretation which fill up the margins of my bible. But in spite of all Jeremias's references to the catastrophic crisis Jesus so urgently warned his people about in his parables, I never learned anything concrete from Jeremias about that larger crisis.

Jeremias called it "the eschatological crisis," a crisis "marked by the sudden irruption of the time of tribulation and the revelation of satanic power over the whole earth."[5] This is the kind of theological language many modern theologians besides Joachim Jeremias have used in describing Jesus' crisis—not Jesus' language of history, which was always concrete, vivid, and as Jeremias showed with respect to parable after parable, always in direct response to particular situations. I knew what Jeremias and the other theologians were talking about in their own terms: the crisis preceding the "eschaton" or "end," the end-of-the-world crisis. But what Jeremias had proven beyond doubt by his brilliant analysis of the parables—that Jesus was profoundly a man of his time and history—Jeremias then contradicted by his references to the "eschatological crisis" Jesus was supposedly talking about in so many of these parables, a crisis with no definable historical dimensions. What on earth (not in the abstractions of a modern theologian's mind) was the terribly urgent crisis in first-century Palestine that lay behind an "awe-inspiring number" of Jesus' parables? What on earth, in his own history, was Jesus talking about? What was he pleading to his people about? What was he struggling to convey through these parables of crisis, whose fine details modern theologians can explore so perceptively and exhaustively while coming up blank on their underlying purpose?

During my time in prison, as I pondered this question of Jesus' urgent but enigmatic crisis, I only vaguely connected his crisis and our own twentieth-century crisis: our crisis of nuclear weapons and global oppression of the poor, a two-sided crisis which is destroying humanity and the earth. I recognized the "end-time" connection: that Jesus was warning about a coming terrible end, and that we today are experiencing such an end. But again, Jesus' end was, in my theologically brainwashed mind, the "eschatological crisis"—an abstraction, not history. There was nothing abstract about the nuclear crisis when I stood praying in front of massive bunkers which contained Trident hydrogen bombs that could incinerate millions. Nuclear weapons were not only on the earth, but also under the earth and the sea, poised for total destruction, simply to maintain to the end of the world the profoundly evil wealth and power of a few individuals and institutions—an identifiable, historical crisis.

The nuclear crisis was even an "eschatological crisis" in that it threatened the end of history. What, then, in historical terms was Jesus' "eschatological crisis"? And how did he respond to it?

THE PRISON OF FIRST-CENTURY PALESTINE

When I think back now to my prison reflections concerning Jesus' mysterious crisis, which theologians could not explain to me, I recall also Martin Buber's retelling of the classic Hasidic tale of the place where one stands:

Rabbi Bunam used to tell young men who came to him for the first time the story of Rabbi Eizik, son of Rabbi Yekel of Cracow. After many years of great poverty which had never shaken his faith in God, he dreamed someone bade him look for a treasure in Prague, under the bridge which leads to the king's palace. When the dream recurred a third time, Rabbi Eizik prepared for the journey and set out for Prague. But the bridge was guarded day and night and he did not dare to start digging. Nevertheless he went to the bridge every morning and kept walking around it until evening. Finally the captain of the guards, who had been watching him, asked in a kindly way whether he was looking for something or waiting for somebody. Rabbi Eizik told him of the dream which had brought him here from a faraway country. The captain laughed: "And so to please the dream, you poor fellow wore out your shoes to come here! As for having faith in dreams, if I had had it, I should have had to get going when a dream once told me to go to Cracow and dig for treasure under the stove in the room of a Jew—Eizik, son of Yekel, that was the name! Eizik, son of Yekel! I can just imagine what it would be like, how I should have to try every house over there, where one half of the Jews are named Eizik and the other Yekel! And he laughed again. Rabbi Eizik bowed, travelled home, dug up the treasure from under the stove, and built the House of Prayer which is called "Reb Eizik Reb Yekel's Shul."

"Take this story to heart," Rabbi Bunam used to add, "and make what it says your own: There is something you cannot find anywhere in the world, not even at the zaddik's, and there is, nevertheless, a place where you can find it."[6]

The treasure of understanding Jesus' and his people's crisis (for they are one and the same) was to be found, as I gradually came to realize, not by traveling across the world in the minds of European theologians, but by seeing Jesus standing in the place where I stood, in prison. As a first-century Palestinian Jew, Jesus was in prison, a Roman prison about to explode. Jesus stood in that place where the wretched of the earth stand now. The crisis he experienced is the crisis experienced by hundreds of millions of colonized people who today live in prison — blacks in South Africa, students in China, peasants in Latin America *favelas*, Native Americans in reservations, Tibetan Buddhists in Tibet, Jews in the Soviet Union, Palestinians in Gaza and the West Bank . . . Jesus was in prison, as they today are in prison.

Jesus' prison, like each of these prisons, had economic, cultural, and political dimensions.[7] The land in which Jesus lived was controlled by Rome for a strategic reason. Rome's imperial strategy in the first century saw Palestine as a necessary barrier against Parthia, still a dangerous enemy to Rome, whose Tigris-Euphrates frontier was "a mere few hundred miles from Palestine, separated by a desert no one could control. If the Parthians could take Palestine, Egypt would fall into their hands."[8] Palestine was therefore a critically important area for Rome, analogous in importance to Afghanistan for the Soviet Union or Central America for the United States. The Roman Empire was not about to withdraw from Palestine, however strongly Jews felt about their freedom.

Rome exploited its Jewish subjects by heavy taxation, ranging from the standard tribute to numerous tolls collected by the local tax collectors, as seen in the gospels. A failure to render tribute to Rome was seen as rebellion. Refusal to pay taxes was, in fact, one of the decisive causes of the Jewish-Roman War.[9]

Colonialism works through the power of indigenous ruling classes. Rome made skillful use of Israel's client-kings and priestly aristocracy. Besides its own procurators, Rome appointed Herodian client-kings to rule pieces of the divided land of Palestine. From 6 to 41 C.E. the high priests of the Temple in Jerusalem were also "appointed by the representatives of the enemy and oppressor, and they could retain their position only by keeping in their good books."[10] The peasantry, who made up the great majority of the Jewish people, were thus controlled in political, economic, and cultural ways by Rome's procurators, client-kings, and the high priestly administration based in Jerusalem.

In Jesus' time much of the land in Galilee was owned by the ruler Antipas.[11] The rest was controlled increasingly by a native aristocracy of priestly families centered in Jerusalem.

A lament in the Talmud recalls the repression of the people by four of the corrupt priestly families of this time:

> Woe unto me because of the House of Boethus;
> woe unto me because of their staves!
> Woe unto me because of the House of Kadros;

> woe unto me because of their pens!
> Woe unto me because of the House of (El) Hanan;
> woe unto me because of their whisperings!
> Woe unto me because of the House of Ishmael ben
>   Phiabi;
> woe unto me because of their fists!
> For the high priests and their sons are Temple treas-
>   urers,
> and their sons-in-law are trustees;
> and their servants beat the people with staves
>   (Pes. 57a).[12]

The House of Kadros named in this first-century lament has, in a literal sense, been rediscovered recently by archaeologists. Excavations in the Old City of Jerusalem have unearthed a once-luxurious dwelling archaeologists have named "The Mansion" and have identified as belonging to the priestly family of Kadros (or Kathros) by a stone weight inscribed "Bar Kathros."[13] The luxury of "The Mansion" can be attributed to the ruinous tithes and rents these priests imposed upon the Jewish peasantry.

The Jerusalem Temple, built by Herod the Great, was the focus of both devout worship by the Jewish population and of the power of the priestly aristocracy. The Temple treasury, controlled by the priests of the families named above, tithed the annual production of a farmer by more than twenty percent. This was in addition to Roman taxation of fifteen to twenty percent making a combined total of thirty-five to forty percent of a farmer's production lost to taxation.[14]

In his political history based on the writings of Josephus, *Israel in Revolution 6-74* C.E., David M. Rhoads has pointed out that the Jewish-Roman War was both a civil and class war, as well as an anti-imperialist war:

> Most of the revolutionary groups had their origins in the ills of the lower classes among the Jews. The Sicarii at the opening of the war burned the archives in which the record of debts was kept in order to rid the records of their own debts and to encourage an uprising of the poor against the rich. The Zealot party was composed of dissident peasants from Judea and lower priests in Jerusalem who had been oppressed by the chief priests in the decade before the war. . . . The vengeance with which both the Zealots and the Idumaeans treated the Jewish aristocracy can best be understood as the expression of accumulated frustration resulting from grievances against the wealthy and traditional authorities.[15]

Given Rome's exploitation of these already existing divisions within Jewish society, it is not surprising that a Jewish war of liberation would be fought against both foreign and indigenous authorities: "The majority of revolutionaries saw the war as an opportunity not only to exclude the foreign power, but also to overthrow the traditional aristocratic Jewish government. And that is exactly what they did."[16] But the violent civil and class struggle within the Jewish nation also served to expedite the Roman victory and the destruction of Jerusalem.

The revolutionaries' immediate burning of the debt archives, which were kept by the high priests in Jerusalem, indicates a deep root of the conflict: economic exploitation of the Jewish poor by the Roman-client-kings high-priest power system. The cumulative effect of that exploitation on the farming population throughout the first century was disastrous. Small farmers were devastated by double taxation, rising debt, loans they could not repay, and eventual confiscation of their land. Large estates held by absentee landholders grew rapidly, absorbing the many family farms lost through debt.

Once the peasants had lost their family farms, their downward spiral continued as they became tenant farmers or day laborers. Besides a minimum of thirty-five percent taxation/tithe on production, a tenant farmer would have to pay twenty-five percent more to the new landowner. Any unexpected expense or a bad crop would mean another fall into debt. Farmers went from the cycle of self-subsistent family farms, increasing debt, and loss of their land to the even worse cycle of tenant-farming, further debt, and finally debt bondage for themselves and their families under the large landholders. Might not peasants in twentieth-century Mexico or Brazil see similarities between Jesus' time and their own?

Some farmers withdrew from these cycles of destruction and joined the growing number of social bandits or "brigands" in the hills.[17] There they were hunted down by the Roman authorities, who "not only took action against the brigands themselves but also intimidated and punished the villagers suspected of protecting the outlaws. The effect of such repressive violence was clearly to bring more people into opposition to the Roman-imposed order."[18] Does any of this sound strangely familiar in our world where guerrilla revolts arise from civil strife and famine? Vietnam, El Salvador, Afghanistan, Peru . . .

Under the system of double taxation, many farmers felt compelled to become "nonobservant" Jews by not paying Temple tithes. "The original reason for tithing, as given in the Torah [Num. 18:21-24], was that the Levite for whom it was levied owned no land and was entirely dedicated to divine service."[19] These offerings for cultic ministers were then ordered to be brought to Jerusalem (Deut. 12:6; 14:22; 18:1-6), "thereby increasing the economic strength of the temple clergy and impoverishing the country priests."[20] As Jerusalem priests and Levites became prominent landowners, Galilean peasants were being tithed to support the same upper-class clergy who already lived off their work on the land.[21]

Whereas Roman taxes were enforced by police power, the tithes commanded by the Torah were not. But farmers refusing to pay Temple tithes, for the sake of economic survival, experienced the inner crisis of neglecting religious duties, while they were severely judged for their apparent failure to support the Jewish social and religious world.[22]

Systematic repression on all sides built up resentment in those too fearful to protest or noncooperate. "One result of such a tightly repressive and controlled situation, which we are familiar with in second Temple Jewish society, was the sense among many people that the situation was in the control of Satan and that one's own personal disintegration was due to demonic possession."[23]

Given these complex conditions over-all, Galilee, where Jesus conducted most of his ministry, was a world sharply divided into two classes, the very (often remote) rich and the very poor, as we meet them in Jesus' parables. In the parables there are the wealthy and the impoverished: the rich man with his steward who, if dismissed, has only the alternatives of digging or begging (Luke 16:1-3); the rich man wearing purple and fine linen and Lazarus covered with sores lying at his gate (Luke 16:19-20); the prince setting off for his kingdom who entrusts to his servants only a trifling sum of money (Luke 19:13);[24] the poor woman searching her house for a single precious coin (Luke 15:8-10); the poor widow pleading with the unjust judge for her rights (Luke 18:1-5); the rich man with his great harvest who plans to build bigger barns (Luke 12:16-20). Jesus' parables are peopled, on the one hand, with kings, masters, and vineyard owners, and on the other, with tenant farmers, day laborers, and slaves.[25] Taken together, the divisions and conflicts in Jesus' parables reveal a world in crisis, on the edge of total violence.

With its legions waiting to strike if necessary, Rome ruled this world of exploiters and exploited through its Herodian client-kings (whom it gradually replaced with Roman governors) and through the priestly aristocracy it maintained in power up to the Jewish War. These collaborators and increasingly wealthy landholders tried in turn to discourage a peasant revolt, but it finally erupted in 66 C.E., which resulted in the Temple's and Jerusalem's destruction in 70.

This was the explosive political, economic, and cultural prison of the Jewish people — their concrete "eschatological crisis" — which Jesus lived in from Nazareth to Jerusalem. It is this life situation, this *Sitz im Leben* of total crisis, in which we must place his proclamation that the kingdom of God was at hand, or within one's power, if we are fully to comprehend that proclamation.

THE PARABLE OF THE GOOD ENEMY

Jesus' Parable of the Good Samaritan can more appropriately be titled "The Parable of the Good Communist" in the world of total crisis we are experiencing today. What the Parable of the Good Communist teaches us is that God breaks into our world of ultimate violence in a way that utterly transcends our expectations.[26]

Like all of Jesus' parables, the Parable of the Good Samaritan is about the kingdom of God. Every parable Jesus told gives us a new and startling suggestion of what the kingdom of God is like. The kingdom of God, like the Human Being, was a symbol Jesus used to describe the breakthrough of Love in history, in the creation of a New Humanity. A breaking in of the kingdom of God is nothing that we can reasonably expect, though we can hope for it. Jesus suggests that the kingdom's shattering breakthrough into our lives may in fact be nothing that we want.

The natural assumption of Jesus, and of those who heard his Parable of the Good Samaritan, was that the man thrown into the ditch by robbers was a Jew. Jesus' audience was composed of Jews. That meant they had nothing to do with Samaritans. As we have seen in the previous chapter, the relation between Jews and Samaritans was one of mutual hatred, which deepened understandably on the Jewish side in response to such hostile Samaritan acts in Jesus' time (reported by Josephus) as the deliberate defilement of the Temple during a Passover by the scattering of dead people's bones.[27] As one parable commentator has put it, "A Jew in the days of Jesus might rather die in a ditch, bleeding slowly to death in the cold night, than be rescued by a Samaritan."[28]

To understand Jesus' parable we have to begin, then, by realizing that the man in the ditch had a deep hatred and suspicion, nourished by his history and culture, for the man who out of compassion rescued him. Samaritans were hated enemies. Jesus is saying in his parable that the kingdom of God is like being saved from death by a hated enemy. The kingdom of God breaks into our lives in a form that we may not expect, in a form that we may in fact loath and want to destroy.

We can recall that in the chapter of Luke's gospel just before the Parable of the Good Samaritan, James and John wanted Jesus' approval to call down on a hostile Samaritan village "fire from heaven to burn them up" (Luke 9:54). But Jesus had rebuked them. Thus, in Jesus' parable, the disciples' object of hatred and destruction becomes a source of salvation.

When we understand it in Jesus' context, the Parable of the Good Samaritan initially moves us to thank God that we, at least, are not lying in a ditch where we have to be saved from death by our enemy. But that is exactly what our situation is: We can only be saved from death by our enemy, and only if we believe in that enemy and are willing to be saved by him. Our enemy has been not a Samaritan, but a Communist. We are in the ditch of nuclear death, and during a now forgotten period of our recent history, Mikhail Gorbachev was the Good Communist attempting to rescue us from that death.

In July 1985 Mikhail Gorbachev made a public commitment to halt all nuclear tests from August 6, 1985, to January 1, 1986, even if the United States continued an active nuclear test program—as in fact we did. After the time expired Gorbachev extended the Soviet Union's nuclear test moratorium three times, to a total of eighteen months. In each case the United States continued its underground tests. Gorbachev repeatedly made the further commitment *never* to test a nuclear weapon again, if the United States would cease testing. In other words, the Soviet Union unilaterally stopped its testing of new weapons and allowed the United States an eighteen month advantage and twenty-five unanswered tests, with the explicit goal of signing a comprehensive test ban treaty. In effect, Gorbachev was initiating an end to the nuclear arms race. The United States government was not, however, willing to reciprocate. As a result, the U.S.S.R. announced its resumption of testing in February 1987. Our steady drift toward annihilation continues.

The United States treaty with the Soviets to eliminate intermediate-range nuclear forces from Europe was, as a response to Gorbachev's diplomacy, a disappointing step. Only about four percent of the world's nuclear weapons were affected by the Intermediate-Range Nuclear Forces Treaty. President Bush's September 27, 1991 proposal to Gorbachev for the elimination of all multiple-warhead *land*-based missiles would retain a huge United States advantage over the Soviets at *sea* as a result of the more numerous, more accurate Trident warheads. The "modernization" of other nuclear weapons critical to a United States first-strike policy would be allowed to continue under the Bush proposal. In spite of the Good Communist's efforts to help, we have refused to leave the ditch.

As the president of a disintegrating empire, beset on all sides by growing freedom movements, Mikhail Gorbachev has on at least six occasions used tanks and lethal force against civilian dissenters, resulting in some 200 deaths: in Kazakhstan in December 1986, in Georgia in April 1989, in Uzbekistan in June 1989, in Azerbaijan in January 1990, in Tadzhikistan in February 1990, and in Lithuania in January 1991.[29] Jesus' parable assumes that the Samaritan—or in our case, the Communist—has a history and capability of violence which rightly (and righteously) preconditions our attitude towards him. Neither the Samaritan nor the Communist is a saint. On the contrary, the point of the parable is in fact the shocking reality, in our eyes, of a well-proven enemy with a violent history acting in a redemptive way toward us—and if we refuse that redemptive action, the impossibility of our being saved from our own situation. Because the rejected Good Samaritan/Communist will then revert to our worst expectations of him as our enemy and will in turn use our violence to cover his own, as in Gorbachev's repression of Lithuania in January 1991, simultaneous with President Bush's triggering of the Persian Gulf War.

We are all in need, it seems, of enemies. Our government needs them in the Middle East to justify a last stand of United States economic and military control over the world. The peace and justice movement also needs enemies. What Saddam Hussein does for the ideology of George Bush, George Bush does in turn for our ideology as activists. He offers us a target for our righteousness, a public contrast to our presumed innocence, a rationale for our projection of evil. But in the nuclear age especially, we must be saved by our enemies. George Bush must be saved by Saddam Hussein (and vice versa). Peace and justice activists must be saved by George Bush (and vice versa) and by those others whom we identify with the policies we oppose—opponents in the government, in corporations, in the military, and in the police forces which arrest us. "Love your enemies," we are told, not as an impossible demand but as a way of saving us from our righteousness and from our self-destructive, world-destructive violence.

As Jesus' parable teaches us, we cannot be rescued from the ditch in which we are lying helpless unless we are willing to accept salvation from our enemy—whether that enemy be Samaritan, Roman, Communist, Iraqi, Capitalist, or Third-World Terrorist.

Because the Cold War has ended, the United States has lost its classic Communist enemy. We also lost a series of historic opportunities to cooperate with Mikhail Gorbachev in mutual test ban and disarmament pacts. Our leaders have been quick to identify new enemies in the Third World to justify omnicidal weapons: the Iraqi forces of Saddam Hussein, and beyond them, "terrorists." Thus the Parable of the Good Communist becomes the Parable of the Good Iraqi or the Parable of the Good Terrorist. As the identity of our enemy shifts, so too does the particular human mediator of our salvation from our violence. The enemy we are given, or whom we make by our own aggression, becomes the Samaritan who alone can save us.

According to the national security study *Discriminate Deterrence*, which in 1988 formulated long-term United States military strategy, our real enemy has been, and will continue to be, in the Third World:

> In the past forty years all the wars in which the United States has been involved have occurred in the Third World. . . .
> . . . To defend its interests properly in the Third World, the United States will have to take low intensity conflict much more seriously. It is a form of warfare in which "the enemy" is more or less omnipresent and unlikely ever to surrender.[30]

Our omnipresent enemy in the Third World, "unlikely ever to surrender," is the Samaritan whom we will be taught increasingly by propaganda to fear and hate—as "terrorist." Yet that enemy "terrorist" is already performing a mission of the Good Samaritan, feeding and clothing us. The clothes we United States citizens wear, and the food we prepare in our kitchens all too often come from the ill-paid labor of third-world peoples. But those who feed and clothe us today, while living in great injustice to themselves and their families, can be expected to rise up against us tomorrow—becoming our hated Samaritans, "terrorists." The third-world "terrorists" of the future have stitched the shirts and pants we wear, have

harvested the coffee and bananas we enjoy. When those now-invisible servants of ours revolt and thus become visible "terrorists," will we see in their
revolutions the divine offer of the Good Samaritan, or Good Terrorist, to
save us from the ditch of our own injustice and violence?

When Jesus said, "Love your enemies, do good to those who hate you,
bless those who curse you, pray for those who abuse you" (Luke 6:27-28),
perhaps he was not so much giving an order as describing the nature of
salvation in the midst of a final crisis of violence parallel to our own. Only
by loving our enemies can we hope to experience a transcendent reality
breaking into the world and saving that world from total death.

In Jesus' world, the particular enmity that existed between Jews and
Samaritans was to become a major cause of the Jewish-Roman War. Samaritans and Jews attacked and counter-attacked one another, creating further
conflicts with the Roman authorities, to which both sides appealed — and
by which both were, in turn, killed and enslaved. One such incident
occurred in 51 C.E., when Jewish crowds led by bandit revolutionaries
burned Samaritan villages and slaughtered their inhabitants in retaliation
for the Samaritan killing of some Galilean Jews. Roman forces pursued the
Jews, killing and capturing many, and later crucifying the captives.[31] This
Samaritan-Jewish-Roman violence "was a turning point in the Jewish relationship with Rome, for the assertion of liberty and the direct clash with
Roman soldiers in Judea stirred up all the dissatisfied elements throughout
the countryside."[32]

But neither the destruction of Jerusalem then, nor the destruction of
the world now, had or has to happen. We can choose to love our enemy.
We can even risk being pulled by that enemy from the ditch of our own
violence.

Jesus' Parable of the Good Samaritan, like his teaching "love your enemies," confronts an impasse of total violence in his time by transforming it
into the kingdom of God. Love your enemy — a hard saying — because there
is no other salvation in an age of violence than the God who comes to us
through our enemies, the God of Nonviolent Transformation. The end of
the world is transformed into the beginning of a new world by accepting
the truth of my enemy.

THE LEAVEN

How, then, does one tell a story of transformation? Jesus did it simply
in his Parable of the Leaven: "To what shall I compare the kingdom of
God? It is like leaven which a woman took and hid in three measures of
flour, till it was all leavened" (Luke 13:20-21; par. Matt. 13:33).

To those who first heard Jesus' parable, leaven was a symbol of moral
corruption. "In the view of all antiquity, Semitic and non-Semitic, panary
fermentation represented a process of corruption and putrefaction in the
mass of dough."[33] Another commentator adds: "The physical characteristics

of leaven support the metaphor for corrupting. Leaven is made by taking a piece of bread and storing it in a damp, dark place until mold forms. The bread rots and decays, unlike modern yeast, which is domesticated."[34]

In Exodus leaven symbolizes the unholy (Exod. 12:19). It was banned from every household during the holy season of Passover (Exod. 12:15-16). For Paul, leaven is the morally corrupt. He twice cites a proverb, "A little leaven leavens the whole lump" (Gal. 5:9; 1 Cor. 5:6-8) whose meaning by his application is the same as our own, "One rotten apple spoils the whole barrel." A little leaven will corrupt the whole. Following the same proverbial understanding of leaven as corruption, Jesus warns of the leaven of the Pharisees and of Herod (Mark 8:15).

Jesus' Parable of the Leaven assumes this identification of leaven with moral corruption. It also assumes we know that three measures are an immense quantity of flour, enough to make a meal for over one hundred people.[35] The poor social status of the character of Jesus' parable, a woman, further subverts the sense of the kingdom of God, turning the kingdom upside down — as does her furtive action: She *hides* the corrupt leaven in the mass of flour. In each of its components, Jesus' parable is subversive to his and our societies. It tells us that a tiny, corrupt substance, hidden in the flour by a woman, accomplished an unseen, massive transformation. Like the kingdom of God.

My parable of transformation is about a series of events which occurred in Rome at the periphery of the Second Vatican Council (1962-65), while the bishops of the Catholic Church struggled with the question of nuclear war. The story begins, however, not in Rome but five years earlier in New York and California. It begins with a leaven, Dorothy Day and the Catholic Worker movement, which an English professor hid in the lives of his students.

The introduction of the leaven in my life took place, unknown to Dorothy Day, in a classroom at Santa Clara University in 1957. Dorothy had become a leaven for the nation in New York City by remaining in a park with twenty-eight friends while millions of other New Yorkers took shelter in basements and subways from an hypothetical hydrogen bomb during a compulsory civil defense drill. The twenty-nine people in the park were, as in Jesus' parable, a tiny, corrupt substance in the consciousness of the nation. They also accomplished a massive transformation, growing in number and stopping the annual civil defense drill in three years.

For her particular act of noncooperation with nuclear war, Dorothy Day went to jail. *Commonweal* published an article on why she did so. I read the article at Santa Clara because my English professor, Herbert Burke, had passed it out to our class. I recall Dr. Burke leaning back against the blackboard, a question mark of a professor, observing us over his glasses as we finished reading the subversive article.

He soon learned that the leaven had been uniformly rejected. All of his students thought Dorothy Day was crazy. We suspected that our slyly ques-

tioning professor thought differently, as he reintroduced the leaven in
Socratic fashion back into our lives.

Looking back now, three decades later, I remember that spring at Santa
Clara as one long meditation on Dorothy Day, her friends in the park, and
the world's threatened destruction by nuclear war. I began reading Dorothy
Day's newspaper, *The Catholic Worker*. There I discovered that resisting
nuclear war preparations was for the Catholic Worker movement all of a
piece with feeding the hungry, sheltering the homeless, and resisting every
kind of injustice. All of it was building a new society, the kingdom of God,
within the shell of the old. Jesus' vision of God's kingdom is why Dorothy
Day had gone to the park and to jail.

My thoughts took a new direction: How could one believe in the kingdom
of God and not respond to the threat of the world's destruction?

But the leaven in my story is not only Dorothy Day. It is also a philosopher of nuclear war, my Santa Clara ethics professor, Father Austin
Fagothey.

In a sense, Father Fagothey was truer to Jesus' Parable of the Leaven
than Dorothy Day was. By converting me to her vision, Dorothy had become
a holy burr in my conscience, prickly but saintly. Father Fagothey's thinking
on nuclear war was, on the other hand, a blasphemy. It was alien, unholy,
transforming — a true leaven. Nuclear war was my enemy, and Father
Fagothey as my ethics professor justified it with a serene logic. By teaching
me skillfully an idea I hated (and still do), Father Fagothey provoked me
into thinking it through.

Is the kingdom of God my enemy's truth?

Father Fagothey taught courses on ethics and the history of philosophy.
He was a small Jesuit priest in his late 50s, with the mental ability to abstract
the essence of every philosopher in history and set them all down in a series
of propositions our class could remember. The history of philosophy was a
marvelous march of Father Fagothey's diagrams and propositions across
our blackboard. Besides the power of abstraction, Father Fagothey had a
knack for comic relief. In the middle of a lecture he would sometimes pause
with intensity and cross his eyes at the class. He also had a photographic
memory. He took roll at the start of each class by scanning the rows of
students before him and jotting down the names he carried in his head that
corresponded to the vacant seats. Father Fagothey's mind seemed to have
the world under control.

It was in his ethics course that we came into conflict. The course was
based on *Right and Reason*, the ethics textbook Father Fagothey had written; the book was used at many Catholic universities. In light of the just-
war doctrine formulated by Augustine and Aquinas, Father Fagothey had
in *Right and Reason* begun to develop a concept of total war that would
justify the massive use of nuclear weapons. It rested (I thought, untenably)
on the assumption of an enemy nation so militarizing its society that it
would lose "all right to a distinction between military and non-military

objectives."[36] Father Fagothey's language was cautious and clinical, but what it aroused in my mind, thanks to Dorothy Day, was the vision of a total evil chosen by ourselves: the death and suffering of entire societies, if not of the world. Father Fagothey and I were destined to spend years of our lives struggling on opposite sides of his concept of a just total war, an idea he would develop at length as a revision of traditional moral restraints upon war.

Pushed on different levels by Dorothy Day and Austin Fagothey, I wrote an article for *The Catholic Worker* and the Santa Clara literary magazine, using the just-war conditions Father Fagothey had helped me understand, to make a case for nuclear pacifism. Father Fagothey responded with a critique of my article, which also appeared in the literary magazine. Perhaps pushed further by my continuing criticisms, he developed his just nuclear war position in a public lecture at Santa Clara. I raised critical questions from the audience. Our extended debate ceased when I graduated from Santa Clara. Thanks to the fellowships Father Fagothey had recommended me for, I moved on to graduate school. We parted as friends in conflict. I had come to respect him deeply but rejected with all my heart and mind his thinking on nuclear war.

After two years of graduate studies I moved to Rome to study the theology of war and peace at the Gregorian University, one of the oldest Catholic institutions in the world. My family and I arrived in Rome in September 1962, at the same time as twenty-three hundred bishops from all over the world for the opening of the Second Vatican Council, which would eventually take up the same question as my focus of study.

One day between classes at the Gregorian, I was startled to run into Father Fagothey. What, I asked, was he doing there? Father Fagothey explained that he had come to Rome at a late stage in his career to get a doctorate in theology. (He already had one in philosophy.) My friend looked at me with the ever-present gleam in his eye. He would be doing his dissertation, he said, on a topic that would interest me: the justification of total nuclear war in Catholic teaching.

I was stunned. I managed to ask if he would share his research with me. Father Fagothey said he would be glad to.

What I began to understand through his developing dissertation was that Father Fagothey had a piece of the truth. He had been honest enough to recognize that a limited nuclear war was a contradiction in terms. Yet it was precisely this abstraction of a strictly limited nuclear war that the United States Catholic church's foremost ethicist, Father John Courtney Murray, had used to justify nuclear weapons during the Kennedy era. The argument for limited nuclear war, as made on strategic grounds by Henry Kissinger, was also taken up and developed by Defense Secretary Robert McNamara into a "surgical strike" (first strike) doctrine that every subsequent administration has further refined. Today its prime example is Trident.[37]

But Father Fagothey looked at Father Murray's "limited nuclear war" and rejected it. The idea was a fantasy. Yet since, like Murray, he could see no alternative to a Communist takeover except nuclear deterrence, Father Fagothey decided in his logical fashion to justify *total* nuclear war.

The case he argued at the Gregorian was possible because of the vacuum left by the ambiguities of papal statements on modern war. Father Fagothey thought no pope or church council had ever been definitive enough in statements against total war to rule out its admissibility in Catholic teaching. Thus he could introduce total war in its ultimate, nuclear form as a reality he thought implicit in the just-war doctrine. Father Fagothey's dissertation advisor approved this proposal.

What alarmed me most about Father Fagothey's new project in Rome was that he was no longer presenting his case to Santa Clara students. Now his audience was the most prestigious Catholic theological faculty in the world, one which the Vatican drew upon for its teaching. To sacrifice the distinction between combatants and civilians to a total war necessity, as Father Fagothey proposed doing, was to break through the just-war doctrine's (and the church's) strongest ethical barrier to nuclear war. Father Fagothey had the mind and credentials for such a project. Now he also had the situation in Rome where he could effectively change the Catholic church's teaching on war to the point of sanctioning the destruction of humanity. I thought my friend had become one of the most dangerous people on earth.

After a year's work at the Gregorian, Father Fagothey returned to Santa Clara to finish writing his dissertation, which he then hoped to have published in the United States—another chilling thought in terms of its possible consequences.

Helped by Austin Fagothey's insights into the contradictions and ambiguities of Catholic thought on war, I committed my life in Rome for the duration of the Council to a project opposite to his: a lobbying effort to encourage the Council fathers to make that definitive Catholic condemnation of total war that Father Fagothey had perceived was lacking.

The next two years in Rome, 1963-65, were filled with grace. A series of extraordinary pilgrims created the "peace lobby" at the Vatican Council; among them Eileen Egan, Jean and Hildegard Goss-Mayr, Gordon Zahn, Dick Carbray, Thomas Merton (in his correspondence with bishops), Daniel Berrigan, William J. Nagle, Lanza del Vasto, Hermene and Joe Evans, and Dorothy Day herself. Dorothy came twice to Rome, once on a pilgrimage to Pope John XXIII and again in the final session of the Council to fast with other women as a personal appeal to the church fathers for a strong statement on war and peace.

The ten-day fast of the twenty women in Rome in October 1965 was, I believe, the most profoundly transforming leaven of the final session of the Vatican Council, when the bishops concluded their deliberations on war and peace. The women's fast, and Dorothy Day's in particular, went to the heart of the total war question: the hunger of the world's destitute beneath the waste and terror of the arms race. Dorothy wrote: "I had offered my fast in part for the victims of famine all over the world, and it seemed to me that I had very special pains. . . . [They] seemed to reach into my very bones, and I could only feel that I had been given some little intimation of the hunger of the world."[38]

Moved again by Dorothy Day and Austin Fagothey, but now with the unique situation of living in Rome, in 1963-65 I spoke with every bishop who would listen to a young lay theology student obsessed with the idea that the Council must condemn total war and support the right of conscientious objection. I circulated a document to that effect, influenced by the counter insights of an old professor of mine. Several bishops used it as a basis for their speeches at the Council urging that the church take a clear stand against total war.[39]

In December 1965, nearing its conclusion, the Second Vatican Council issued the only condemnation during its four sessions on any subject, a definitive condemnation of total war.

"Any act of war aimed indiscriminately at the destruction of entire cities or of extensive areas along with their population is a crime against God and humanity itself. It merits unequivocal and unhesitating condemnation" (*The Pastoral Constitution on the Church in the Modern World, Gaudium et Spes*, promulgated December 7, 1965).

Twenty-two years later, in the fall of 1987, I spent a morning at the archives of the Jesuit Center in Los Gatos, California, reading the letters and papers of Father Fagothey, who died in 1975. In the span of years between the Vatican Council's declaration and Father Fagothey's death, we had seen each other on only one occasion, at the scene of our old debates, when I was invited back to Santa Clara to give a talk on nonviolence.

We had sat next to each other at dinner, but with the press of conversation from other friends, we had little opportunity to talk together. I did ask Father Fagothey what had become of his dissertation. He said only that he had not been able to complete the project.

Reading through his correspondence with his dissertation advisor twelve years after Father Fagothey's death, I could see the frustrations of an extraordinary mind confronted by the changing tide on peace of a church he thought he understood. The advisor finally told Father Fagothey to forget the idea of ever having his dissertation on total war approved for a doctorate in theology at the Gregorian University. He suggested instead using his material for a book and trying to find a publisher in the United States.

Other letters revealed that Father Fagothey's proposal for such a book was seriously considered for several months by a leading United States Catholic publisher. The editor finally wrote back a rejection in the fall of 1965, explaining that between the completion of Father Fagothey's research and the present time "there have been some notable shifts in the thinking of the Church on almost every level on the moral implications of total war."[40]

Reading that sentence, I thought first of Pope John's encyclical *Pacem in Terris*, the most revolutionary source of change, a leaven coming from the papacy itself. I thought, too, of the man who wrote the letter rejecting Father Fagothey's book, Philip Scharper, then editor of Sheed and Ward, soon to be a founder of Orbis Books and instrumental before his death in 1984 in bringing a wave of liberation theology to the United States, another "notable shift in the thinking of the Church." Philip Scharper had also been one of the pilgrims among the "peace lobby" in Rome, helping to create the Council's condemnation of total war and support of conscientious objection.

And for the rest of that day, and on many days since then, I thought of Austin Fagothey, who had spent many of his days arguing a counter position to those changes . . . and thereby helped create them. Through the "clarification of thought" he brought about in the peace lobby, as Dorothy Day liked to say of illuminating conflicts, Father Fagothey had been a leaven in the leaven.

Gandhi was once confronted by a government official who questioned his belief in the power of truth. Their dialogue is a simple revelation of what I also learned from Father Fagothey:

Official: "However honestly a person may strive in the search for truth, that person's notions of truth may be different from the notions of others. Who then is to determine the truth?"
Gandhi: "The individual would determine that."
Official: "Different individuals would have different views as to truth. Would that not lead to confusion?"
Gandhi: "I do not think so."[41]

The purity of Gandhi's response to the skeptical government official has echoed in my heart for years. However different our paths may be, the truth is one. Each of us has a piece of the truth. Those pieces can and will eventually come together in a deeper unity. The power of truth and love, acting together, will see to that.

Father Fagothey pursued a truth that I believed profoundly wrong in the effect it might have upon the world. I thought it a profound corruption of theology and ethics, a leaven which could further corrupt a church, a society, and a world. He thought the truth I was pursuing was equally misguided in its implications for humanity. Thus we struggled. But in spite of our blindness to the redemptive dimensions of the other's truth, God had introduced another factor between us: friendship and respect. As we struggled, the apparently conflicting truths deepened and in a more unified way reached the lives of others.

In the course of writing this story I have continued to debate internally with Father Fagothey. He is still my teacher, friend, and opponent — still the leaven.

PARABLES THAT TRANSFORM POWER

Jesus' parables are keys for opening a people's prison into the kingdom of God.

When an entire people comes to realize that it is living in a prison, as Jesus' people did, it cannot collectively engineer a secret escape. To break free collectively, the mass of prisoners would have to overwhelm their jailers by show of superior force. A prison rebellion may achieve a short-term success, as the rebellious Jewish nation did from 66 to 70. But prison authorities can always call on massive reinforcements from outside the walls, as the Romans did in finally destroying Jerusalem in 70.

Jesus recognized that any semblance of "successful" violence against Rome would lead to another Sepphoris: "All who take the sword will perish by the sword" (Matt. 26:52).[42] His Parable of the Tenants (Mark 12:1-12; par. Matt. 21:33-46, Luke 20:9-19) reflects his understanding of the deep enmity between landlord and tenants, "the logical outcome of which is the readiness on the part of the latter to kill the proprietor's heir and to take over his property. From this situation to the events of 66-70 a direct line can be drawn."[43]

We have seen Jesus' awareness, in the tradition of the prophets and of John the Baptist, that the Roman ax through a divine judgment would certainly fall on the nation unless it could overcome the violent injustices within its own people. And he sought a nonviolent way for responding to this terrible crisis: his proclamation of God's transforming kingdom.

Because their prison system was controlled imperially by Rome, and locally by a client-king and absentee landlords, the exploited people of the Galilean countryside supposed the keys to open their prison lay remote from them. The keys to their prison seemed like the treasure in Rabbi Eizik's dream in the Hasidic tale Martin Buber told: a treasure remote from the dreamer, a treasure distant from Galilean peasants.

Jesus discovered that treasure in his own hands and in the hands of the poor. He told the poor that the key to freedom, which he called the kingdom of God, was at hand, within their power. Their freedom was not dependent on decisions made by others in Rome or Jerusalem, or dependent on their killing such decision-makers, killings sure to bring retaliatory killings. Liberation was, like Rabbi Eizik's real treasure, a treasure waiting to be discovered on the land where they lived, the ground of Galilee. It was in fact even nearer than that. Liberation was in their very hands. Liberation was to come through their own transformation.

In the Parable of the Good Samaritan Jesus transformed a violent perception of the hated Samaritan into a symbol of the kingdom of God. Those who first heard his parable were shocked by its profane comparison. When an enemy race is portrayed as a symbol of the divine, the subterranean sources of power in the psyche are being radically challenged. In such a comparison the psychic roots of injustice are transformed by shock and reversal. In other parables as well Jesus transformed the assumptions of power by reversing the accepted roles of symbolic characters.

In the Parable of the Lost Sheep, a shepherd, a member of a socially outcast group, risks everything he has, his ninety-nine sheep, for the sake of a single, lost sheep. By doing so he becomes a comparison to God (Matt. 18:12-14; Luke 15:4-7); the God present in each of us, including the outcast (the shepherd), is enlivened by the risk of everything for the one lost being (sheep or human). Jesus lived out his Parable of the Lost Sheep by his daily association with many of the outcast, women, tax collectors, sinners, and the shunned.[44] Translated into our context, the Parable of the Lost Sheep might read: The kingdom of God is like one prisoner taking the place of another on the way to the electric chair.

In Jesus' Parable of the Pharisee and the Publican (Luke 18:10-14), two men, a revered religious leader and a notorious sinner, have gone up to the Temple to pray. There they have their status reversed by God's response to their prayers. A sense of the parable's first impact might be gained by imagining a Catholic priest saying from his pulpit, "A pope and a pimp went into St. Peter's to pray."[45]

In the Parable of the Unjust Judge (Luke 18:2-8), "a complacent and fearless judge is pummeled like a faltering boxer"[46] by a presumably powerless widow fighting for her subsistence rights. A friend remarks, "Surely the widow's complaint is the same as that of those whose adversary is hunger and the system which perpetuates it."[47] Against all expectations about the dominance of power the persistent widow prevails — as does, Jesus teaches, the God present in all of the world's struggling poor. "Blessed are you poor, for yours is the kingdom of God" (Luke 6:20).

Given the context of a patriarchal society, the father in the Parable of the Prodigal Son acts like nothing so much as a mother. With a totally forgiving love he runs joyfully to embrace a son who has disowned him and dissipated his property. "In oriental culture the idea of the *paterfamilias* (i.e., male head of the house) running for any reason would occasion ludicrous shock."[48] This non-patriarchal patriarch shocks Jesus' listeners a second time when he leaves the celebration being given for the returned, younger son and humbles himself before the angry, older son by begging him to join them. "The father combines in himself the maternal and paternal roles. As a father he is a failure, but as a mother he is a success. It is his forgiving, nourishing character that has entranced generations of hearers and readers."[49]

The teller of this parable is suggesting beneath its surface that a divine *Abba* ("Papa") has the tender, compassionate love of a divine *Ima* ("Mama"). Thus the nuances of Jesus' teaching, from love of enemies to parables of compassion, bring us to understand that the prayer he taught the disciples began, in essence, *"Abba-Ima"* ("Papa-Mama"). What profound effect would have followed had the church recognized from the very beginning this dimension of Jesus' teaching, by expressing the first line of the Lord's Prayer as "Our *Abba-Ima* who is in heaven"?

The transformation of power, both human and divine, is a basic theme running through Jesus' parables. Because the nature of power can be transformed by a people realizing its own divine power, in the replacement of violent attitudes and injustices with the kingdom of God, the military power of Rome was irrelevant to Jewish freedom. Nonviolent liberation was in the hands of the Jewish people. Today nonviolent liberation is in the hands of every people.

This is the meaning of that bedrock text of the Jesus tradition, Luke 17:20-21: "The kingdom of God is not coming with signs to be observed; nor will they say, 'Lo, here it is!' or 'There!' for behold, the kingdom of God is within your power [*entos humōn*]."

In the first place, Jesus rejected any false, prophetic claims to predict by signs when the kingdom of God would come, coming presumably to overwhelm the Romans and free the Jewish nation. Seeking signs of foreordained futures and victories was "an effort to manipulate God's open future."[50]

Moreover, the kingdom of God is not simply "within" or "among" you, common translations for *entos*. From a study of classic Greek and Patristic parallels to the Lucan *entos*, Colin Roberts concludes:

> [The kingdom of God] is with you, in your possession, if you want it, now. ... It is a present reality, but only if you wish it to be so. The misconception to be removed is that the Kingdom is something external to people, independent of their volitions and actions; it is a conditional possession.[51]

For Jesus, the kingdom of God encompassed both "within you" and "among you," but in a far more comprehensive grasp of liberation or better, transformation, than either of these understandings allowed. What Jesus proclaimed to oppressed Galilean peasants was that the kingdom of God is *"within your power,"* a divine power that is both within and among humanity.[52] What he said, and practiced, was that the power of freedom for all the people in that Roman prison was in their very hands, if they could only realize its divine presence. The alternative to that realization was destruction.

THE PARABLE OF THE UNMERCIFUL NATION

Transposing Jesus' Parable of the Unmerciful Servant (Matt. 18:23-35) into our time produces the following reading:

Compare the kingdom of God to a financial lord who wished to settle accounts with his debtor nations. When he began the reckoning, they brought to him one who was the president of a nation that owed him three trillion dollars, the United States. And as the nation could not pay, the lord ordered that austerity measures be adopted by its government. Henceforth all government services were to be cancelled, millions of employees were to be dismissed, and all health, welfare, and social security payments were to be suspended until the United States debt was paid. Every available resource was to go toward mounting debt-service payments.

So the president of the United States fell on his knees before the financial lord, imploring him, "Lord, have patience with us, and we will pay you everything." And out of pity for him and his people, the lord of that president released him and forgave him the debt.

But that same president, as he went out, came upon the president of a small African country that owed the United States 100 million dollars; seizing him by the lapel, he said, "Pay what you owe." So his fellow president fell to his knees and besought him, "Have patience with us, and we will pay you everything." He refused and his economic advisors forced austerity measures on the African country, whose people died of malnutrition while their own resources were used up to service the debt.

When the presidents of other debtor countries saw what had taken place, because of their great distress they were moved to solidarity. And they went and reported to the financial lord all that had happened and their resolve to stand together: "We shall not pay our foreign debt with the hunger of our people."[53]

Then the lord summoned the United States president and said to him, "You stupid man, I forgave you and your people all that debt because you besought me; and should not you have had mercy on your fellow president, as I had mercy on you? And look what you have done now! Those nations are in solidarity, and all of us who have held them in debt will be ruined!" And in anger his lord delivered him and his nation to austerity measures and a great depression, and both president and lord then fell from wealth and power.[54]

The world's largest debtor is not Brazil. Nor is it any of the other third-world countries whose people are being starved by the austerity measures imposed by the International Monetary Fund. The greatest debtor in history is the militarily most powerful nation in history, the United States. These two characteristics, military might and trillion-dollar debt, go together. It is no accident that during its two trillion dollar military buildup of the 1980s, the United States added a corresponding two trillion dollars to its federal debt.

So far, the United States has been a uniquely privileged debtor. Its privileged status derives from a meeting in July 1944 at Bretton Woods, New Hampshire, attended by delegates from forty-four of the world's nations. The purpose of the Bretton Woods meeting was to agree on mechanisms for normalizing post-war international economic relations. It set up the International Monetary Fund (IMF) and the International Bank for Reconstruction and Development (the World Bank), both with the avowed purpose of assisting "developing countries." Voting rights in the IMF and the World Bank were allocated, however, in proportion to the financial strength of the member states. Thus, from the beginning the third-world nations were excluded from any real influence upon these institutions, ostensibly set up for their benefit in the international economic order.

The United States, on the other hand, in addition to being given a dominant voting power, gained a unique privilege. Rather than adopting a neutral international currency, the Bretton Woods meeting chose to let the U.S. dollar remain the only currency used worldwide. Other currencies were to be pegged at a fixed exchange rate to the dollar. As a result of the dollar's privileged status, the United States has benefitted from not only a domestic demand for U.S. currency but a large international demand as well. We are thereby freer than other countries to print more money, which can then be absorbed in the international demand for it. This is one way in which the United States can transfer its huge budget deficit to the rest of the world, so long as our wealthy clients keep taking dollars. The main source of this deficit has been military spending, carried out to protect the same economic privilege that is expressed in the deficit and is embodied in the economic system behind it.

In *Bad Samaritans: First World Ethics and Third World Debt* Paul Vallely sums up this mammoth structure of evil:

> Through [its budget deficit] the United States has been living beyond its means and sending the bill to the rest of the world. Much of the burden has fallen on that billion people who spend part, if not the whole, of each year in hunger.
>
> It is, in truth, the United States which needs more than any other nation, a rigorous programme of adjustment. It is because of the gigantic budget deficit—which is twice the size of the entire debt of all Third World nations put together—that the United States has had to keep interest rates so high, to attract in the money it needs to finance the deficit. It is borrowing to consume.[55]

In the debt war being waged against the Third World, the main weapon is interest, whose rates are controlled in the first world. A critical connection exists between the interest rates set by the United States to finance its own deficit from military spending and the interest rates on third-world debt. To see that connection, we need to respond to two prior questions.[56]

To whom exactly is our inconceivably high debt owed?

The $3.1 trillion gross federal debt for 1990 derives from two sources:

1) The smaller part of the debt, $822.4 billion, has come from borrowing

out of other government reserves, such as the Social Security and unemployment trust funds. The government is borrowing here from our children's future. These debt-depleted government funds are becoming incapable of meeting the human needs for which they were created.

2) The larger part of our debt, $2,285.8 billion, has been run up by borrowing from banks, large corporations, investment firms, foreign governments, and extremely wealthy people. Affluent institutions and individuals have purchased U.S. Treasury bonds because they yield high interest rates and have virtually zero risk. To borrow the billions for the debt, the United States government must offer a higher interest rate to such investors. In 1990 alone, the interest being paid by United States taxpayers to these already well-heeled creditors of our federal debt amounted to $170 billion, the third largest item in the budget, following only defense and Social Security.

As each federal deficit pushes higher, so does our debt and the annual interest we are paying on it. Economists warn of a clock ticking ever more ominously toward a day of reckoning.

Why are our political leaders committed to such a self-destructive economic policy?

An already disastrous United States debt continues to grow so that the government can pay for the military power required to enforce the unfair trade practices which U.S.-based corporations enjoy over third-world nations. Hundreds of millions of people cannot be expected to starve voluntarily while watching less numerous neighbors in the United States, Europe, and Japan thrive on produce and products from the former's fields and labor. The privileged need their trillion-dollar sword to defend a banquet in the midst of austerity. Thus United States citizens, many of them poor themselves, hear a constant drumbeat from their more privileged leaders for the need to remain strong in the world, at a cost of two trillion dollars for the military during the Reagan presidency alone, sending the country two trillion dollars further into debt.

To finance the military power needed to protect trade privileges, the United States government has come to rely heavily on foreign creditors in Japan and Germany—who themselves enjoy similar privileges over the poor and are therefore also in need of United States military protection. As the United States Treasury Department has increased the interest rates on its bonds to draw such investment, third-world countries in debt to the first world have been subjected to a corresponding rise in the floating interest rates on their already unpayable debts. It is, then, the annual third-world nations' servicing of their debts, at ever-increasing rates, derived ultimately from the United States government's need to finance military power over the very same nations, which in turn causes millions at the bottom of this vicious circle to suffer and die under tightening austerity measures. Thus the upper classes of one nation, along with its economic allies and client elites, have been able to exploit, bill, and kill the poor of the world.

The Parable of the Unmerciful Servant shows that transformation is both possible and necessary. The "just payment" and "fiscal responsibility" that our government now demands of exploited debtor nations will eventually be demanded of the greatest debtor of all, the United States, at inconceivable human cost. On the other hand, the economic privilege that our nation has enjoyed beyond any possible justification can be used redemptively to transform us to the point of forgiving our debtors, as we have been forgiven in abundance. Privilege can be transformed nonviolently into mercy and a just economic order. The alternative in history to choosing forgiveness, mercy, and real justice is graphically portrayed in the original parable's conclusion. The unforgiving debtor is tortured. A literal translation of the Greek text reads: "And in anger his lord delivered him to the torturers [not jailers as it is often euphemistically translated], till he should pay all his debt" (Matt. 18:34).[57]

The parables of Jesus reflect the same historical realism as do his prophecies: a choice between nonviolent transformation and a future of torture for ourselves and our children. What we sow we reap.

"FORGIVE US OUR DEBTS"

At the heart of Jesus' teaching stands the central petition of the Lord's Prayer, spoken every day by millions of Christians to their God,

> "And forgive us our debts,
> As we also have forgiven our debtors"
> (Matt. 6:12; par. Luke 11:4).

Norman Perrin reminds us that "no saying in the tradition has a higher claim to authenticity than this petition, nor is any saying more important to an understanding of the teaching of Jesus."[58] These words of Jesus are, indeed, among the best-known phrases in the English language, as are their equivalents in other languages. It is baffling, therefore, to find that so little attention has been paid to what they say and mean.

To debt-ridden, debt-impoverished Galilean peasants of the first century, the words "forgive us our debts, as we also have forgiven our debtors" meant "forgive us our debts, as we also have forgiven our debtors." Jeremias and Perrin have shown that the Aramaic word, *hobā*, behind the gospel text means "debt/sin," suggesting there is a word play on the double meaning of the term, as Jesus spoke it.[59] In a desperate Galilean countryside besieged by debt, the term *debt* was understood by Jesus' audience first in the root meaning of the word. Deepening debt was experienced by the farming poor every day of their lives. To farmers economically enslaved by debt, praying to God for relief meant just that: forgiveness and cancellation of all debts, in a situation that was culturally attributed to their sins (the other sense of *hobā*). In Jesus' prayer the Galilean poor were begging God for their survival through a divinely initiated debt revolution, a forgiveness and cancellation of all their sinful debts and debt-ridden sins. "Forgive us our debts" was the plea of Galilean peasants to God for that miracle that would allow them and their families to survive.

As we have already seen, it was double taxation under the Roman high priest system which drove the Jewish peasants into debt: at least fifteen to twenty percent to Rome; twenty percent to the Temple, much further enriching the priestly owners of the land the peasants worked. The double burden was an economic impossibility for most peasants. Antipas' soldiers physically enforced the empire's taxes. The Temple authorities enforced their tithes through religious and social pressures. The priestly sanctions worked in terms of sin: Not to pay the Temple tithes was to become a "nonobservant" Jew, a sinner in the eyes of that society and presumably in the eyes of God.

The prayer Jesus taught the people was a prayer to a God who forgave any debt-sins incurred by farmers unable to pay their Temple tithes. The prayer meant forgiveness of an economically crippling, religious duty: Forgive us our Temple-tithe debts which we owe to you, as we in turn forgive our debtors. And this was a prayer of revolutionary forgiveness. Thus, Jesus' *Abba* who is *Ima*, out of justice and compassion, released the Jewish peasants from an unbearable religious and economic burden. They in turn were to release any brother or sister Jews who bore debt burdens toward them. As we saw, Jesus emphasized this reciprocity in his Parable of the Unmerciful Servant, where a king—or our modern equivalent, a financial lord— cancels his servant's huge debt but is dismayed at the servant's refusal to cancel a small debt owed him by a fellow servant. The forgiveness embodied in the revolutionary debt prayer was to pass from God down through the greatest to the smallest debt-burdened members of the society, releasing everyone from economic bondage.

Jesus taught the day laborers of the Galilean countryside, stripped of their land, to rely on God within their midst for that daily bread which their land would no longer provide: "Give us this day our daily bread." A widening communal sharing would be the means of God's Providence: "And I tell you, Ask, and it will be given you; seek and you will find; knock, and it will be opened to you" (Luke 11:9). For that "knocking" prayer to be answered in Galilee, peasant families had to open real doors to one another's hunger and thereby experience God's multiplication of their loaves: "Give us this day our daily bread." Jesus' kingdom of God was within the power of poor Galileans, because it was an upside-down kingdom[60] in which power resided not on a distant throne but in the loving care of one's own divinely empowered community—as in the self-subsistent village communities of Gandhi's nonviolent revolution in India.

Is that upside-down kingdom being created today?

In her analysis of the debt crisis, *Dialogue on Debt*, George Ann Potter observes:

Throughout the Third World, a silent revolution is taking place as poor and working class people drop out of the market economy. They are abandoning the capitalist system that has forsaken them and creating what has come to be known as the "informal sector." In cities throughout Asia, Africa and Latin America, where formal unemployment is endemic, street vendors and home based micro-enterprises are proliferating everywhere. Self-subsistence rural agriculture, producing barely enough for one's own family and perhaps marginally more with which to barter for non-locally produced necessities, is increasing. Community-organized soup kitchens and even alternative health care services are partly filling the gaps created by IMF-created, Third World government austerity programs.[61]

"The kingdom of God is within your power" (Luke 17:21). For the Galilean poor, it was the divine possibility of their own lives. Theirs was God's new community, within their power, if they believed and acted, acted and believed, deeply enough in its reality. That same possibility is ours.

THE PARABLE OF THE DISHONEST BANK MANAGER

Besides the Unmerciful Servant, Jesus told another parable about debt which can be translated into our time. His Parable of the Dishonest Steward (Luke 16:1-9) has puzzled churchgoers for centuries. What is the moral of a story which seems to praise a dishonest character? But perhaps this strange parable speaks about the transformation of power in a way that can make sense to Brazilians or Peruvians in the twentieth century, as it once did to Galileans in the first.

The president of the World Bank had a manager, against whom allegations were made that he was wasting opportunities by not negotiating new loans.

And the president phoned his manager and said to him, "What's this I hear about you? Turn in your accounts, for you can no longer be manager."

And as the manager hung up the phone, he said to himself, "What shall I do, since my boss is firing me? I am too old to begin a new career, and I am ashamed to beg for charity from friends. Ah, I know what I'll do, so that people may receive me into their homes when I'm put out of this position!"

So summoning representatives of debtor nations one by one, he said to the first, "How much does your nation owe the bank?"

He said, "A hundred billion dollars."

And he said to him, "Take your bill, and sit down quickly and write fifty."

Then he said to another, "And how much does your nation owe the bank?"

He said to him, "Fifty billion dollars, and our people are starving."

And he said to him, "Take your bill, and write zero."

And as the president of the World Bank received congratulations from around the world for an enlightened policy, rather than pressing charges he commended the dishonest manager for his shrewdness.

How is the murderous power of systemic evil transformed? Jesus' parables suggest that what most needs to be transformed is our own sense of reality, and of evil in particular.

Who can save us from violence? Our enemy—the Samaritan, the Iraqi, the terrorist, whomever it is we feel the greatest fear and violence toward and are least willing to accept as the divinely given means of our salvation. In the kingdom of God which is within our power, the object of our fear and loathing becomes, through *Abba-Ima* who loves enemies, the source of our hope.

How does the kingdom come? Through the leaven of a truth so alien and corrupt, to my judgmental way of thinking, that it must be "hidden" in my consciousness—or the consciousness of my society—for an unseen, nonviolent transformation to occur. Both Jesus and Gandhi suggest that the kingdom of God may be my enemy's truth.

How, then, does the transformation of this strange kingdom occur in a people living under structures of massive injustice? By realizing, first of all, that the kingdom of God is at hand, in our hands, within the power of our own community, independent of what any ruling authority may impose upon us. No government or corporation on earth can kill or suppress a nonviolent movement whose members are determined to love their enemies and give their lives for the truth. Through that graceful realization of an infinitely loving power in ourselves and our community, God moves in astounding ways.

What is the alternative to such a strange way of transforming power—loving enemies, forgiving debtors, recognizing outcasts as God's chosen ones, discovering truth in the opponent, seeing the infinite presence of God in our own fallible community? We would like to believe that the alternative is to continue along a more familiar, more comfortable way (supported by a murderous, institutionalized violence) without turning to our Nonviolent God.

The parables and prophecies of Jesus proclaim that in fact we have two choices: transformation or annihilation. The realities of our nuclear world confirm that ancient proclamation.

5

JESUS, JERUSALEM, AND THE END OF THE WORLD

I am holding in my left hand a document which calls to mind Jesus' weeping over Jerusalem because it did not know "the things that make for peace" (Luke 19:42).

The document that summons this vision of Jesus weeping is a U.S. government bill of lading for a railroad car. I have been reading it slowly, carefully, absorbing the words. The shipment that it authorizes is identified as a "special car." Where have I seen that term before?

I read on. Across the bill of lading for this special car has been stamped the word "EXPLOSIVES." A box below is more specific: "Rocket Motor Class A Explosive; net explosive weight: 105,824.3 pounds."

What I am reading is the bill of lading for the first Trident-2 missile-propellant shipment sent by rail, in September 1988, to the Trident submarine base at Kings Bay, Georgia. I have received it in the mail from a friend who obtained it from the government through the Freedom of Information Act. Enclosed with it was a newspaper article to underline the document's significance.

The article states that a fleet of Trident submarines, with missiles such as the one in the "special car," would constitute an arsenal of more than five thousand nuclear warheads with a "hard-target" kill capability against underground missile silos or command posts. The article cites the cautiously worded warning of a U.S. defense analyst: "Under these conditions, the Soviets must consider the possibility of a U.S. pre-emptive first strike."

I pull an article from a drawer, "German Railroads / Jewish Souls" by Holocaust author Raul Hilberg. The term is there: "special trains." That was the way in which the *Deutsche Reichsbahn,* the German railroad system, referred on its bills of lading to the trains of Jewish people it sent to Auschwitz and Treblinka: "special trains" (*Sonderzüge*).[1]

Those trains, which delivered the people to the ovens, and our trains, which deliver the ovens to the people, have both been designated "special" by their respective governments.

The friend who sent me the bill of lading for the first "special car" to the Kings Bay base, Glen Milner, has understood its significance. Glen has been arrested for sitting in front of a White Train at the Bangor Trident base. With the bill of lading is a note from Glen that says simply, "All we can do is try."[2]

All we can do is try to be transformed.

In these minutes before midnight, the question that confronts us all — from the engineers of "special trains" to the taxpaying millions who finance and consent to their passage — is the question of nonviolent transformation.

Will we be transformed?

All we can do is try.

THE THINGS THAT MAKE FOR PEACE

The sorrow that Jesus once felt while entering a city he loved, Jerusalem, is reflected today in the sorrow of those who love this world and fear for its future:

"And when Jesus drew near and saw the city [the world] he wept over it, saying, 'Would that even today you knew the things that make for peace!' " (Luke 19:41-42).

The political-economic system ruling the planet today is engaged in a total violence that seems beyond our capacity to change. Nations and corporations linked by the logic of death make up this runaway train. Beneath its wheels are the bodies of the world's poor, most of them in the Third World, most of them children; forty thousand children die of starvation each day in the Third World.

"And when Jesus drew near and saw the city [the world] he wept over it, saying, 'Would that even today you knew the things that make for peace! But now they are hid from your eyes' " (Luke 19:41-42).

Let us contemplate what things that make for war are hidden from our eyes, so that we might begin to see the things that make for peace. Imagine that one of the forty thousand children dying today of starvation is a member of your family. Imagine that child you know and love sinking into death. Were we to suffer through this imagined experience, it might make a bridge for us to the inconceivable truth of our situation. All forty thousand children starving to death today are our sisters and brothers. The children at the heart of the world's suffering are all members of our family. The things that make for peace begin with justice and love for the world's children.

"And when Jesus drew near and saw the city [the world] he wept over it, saying, 'Would that even today you knew the things that make for peace! But now they are hid from your eyes. For the days shall come upon you when your enemies will raise fortifications all around you [encircle you with nuclear missiles], and hem you in on every side [hold your cities hostage with terrorist bombs] . . .' " (Luke 19:41-43).

Our brothers and sisters who live in terror and oppression in third-world countries will not always tolerate the intolerable. More and more they will counter the terrorism of our "extended deterrent" with their own terrorism, assisted by the nuclear technology of supportive nations. Counter-terrorism is seen by them as self-defense. They and their children are being decimated by a political-economic machine which meshes with the ultimate threat to annihilate all life on earth by nuclear weapons. What terror, they might say, can compare with that threat?

"And when Jesus drew near and saw the city [the world] he wept over it, saying, 'Would that even today you knew the things that make for peace! But now they are hid from your eyes. For the days shall come upon you when your enemies will raise fortifications all around you [encircle you with nuclear missiles], and hem you in on every side [hold your cities hostage with terrorist bombs], and dash you to the ground, you and your children within you [blow up your cities, radiate your children], and they will not leave one stone upon another in you [will not leave one speck of earth without radiation]; because you did not repent on the day before your death!' " (Luke 19:41-44).[3]

THE LAST HOURS OF JERUSALEM

"Jesus wept over it." I believe these words of Luke preserve an indispensable basis for understanding Jesus' life. That Jesus wept over the future of the city provides a transforming insight into a fundamental purpose of his life: to save the city and its people from destruction.

The city that Jesus wept over, Jerusalem, was not saved. In the third decade of the first century, Jesus had seen Jerusalem threatened by internal violence, the people's rising hatred of Rome, and a coming judgment in the form of Roman legions. Following the tradition of Jewish prophets, and his precursor, John the Baptist, Jesus tried to save the people of Jerusalem by proclaiming and initiating "the things that make for peace." As a result, he was sentenced to death by the Roman governor and executed by Roman soldiers. Four decades later, at the end of a bitter civil and revolutionary war, Jerusalem was burned to the ground by Roman legions.

The varied interpretations of that terrible event, the fall of Jerusalem in 70 C.E., as given by the three evangelists, Matthew, Mark, and Luke, have placed an unnoticed lens between our eyes and Jesus when we read the gospels. We tend to forget that the synoptic gospels were written just before, or a few years after, the destruction of Jerusalem and its Temple. The catastrophe of Jerusalem helped create the earthquake of consciousness which produced the gospels. Among the tragedies of Jerusalem's end was the demise of the Jerusalem church, then center of the Christian church.[4] To the modern reader the impact of these events, contemporary to the creation of the gospels, seems to receive little or no recognition in the evangelists' depictions of Jesus' life, which had in fact ended a generation before. However, when the gospels are interpreted in the context of their own proximity to Jerusalem's fall, then the shock waves can be distinctly felt in their respective narratives of Jesus' life, especially as his life reaches a climax corresponding to Jerusalem's end: the cross. In the gospels Jesus is shown being executed as a revolutionary by Rome, just outside the sacred city whose people would be slaughtered as revolutionaries by Rome forty years later. Such startling parallels between prophet and people, which were deeply disturbing to the evangelists and the early church, today go unrecognized.

Only in the context of these parallels can we understand such a passage as Jesus' final words to the women of Jerusalem:

> "Daughters of Jerusalem, do not weep for me, but weep for yourselves and for your children. For behold, the days are coming when they will say, 'Blessed are the barren, and the wombs that never bore, and the breasts that never gave suck!' Then they will begin to say to the mountains, 'Fall on us'; and to the hills, 'Cover us.' For if they do this when the wood is green, what will happen when it is dry?" (Luke 23:28-31).

If the Romans thus burn the green wood of a nonviolent Jew, what will they do with the dry wood of a violent revolution? The readers of Luke after 70 C.E. knew only too well the horrible answer. Dry wood burns readily, igniting everything surrounding it. That would include the daughters of Jerusalem and their children.

What in fact happened to the "dry wood" of a Jerusalem in revolt when the imperial torch was flung on it was recorded by Flavius Josephus, an eyewitness to the city's last days, in his history, *The Jewish War.* Josephus's stark descriptions of the suffering and death of Jerusalem will serve as counterpoint in this chapter to the gospel interpretations of the same reality:

> As the legions charged in [the Temple], neither persuasion nor threat could check their impetuosity: passion alone was in command. . . . Most of the victims were peaceful citizens, weak and unarmed, butchered wherever they were caught. Round the Altar the heap of corpses grew higher and higher, while down the Sanctuary steps poured a river of blood and the bodies of those killed at the top slithered to the bottom.
>
> . . . Next [the Romans] came to the last surviving colonnade of the outer court. On this women and children and a mixed crowd of citizens had found a refuge — 6,000 in all. Before Caesar could reach a decision about them or instruct his officers, the soldiers, carried away by their fury, fired the colonnade from below; as a result some flung themselves out of the flames to their death, others perished in the blaze: of that vast number there escaped not one.[5]

"Daughters of Jerusalem, do not weep for me, but weep for yourselves and for your children." Unlike later Christian preaching, Jesus turned the concern away from his own death toward the suffering and death that lay ahead for his people. The women's tears should be shed instead, as his own were on entering Jerusalem, at that prospect. Implicit here is the truth that they, the women of Jerusalem, might still make a difference in saving themselves and their children from a violent disaster not of their own choosing. A twentieth-century parallel to Jesus' hope may be seen in the weekly vigil in downtown Jerusalem of the "Women in Black," one hundred women opposing Israel's occupation of the West Bank and Gaza, who turn out week after week to stand at a busy intersection, dressed in black and holding signs that say simply, "Stop the Occupation." These modern "daughters of Jerusalem" represent a nonviolent alternative to both injustice against Palestinians and the threat of yet another destruction of Jerusalem.

In the 70s, after Jerusalem perished, the agony of its last hours was a story retold from synagogue to synagogue and church to church across the empire. Christians struggled to comprehend Jerusalem's tragedy in the strangely similar paradigm of Jesus' cross. In prophetic solidarity with his people and their city of Jerusalem, Jesus had been executed by the Roman Empire. Christian efforts to interpret the meaning of the fall of Jerusalem within divine providence, in light of Jesus' prophecies, and under the impact of his own Jerusalem crucifixion, are embedded in the eschatology of the synoptic gospels. In that emerging gospel vision the deaths of Jesus, Jerusalem, and the world became bound up with one another in a theological tangle that would have tragic consequences.

To enter the gospel interpretations of the fall of Jerusalem is to begin a journey into the life of Jesus, whom we can rediscover in history as the one who tried to save his people and their holy city from a terminal tragedy. But to see even the initial steps of this journey, we must first become aware of the historical dynamism of these gospel tests and the contrasting visions of their authors.

Years ago Shelley and I were taking turns every other night reading a bedtime story to our then 5-year-old son, Tom. It was a children's mystery story, whose plot we had thought was not too complex for Tom's level of comprehension. At the final reading we found out we were wrong.

Sitting with Tom on his bed that last night, I finished reading the concluding chapter, with its solution to the mystery, and closed the book.

Tom was silent.

"So that's the answer," I said.

My son looked up in bewilderment and frustration and said, "But what's the question?"

The question of Jerusalem's destruction lies behind the answers of the synoptic gospels. Recognizing this unspoken question of Jerusalem behind the texts of Matthew, Mark, and Luke is essential to understanding many of the answers given by the evangelists in their portraits of Jesus.

In analyzing these sacred texts, I pray that I will be as faithful as my limitations permit both to the deepest meaning of the gospels and to the present redemptive power of the many who have been killed because of some of the gospels' answers.

MARK AND THE QUESTION OF JERUSALEM

Let us begin with the earliest of the three synoptic gospels, Mark.

For Mark, the question of Jerusalem arose before the city's destruction. Most scholars agree that Mark's gospel was composed sometime in the years 64-70, just before or during the Jewish-Roman War.[6] Locating it geographically is a further key to its meaning. By situating the gospel in Galilee within the years 67-69 c.e., Ched Myers has been able to make sense of the text from beginning to end in his remarkable commentary on Mark, *Binding the Strong Man.* Myers' hypothesis is:

The immediate and specific issue occasioning the Gospel was the challenge of rebel recruiters in Galilee [between the first and second Roman sieges of Jerusalem], who were trying to drum up support for the resistance around Palestine, and no doubt demanding that Mark's community "choose sides." Though sympathetic to the socio-economic and political grievances of the rebels, Mark was compelled to repudiate their call to a defense of Jerusalem. This was because, according to his understanding of the teaching and practice of a Nazarene prophet, executed by Rome some thirty-five years earlier, the means (military) and ends (restorationist) of the "liberation" struggle were fundamentally counterrevolutionary.[7]

The historical moment for Mark's composition, then, grew out of the persecution of his "radical and non-aligned" community, by both imperial and rebel forces, in Roman-occupied Galilee. The Markan community's situation was "not unlike villagers today in El Salvador or Angola in areas that seesaw back and forth between guerilla and army control. Even if one has clear sympathies [as Mark did toward the rebel side], a refusal to publicly align is regarded as apostasy by both sides."[8]

This historical moment in the midst of the Jewish-Roman War coincides with the narrative moment of Mark's text when Jesus gives his "sermon on revolutionary patience" (the apocalyptic discourse), perhaps the most puzzling chapter in the synoptic gospels. Because Mark speaks directly to his historical situation here, we are given the clues necessary to unravel the meaning of the entire gospel, as Myers does in illuminating detail, emphasizing Jesus' prophetic break with an oppressive Temple state.

Jesus' disruption of the Temple market, which exploits the poor and cultically unclean, symbolizes the break. He interprets this action in terms of the prophets Isaiah and Jeremiah (Mark 11:17). Isaiah had insisted that the Temple be a house of prayer for all peoples, including foreigners and Israel's outcasts (Isa. 56:1-8). Jeremiah had warned against making the Temple a robbers' den, proclaiming in Yahweh's name that unless the Temple ceased exploiting the poor, it would be destroyed (Jer. 7:11-15), as then happened in 587 B.C.E. when Jerusalem was overrun by Babylonian armies. Citing these prophets, Jesus disrupts the priests' market and banking system (Mark 11:15-17) and prophesies the Temple's destruction (Mark 13:2). Because its priestly aristocracy robs the poor of Israel ("you have made it a robbers' den"), the Temple is moving toward destruction.

Mark illustrates the Temple's exploitation of the poor by the story of the widow's coins (Mark 12:41-44). Jesus' attitude to the poor widow's gift of her last resources is not, as is usually assumed, approbation but rather disapproval. His comment is, in fact, a lament that "she out of her poverty has put in everything she had, her whole living" (Mark 12:44). The real point of the story is emphasized by its context. Just preceding it, in Mark as in Luke, is the passage where Jesus condemns those scribes who devour the houses of widows (Mark 12:38-40; Luke 20:45-47). Then there follows immediately, as a perceptive commentator has remarked, "the story of a widow whose house has beyond doubt just been devoured"[9] because she felt compelled to give everything she had to the Temple treasury. In the very next scene, in both Mark and Luke (Mark 13:1-2; Luke 21:5-6), Jesus prophesies the destruction of the Temple to which the widow has just given her entire livelihood — an economic institution that has become devastating to the poor.

In Jesus' apocalyptic discourse, it is this prophesied destruction of the Temple that constitutes the "end of the world." In Mark's use of apocalyptic symbolism the end of the world is the end of that universe of meaning identified with a Temple whose economic practices make widows destitute. Jesus identifies the nonviolent coming of *Bar Enasha*, the New Humanity, with the end of not only the Temple but all the dominant powers on earth, that world of exploitation that seems endless to those who suffer its greatest burdens: "But in those days, after that tribulation [of the Jewish-Roman War], the sun will be darkened, and the moon will not give its light, and the stars will be falling from heaven, and the powers in the heavens will be shaken" (Mark 13:24-25). These cosmic portents allude to the fall of the highest structures of power in history, from Jerusalem to Rome, undermined today and toppled tomorrow by God's nonviolent coming in Jesus and the New Humanity. In the Hebrew Scriptures the darkening of sun and moon is traditionally associated with the fall of a nation.[10] This fall of national powers occurs in the gospel at what appears to be their moment of triumph, at the execution of the Human Being who challenges them. Thus the sun darkens while Jesus is on the cross, and the curtain of the Temple is symbolically torn in two as he dies (Mark 15:33, 38). Mark's narrative reveals Jesus' cross of suffering love as the nonviolent overthrow of the reign of domination in the world, reflected, Mark hopes, in the pattern of faithful suffering in his besieged Galilean community thirty-five years later. This is the transforming way of *Bar Enasha,* as seen first in Jesus, then in the New Humanity of Mark's faith-filled community. As Myers puts it, "The powers will be pulled from the highest places (13:25f) only when and where the power of nonviolence ('to save life, one must lose life') is practiced."[11]

To understand the question of Jerusalem in Mark's gospel, we have to discern his indictment of the Temple's oppression of the Jewish poor. To understand his answer to the question, we have to learn to read his symbolism, whereby the end of the world simply means the end of the Temple state.

Understanding apocalyptic symbols has not been a strong point of gospel exegesis. Some of the best-known scholars of our time have interpreted the gospels' apocalyptic symbols in a literal way, thus ignoring their revolutionary meaning within time and history. But as the great New Testament literary critic Amos Wilder has insisted, the point of these symbols is the hope for a transformation within time: "The eschatological myth dramatizes the transfiguration of the world and is not a mere poetry of an unthinkable a-temporal state."[12]

What these end-of-the-world symbols mean is that a new world is coming on earth, through God's transforming power: "Thy kingdom come, thy will be done *on earth* . . ." The "end" signified by the sun and moon darkening and the stars falling from heaven is simply the end of a dominant unjust order. The sun, moon, and stars are the ideological systems which claim power over our world, identical with the principalities and powers that are the constant theme of Paul's epistles.[13] They are the inner dynamic of the institutions that control humanity, more sophisticated in their modern rule through mass media than were the stars of Mark's time. The "sun, moon, and stars" maintain their power over us until the nonviolent coming of *Bar Enasha,* Jesus and the New Humanity, dethrones them, casting them down from heaven and ending the world as we have known it—the world controlled by these powers. This end translates directly into a new beginning, a new world in this world, as the Hebrew prophetic-apocalyptic traditions envisioned long before Jesus. The "end of the world" is the beginning of the world which the prophets struggle and die for—the world envisioned, for example, by Martin Luther King the night before he died. The "end of the world" means the beginning of that new world of justice and peace.

To see the question of Jerusalem in Mark's prophetic-apocalyptic terms therefore requires enough historical empathy on our part for us to identify with the Jewish poor under a pre-70 Jerusalem Temple state at the height of its power. To the Galilean peasants of Mark's community the Temple seemed in its own way as insurmountable a power as the Roman occupying forces, yet one that religiously and patriotically (the two dimensions were one) claimed their allegiance in spite of its high-priestly corruption. The overwhelming political-symbolic power which they felt from the Temple's presence in their lives is reflected in the gospel scene where a disciple's exclamation of awe at the Temple becomes the occasion for Jesus' prophecy of its destruction:

> And as he came out of the Temple, one of his disciples said to him, "Look, Teacher, what wonderful stones and what wonderful buildings!" And Jesus said to him, "Do you see these great buildings? There will not be left here one stone upon another, that will not be thrown down" (Mark 13:1-2).

From Mark's reading of Jesus, Jerusalem's provisional revolutionary government of the late 60s, which purged the Temple aristocracy and defied Rome, was no solution to the problem. It was simply another violent cycle and a prelude to the ultimate disaster Jesus had warned against earlier. In the apocalyptic discourse Mark therefore interprets Jesus' teaching in such a way as to urge Jesus' followers to refuse rebel recruitment into Jerusalem's defense. Instead, they should abandon the city:

> "But when you see the desolating sacrilege set up where it ought not to be [meaning idolatrous Roman standards taking over the holy city] (let the reader understand) [as Mark the narrator says circumspectly in a Galilee that has been reoccupied under those same Roman standards], then let those who are in Judea flee to the mountains" (Mark 13:14).

The call to abandon Jerusalem is meant both historically and symbolically. This destructive, doomed world of competing powers that dominate subject peoples is to be left behind. Mark declares the end of that world and the beginning of a new one. The new world is symbolized by *Bar Enasha*, the New Humanity of Jesus' vision, who comes as the powers of the old world fall: "And the stars will be falling from heaven, and the powers in the heavens will be shaken. And then they will see *Bar Enasha* coming in clouds with great power and glory" (Mark 13:25-26).

At this point, I suggest that we distance ourselves critically from Mark's radically nonviolent abandonment of Jerusalem in order to reflect on its significance.

In his gospel Mark is calling for a faith in the power of a Nonviolent God, embodied in Jesus and the New Humanity, a faith deep enough to overcome an entrenched system of power, represented in the foreground by the Temple. However, as we know from our own perspective looking back on Mark's, the towering Temple system he is confronting in faith would, in the year 70, be destroyed by the power and might of Roman legions. However imposing that world may have seemed to Galilean peasants before 70—"Look, Teacher, what wonderful stones and what wonderful buildings!"—it was about to be destroyed by the troops of Titus. And by that stroke of imperial power Mark's gospel became ambiguous, because history is ambiguous. The gospel's prophetic and mythological stripping of power, in fidelity to its own Jewish traditions, would now be read outside those traditions in terms of an historical catastrophe to the Jewish people.

We can begin to see in Mark questions that will grow as we consider the other gospels. We should at least note now the tension in our own minds between the two sides of Mark's vision, and between its more positive side and its realization in history. The first tension is between seeing Jerusalem as necessarily doomed and at the same time affirming a faith in the transforming power of *Bar Enasha*. The second tension lies between a faith in the cross of nonviolent, suffering love overcoming the prevailing system and its actually being overcome by Rome instead. These tensions may not have been very noticeable in the first century, but they are today. We become more conscious of these questions to the extent that we take into our lives the lives of those in Jerusalem who were encircled by Roman legions in the year 70. Did Jesus thirty-five years earlier have more hope for Jerusalem than Mark expressed at the eleventh hour?

Josephus can remind us again of what in fact happened to the people of Jerusalem in 70:

> While the Sanctuary was burning, looting went on right and left and all who were caught were put to the sword. There was no pity for age, no regard for rank; little children and old men, laypeople and priests alike were butchered; every class was held in the iron embrace of war, whether they defended themselves or cried for mercy. Through the roar of the flames as they swept relentlessly on could be heard the groans of the falling: such were the height of the hill and the vastness of the blazing edifice that the entire city seemed to be on fire, while as for the noise, nothing could be imagined more shattering or more horrifying. There was the war-cry of the Roman legions as they converged; the yells of the partisans encircled with fire and sword: the panic flight of the people cut off above into the arms of the enemy, and their shrieks as the end approached. The cries from the hill were answered from the crowded streets; and now many who were wasted with hunger and beyond speech found strength to moan and wail when they saw the Sanctuary in flames. Back from Peraea and the mountains round about came the echo in a thunderous bass.
>
> Yet more terrible than the din were the sights that met the eye. The Temple Hill, enveloped in flames from top to bottom, appeared to be boiling up from its very roots; yet the sea of flame was nothing to the ocean of blood, or the companies of killers to the armies of killed; nowhere could the ground be seen between the corpses, and the soldiers climbed over heaps of bodies as they chased the fugitives.[14]

For seven years after the fall of Jerusalem, says the Talmud, "the nations of the world cultivated their vineyards with no other manure than the blood of Israel."[15]

THE TWO SIDES OF MATTHEW

If we open our hearts to the people of Jerusalem in 70, what we have experienced as tensions in Mark's gospel, then become contradictions in Matthew's.

Matthew's gospel has two such diverse sides that a reader is forced to ask how they ever came together in a single document. For practitioners of nonviolence, there has always been the Matthew of the Sermon on the Mount. This is the Matthew that Gandhi loved and identified as the most powerful document in Christianity. This first Matthew is summed up in Jesus' commandment of love of enemies as the heart of his teaching. In the nonviolent Matthew, Jesus proclaims the beatitudes and offers a way of divine reconciliation for humanity: Love your enemies, pray for those who persecute you, so as to be children of your merciful God who makes the "sun rise on the evil and on the good, and sends rain on the just and the unjust" (Matt. 5:44-45).

But there is another side to Matthew's gospel that proclaims a different message, which has also had its impact on history. It is this second Matthew we shall consider now, because it is this side of Matthew that deals with the fall of Jerusalem.

Through Matthew's eyes we see Jerusalem in a completely different historical perspective than we did through Mark's. Matthew wrote his gospel a decade or two after the fall of Jerusalem, probably in Antioch, Syria.[16] In form and content Matthew is often characterized as the most Jewish of the gospels. The author is seen as a Christian scribe, "who drew up the sayings of Jesus as a guide to conduct much as Jewish scribes formulated a code of conduct on the basis of the law."[17] In a hypothesis that many scholars have accepted, W. D. Davies has suggested that Matthew's gospel should be seen in a relationship of rivalry to the school of rabbinic Judaism which arose under the leadership of Rabbi Yohanan ben Zakkai in the Palestinian village of Yavneh after the Jewish-Roman War. The form of Matthew's gospel, in particular the Sermon on the Mount, suggests "a kind of Christian, mishnaic counterpart to the formulation taking place"[18] at Yavneh. But we shall find reasons within this gospel to question the assumption that the redactor we call Matthew was a Jewish convert to Christianity.

In entering Matthew's text we shall be guided by the work of David Flusser of the Hebrew University in Jerusalem, who has illuminated the teachings of Jesus by his linguistic studies and by comparisons of the gospels with rabbinic texts. Flusser has analyzed carefully the editorial methods behind Matthew's gospel.[19] What he has discovered will allow us to distinguish the "second Matthew," as he approaches through his gospel the very different post-70 question of Jerusalem.

Flusser shows Matthew's editorial philosophy in the story of Jesus' healing of the centurion's servant (Matt. 8:5-13; Luke 7:1-10; John 4:45-54). As Matthew and Luke tell the story, the God-fearing centurion assumes that Jesus as a pious Jew will not enter his house lest he be polluted by the impurity of Gentiles. So in order to save his servant, the centurion says to Jesus, "Lord, I am not worthy to have you come under my roof; but only say the word, and my servant will be healed" (Matt. 8:8; par. Luke 7:6-7).

In Luke, Jesus marvels at the faith of the centurion and says to his followers, "I tell you, not even in Israel have I found such faith" (Luke 7:9). Matthew, however, drawing on the same collection of Jesus' sayings as does Luke, begins to show his hand with a small but significant change: "Truly, I say to you, *with no one in Israel* have I found such faith" (Matt. 8:10).[20] Matthew's Jesus then goes on to deliver a judgment that is absent from Luke: "I tell you, many will come from east and west and sit at table with Abraham, Isaac, and Jacob in the kingdom of heaven, *while those born of the kingdom will be thrown into the outer darkness*; there people will weep and gnash their teeth" (Matt. 8:12).

According to Matthew, the Gentile centurion had a faith found with no one in Israel. This is a sign, revealing the truth: Those born of the kingdom, the Jewish people, will be thrown into the outer darkness, while believing Gentiles will come to sit down instead with Abraham, Issac, and Jacob in the kingdom of heaven. In Luke's gospel the original condemnation connected with this saying is applied not to Israel in general, but more specifically to false followers of Jesus.

In another example of editorial changes, the Parable of the Tenants, which Mark and Luke apply especially to the power structure, becomes for Matthew the basis for a concluding judgment on Israel: "Therefore I tell you, the kingdom of God will be taken from you *and given to a nation that yields proper fruit*" (Matt. 21:43).

At one time David Flusser accepted the conventional scholarly view that the evangelist was a Jewish Christian, refusing to believe that the "nation that yields proper fruit" was a term designating the Gentiles. Growing more familiar with Matthew, he came to see that any other interpretation was forced.[21] That the kingdom was now to be given to Gentile Christians, in Matthew's vision, was also consistent with his seeing "those born of the kingdom," its Jewish sons and daughters, being thrown into the outer darkness.

Matthew's gospel relates this Jewish outer darkness to a historical hell: the destruction of Jerusalem in 70 C.E. As seen again by a comparison with Luke, Matthew has rewritten the Parable of the Marriage Feast (Matt. 22:2-13; Luke 14:16-24) as an allegory with a new subplot. A king (God) invites his subjects (Israel) to a feast for his son (Jesus). Some disregard the invitation. Others illogically kill the king's servants (the prophets), thus bringing down on themselves the king's judgment: "The king was angry, and he sent his troops and destroyed those murderers and burned their city" (Matt. 22:7). The burned city is Jerusalem. Then the king invites others (Gentiles) to the feast of the kingdom of heaven.[22]

Because of the history between the first two gospels, the question of Jerusalem to which Matthew is responding is very different from Mark's question. Mark had wondered how his Galilean community could remain faithful to the nonviolent way of Jesus when challenged in the late 60s by the Jerusalem Temple state, Roman occupation, and the crisis of the Jewish-Roman War. To Matthew in the 80s, after Rome's triumph, the devastation of Jerusalem and the Jewish nation called forth instead the stark question: Why? Why did God allow this terrible tragedy to happen? Writing with hindsight in the same prophetic-apocalyptic tradition as Mark, Matthew gave what must have seemed to him an obvious answer: by the destruction of Jerusalem, God was punishing his people.

Matthew, however, does not restrict the responsibility for this divine punishment to the economic injustice of a priestly aristocracy. He omits Mark's story of the widow's coins and draws a much broader picture of culpability to account for the razed city. Matthew's presentation of Jesus' woes against the scribes and Pharisees goes far beyond the conflicts between Jesus and some scribes and Pharisees depicted by Mark and Luke. Matthew enlarges the scope of these conflicts, so that they become the basis for Israel's rejection of Jesus and God's rejection of Israel.

At least two historical crises lie behind the series of theological judgments made on Israel in Matthew's gospel. Besides the crisis of Jerusalem's destruction, Matthew is also responding to a crisis in the Christian church's self-understanding: that community's growing recognition of its failure to convert the Jewish people to a faith in Jesus as the messiah. The Jewish Christian church had believed that God's plan would surely be fulfilled by Israel's acceptance of Jesus. Yet Israel had not responded. By the 80s the hope of a Christian Israel had been frustrated, and the church had instead become increasingly a Gentile faith. How could God's infallible plan account for these two historical tragedies, Israel's lack of response to the church and Rome's destruction of Jerusalem?

Matthew has drawn together in one theological vision these two crises that challenge his view of God's purpose in history: the failure of the Christian mission to Israel; the destruction of the holy city of Jerusalem by Rome. The final editor of Matthew, writing a decade or so after Jerusalem's fall, is using the first crisis, projected back into Jesus' life, to explain the second. He is struggling to explain the shocking event of 70 as a divinely willed punishment on an unbelieving people.

Thus, in his most consequential interpretation Matthew reaches back to Jesus' life to create the terrifying cry from the crowd to Pilate (found in no other gospel), "His blood be on us and on our children!" (Matt. 27:25). Here, in Matthew's view, is the reason why Jerusalem was burned in 70, why the sons and daughters of the kingdom were thrown into the outer darkness of history. It must, he thinks, have been connected somehow with Jesus' death, and he has made such a connection. In telling Jesus' story Matthew's final editor has inserted a theology of history to interpret the recent destruction of Jerusalem. He is portraying Jesus' execution by the Romans in 30 in such a way as to explain the Jewish people's execution by the Romans in 70. He creates a picture of corporate Jewish responsibility in 30 in an effort to explain the terrible divine judgment of 70: "His blood be on us and on our children!"[23] But in trying to understand a first-century holocaust, Matthew is providing a rationale for a twentieth-century holocaust. By his theological reinterpretation of Jesus' death to explain the death of Jesus' people, Matthew was inadvertently contributing to an outer darkness no one could imagine.

THE FUTURE HOLOCAUST

Approximately nineteen hundred years after Matthew finished writing his gospel on the scroll set before him, some villagers are standing outside a Catholic church in Chelmno, Poland. They have just attended Mass and have been joined in front of the church by one of the few surviving Jews of the Nazi extermination camp that had once, as the villagers all knew, been in their midst. The Chelmno death camp had sent its gas vans to the door of this church to collect the hundreds of Jews being held inside.

Now the villagers on the church steps express happiness at the return of the Jewish survivor. Then, in a scene that was captured in the film *Shoah,* they turn to respond to an interviewer's questions. That interview concludes as follows:

> *Interviewer (through interpreter):* "Why do they think all this happened to the Jews?"
>
> *First woman:* "Because they were the richest! Many Poles were also exterminated. Even priests."
>
> *Second woman:* "Mr. Kantarowski will tell us what a friend told him. It happened in Myndjewyce, near Warsaw."
>
> *Interviewer:* "Go on."
>
> *Mr. Kantarowski:* "The Jews there were gathered in a square. The rabbi asked an SS man: 'Can I talk to them?' The SS man said yes. So the rabbi said that around two thousand years ago the Jews condemned the innocent Christ to death. And when they did that, they cried out: 'Let his blood fall on our heads and on our sons' heads.' Then the rabbi told them: 'Perhaps the time has come for that, so let us do nothing, let us go, let us do as we're asked."
>
> *Interviewer:* "He [Mr. Kantarowski] thinks the Jews expiated the death of Christ?"
>
> *Second woman:* "He doesn't think so, or even that Christ sought

revenge. He didn't say that. The rabbi said it. It was God's will, that's all!"

First woman: "So Pilate washed his hands and said: 'Christ is innocent,' and he sent Barrabas. But the Jews cried out: 'Let his blood fall on our heads!' "

Second woman: "That's all; now you know!"[24]

Matthew was trying to understand a past holocaust. His explanation was used to justify a future one. We should not blame Matthew for what centuries of anti-Semitism and an extermination system have made in our eyes of his dramatized explanation of the fall of Jerusalem. But night begins in shadows. We can see the shadows of our twentieth-century night in Matthew's change of perspective on Jesus' prophetic truth. Matthew, in an increasingly Gentile church, is looking back at a Jewish catastrophe that Jesus decades earlier had feared and warned against, as a Jew to other Jews. The danger inherent in Matthew's post-70 point of view is that of using Jesus' prophetic vision to interpret a Jewish tragedy as a Christian triumph. Did Matthew overcome that danger, that temptation to use history against its victims? I fear he did not.

Nor, to this day, have our Christian churches repented the anti-Semitic, Holocaust legacy now inextricably attached to Matthew's worst text and to our Good Friday liturgies which cite it. The blood of six million Jews demands that the cry of Matthew's crowd be silenced forever. Yet "His blood be on us and on our children!" (Matt. 27:25) continues to be recited annually by millions of Christians in the course of Holy Week ceremonies.

THE COMING OF BAR ENASHA *IN ROMAN LEGIONS*

We can see the root of this continuing evil in Matthew's triumphal change of perspective, which is expressed in the eschatological discourse in his reinterpretation of Jesus' coming as *Bar Enasha*. To understand Matthew's version of the eschatological discourse (Matt. 24 and 25), we must read with it, as a single unit, his preceding presentation of Jesus' woes against the scribes and Pharisees (23:13-36) and Jesus' lament over Jerusalem (23:37-39).[25]

The extraordinary significance Matthew gives the denunciation of the scribes and Pharisees is stated at the conclusion of that speech. After the most hostile statements found anywhere in the gospels, Matthew's Jesus ends his seven woes against the scribes and Pharisees by saying:

Therefore I send you prophets and wise men and scribes, some of whom you will kill and crucify, and some you will scourge in your synagogues and persecute from town to town, *that upon you may come all the righteous blood shed on earth,* from the blood of innocent Abel to the blood of Zechariah the son of Barachiah, whom you murdered between the sanctuary and the altar. Truly, I say to you, *all this will come upon this generation"* (Matt. 23:34-36).

In the words I have emphasized (drawn from the sayings source Matthew has in common with Luke but given greater emphasis by Matthew's placement), Matthew's Jesus is here foreshadowing the people's cry to Pilate, which will seal their generation's fate. Thus the guilt of the scribes and Pharisees, which Matthew has already accentuated in the woes, is being extended to the entire Jewish nation. The crimes of the scribes and Pharisees will call down "all the righteous blood shed on earth," not only on themselves — "upon you" — but also "upon this generation." In other words, by the destruction of Jerusalem in 70 C.E., all past murders of the prophets will be avenged "upon this generation."

It is possible that Matthew himself was persecuted in some way by Jewish authorities during that transition period in the Roman Empire when there were still remnants of Jewish power and before Christian power had established itself at the former's expense. If this hypothesis is true, it helps explain the intensity of Matthew's indictment against the scribes and Pharisees in the name of Jesus. The persecuted prophets, on whose behalf Matthew has Jesus speak, may in the evangelist's mind have included himself. Yet the righteous prophet, who speaks so definitively to his oppressors, runs the risk of becoming their children's oppressor. Once history has turned over, a prophecy made on behalf of a beleaguered, minority community can be converted into the voice of established power.

In the next passage Matthew takes another step into his explanation of the destruction of Jerusalem. There Jesus laments over Jerusalem for the same crime of killing the prophets, coupled with its rejection of him, and says, "Behold, your [Jerusalem's] house is forsaken and desolate" (23:38). "Your house" is the Temple, which because of these crimes is now abandoned by God to its enemies.

Finally, to introduce his eschatological discourse, Matthew has Jesus leave the Temple, prophesying its destruction as he symbolically abandons it: "Truly, I say to you, there will not be left here one stone upon another that will not be thrown down" (24:2).

Having already anticipated, explained, and prophesied the destruction of Jerusalem and its Temple, Matthew in his eschatological discourse then focuses on that very event, as it had already occurred a decade or so before the gospel's final editing.

In Matthew's discourse, as in Mark's, "the desolating sacrilege" (24:15) is the invasion of Jerusalem and the Temple by the Roman legions carrying idolatrous standards. Matthew, however, is more explicit than Mark, for he says that the desolating sacrilege will be seen "standing in the holy place" (24:15), that is, within the Temple.

Matthew adds, again from a source of Jesus' sayings, a prophetic symbol of the city's death at the hands of Rome's legions: "Wherever the body is, there the eagles will be gathered together" (24:28). The body is the carcass of Jerusalem. The eagles gathered together are also vultures: Roman eagle-vultures.

The eagle was well-known as Rome's military symbol. The Roman legions carried golden eagles above them, emblazoned on their standards. The legion soldiers worshipped their golden eagles as imperial military gods. To the Jews, Rome's eagles meant idolatry and death. Their language reflected this understanding. In Aramaic and Hebrew the same word was used for eagle and vulture. Thus the saying in Matthew's text unites in one symbol Roman military power and the way it fed on its victims, in this case the dead body of Jerusalem and its people in 70 C.E.: "Wherever the body is, there the eagles [vultures] will be gathered together."[26]

These symbols converged in the burning Temple of the conquered city. Josephus describes the very scene in which the desolating sacrilege of the eagles was seen standing in the holy place:

> As the partisans had fled into the City, and flames were consuming the Sanctuary itself and all its surroundings, the Romans brought their [eagle] standards into the Temple area, and erecting them opposite the East Gate sacrificed to them there, and with thunderous acclamations hailed Titus as *Imperator.*[27]

It is in this immediate context of the desolating sacrilege, with Rome's soldiers pillaging as vultures the dead of Jerusalem, that Matthew has set the coming of *Bar Enasha,* the Human Being: "For as the lightning comes from the east and shines as far as the west, so will be the coming of *Bar Enasha.* Wherever the body is, there the eagles [vultures] will be gathered together" (24:27-28).

The juxtaposition is startling. Matthew knows in retrospect the terrible suffering and death of Jerusalem in 70 C.E. beneath the gathering of the Roman eagles. Yet he has chosen to connect that disaster with the coming of *Bar Enasha.* What he means by this interpretation of the Human Being, Jesus the Messiah, is a Second Coming, this time in judgment. The Human Being, seen as rejected and murdered in Jesus and the prophets, comes in God's lightning judgment upon the Jewish people at the destruction of Jerusalem. Thus a mission that began in Matthew with the Sermon on the Mount is seen as ending in a first-century holocaust.

In that holocaust judgment Matthew also sees the beginning of a new age, the age of the church. The disciples' opening question of chapter 24, to which Matthew's Jesus is responding in his discourse, unites these perspectives: "Tell us, when will this [Jesus' just-predicted destruction of the Temple] be, and what will be the sign of your coming and of the close of the age?" (24:3). The "close of the age" means the end of the age of the Jerusalem Temple. Jesus' coming in judgment marks the close of that age, as seen in the desolating sacrilege of the eagle standards flying over the burning Temple. As the age of the Temple ends, Matthew's new age of the church begins, a beginning identified in verse 30 with *"Bar Enasha* coming on the clouds of heaven with power and great glory."[28]

Thus, in his eschatological discourse, Matthew has identified a Second Coming of Jesus in the new age of the church with a divine judgment expressed in the burning of the Temple and the massacre of the people of Jerusalem by Roman legions.

That this is in fact what Matthew meant by his *parousia* passages, his "coming of the Human Being," I find profoundly disturbing, yet inescapable from the final editing of his gospel. Matthew's "Human Being," Jesus the Messiah, has come in judgment upon Jesus' own people through Roman legions. This is indicated in earlier passages of the gospel, such as one we are familiar with from a previous discussion: "When they persecute you in one town, flee to the next; for truly, I say to you, you will not have gone through all the towns of Israel, before *Bar Enasha* comes" (10:23). I have already said how I believe this saying should be understood in terms of Jesus' own vision and ministry to Israel. Jesus hoped for the revolutionary coming in his time of a faithful, nonviolent people who could expect to experience both persecution and a realization of the kingdom of God.[29] Such a meaning is also possible from the saying's immediate context in Matthew. However, I do not think the final editor of Matthew had that meaning in mind. Following the destruction of Jerusalem, he reinterpreted the saying as a prediction of judgment upon Israel, linking it structurally with Matthew 16:28, which, in its context, shows a *Bar Enasha* coming in judgment:

> For *Bar Enasha* is to come with his angels in the glory of his Father, and then he will repay all people for what they have done. Truly, I say to you, there are some standing here who will not taste death before they see *Bar Enasha* coming in his kingdom (16:27-28).[30]

In the final version of Matthew's gospel, both of these "coming Human Being" statements (10:23 and 16:28) anticipate the conclusion to the woes against the scribes and Pharisees, "Truly, I say to you, all this will come upon this generation" (23:36), which points in turn, in the eschatological discourse, to the coming in judgment of the Human Being in the year 70.[31]

Matthew's post-70 perspective on the destruction of Jerusalem has obscured for succeeding generations Jesus' original hope of nonviolent transformation for Israel and all of humanity. Yet Matthew has also passed down to us the nonviolent charter of the Sermon on the Mount, by which we measure the historical judgments of his own gospel.[32] The Jesus at the heart of Matthew redeems Matthew.[33] It is, therefore, in fidelity both to the heart of Matthew's gospel and to the victims in history of that gospel's worst legacy that we question his dramatized explanation of the destruction of Jerusalem. Matthew gave us the vision to measure all visions in Jesus' command to "love your enemies and pray for those who persecute you, so that you may be children of your merciful God who is in heaven" (Matt. 5:44). It was when Matthew shifted the emphasis of his gospel from love to judgment, so as to explain the failed mission to Israel and the destruction of Jerusalem, that the good news turned bad. Thus foundations were laid in faith for future judgments in history that would contradict the God of Love, whose children, Jesus taught, must love their neighbors as themselves (Matt. 22:37-39).

THE MYSTERY OF Q

In discussing Matthew I have referred in passing to a collection of Jesus' sayings, which Matthew and Luke drew upon independently in composing their gospels. Through a kind of literary archaeology accomplished by scripture scholars, this earlier "Sayings Gospel Q" has been gradually unearthed from the texts of Matthew and Luke, in which it has been imbedded since the first century. "Q," so named from the German word *quelle* meaning "source," has been reconstructed by identifying the sayings of Jesus which, according to the two-source hypothesis, Matthew and Luke drew from a common, written source to fill out the basic outlines of Mark as used in their own gospels. Matthew and Luke thus have two sources in common, Mark and the Sayings Gospel Q. Now recognized as a gospel in its own right, Q is normally dated between 50 and 70 C.E.[34] Judging from the locations cited in Q, its most likely place of composition was northern Galilee or western Syria.[35]

The Sayings Gospel Q has been so edited that its theme is a fiery judgment on "this generation" for its refusal to heed the prophets John the Baptist, Jesus, and the Q preachers. In a way that is as unrecognizable for modern readers as it was unmistakable for first-century Jews, Q's opening line gives immediate notice of a coming judgment by fire: "John came into all the region about the Jordan" (Luke 3:3; par. Matt. 3:1-5).[36] The phrase, "all the region about the Jordan," was used in the Hebrew Scriptures specifically for the setting of Sodom's and Gomorrah's destruction by fire (Gen. 13:10-11).[37] The prophet John, seen against this backdrop of Sodom in flames, then delivers a prophetic message (Matt. 3:7-10; Luke 3:7-9) that draws upon three images of Lot's escape from Sodom: 1) flight ("Who warned you to flee from the coming wrath?"); 2) fiery destruction ("every tree therefore that does not bear good fruit is cut down and thrown into the fire"); and 3) the presumptuous image of Abraham as kin ("Do not presume to say to yourselves, 'We have Abraham as our father' "), which was *not* the reason Lot was saved from Sodom. He was saved by his righteousness. Unless John's listeners turn themselves and their nation around and "bear fruit worthy of repentance," they, too, like the people of Sodom, will be destroyed.

As John Kloppenborg has shown, a key to the unifying structure of Q is the role of the "Coming One."[38] After evoking Sodom, John proclaims the Coming One (Matt. 3:11; Luke 3:16), a terrifying figure who will bring fire on those who fail to repent: "He will baptize you with the Holy Spirit and fire . . . the chaff he will burn with unquenchable fire" (Matt. 3:11-12; Luke 3:16-17). John later sends disciples to ask Jesus if he in fact is the Coming One (Luke 7:18-23; Matt. 11:2-6). Jesus' answer indicates a very different kind of Coming One, not the judge of John's vision but one who frees the oppressed of suffering and gives good news to the poor. Yet, as the Sayings Gospel progresses, the theme of transformation gives way to judgment. "This generation," like fickle children sitting in the marketplace, rejects both John and Jesus (Luke 7:31-35; Matt. 11:16). As a result, the Coming One, in his third and final appearance, is re-identified with judgment but this time by Jesus in a prophecy of Jerusalem's destruction (Luke 13:34-35; Matt. 23:37-39). Thus Jesus finally confirms John's opening message. The gospel of Q ends, as it began, with a text stating the theme of judgment: the prediction of Jesus' followers in the Q community judging the twelve tribes of Israel (Luke 22:28-30; Matt. 19:28).[39]

Critical to an understanding of Q is the distinction between its two main stages of composition, Q1 and Q2, corresponding to two stages of consciousness in the Q community. John Kloppenborg, whose *Formation of Q* has become the classic analysis of the Q layers, sums up the tensions between Q1 and Q2: Whereas in Q1 "only actions which surpass the ordinary expectations of reciprocity are truly meritorious," in Q2 "the condemnation of this generation for rejecting Jesus' preaching is worked out with a simple and deadly calculus."[40] The merciful God who expects mercy toward others in Q1 comes down hard on the unrepentant in Q2. We go from the Creator's loving care for every hair of every creature in Q1 ("even the hairs of your head are all numbered. Fear not; you are worth more than many sparrows": Luke 12:7; Matt. 10:30-31) to fierce judgments upon entire Galilean towns in Q2 (Matt. 11:20-24; Luke 10:13-15). Q1 and Q2 seem to present sharply contrasting visions of divine logic.

THE PURPOSE OF THE Q COMMUNITY

What does the Q gospel tell us about the community reflected in its sayings and layers of composition?

As a gospel of Jesus' sayings, with no reference to his passion or resurrection, Q is rooted in Jesus' ministry in Galilee. Q's geographical references suggest a community growing up in the villages of Galilee from Jesus' ministry before 30, when his sayings began to be collected, until the final editing of the gospel between 50 and 70. In the time between its founding and the completion of its gospel, the Q community underwent a painful experience. We see the suffering and the struggle reflected in the shift of emphasis in the final version of the gospel from nonviolent transformation to prophetic warning and finally judgment. Q scholars have identified the experience behind that shift in the gospel as rejection. As Kloppenborg puts it, "According to the Q people, 'this generation' has failed to recognize that the true Israel is to be found with Jesus' followers. They have not repented."[41] Stunned by the rejection of a message that had transformed them, and probably experiencing a persecution reflected in some of their sayings, the Q community composed a gospel that used the sayings of Jesus and John, and their own, to proclaim a judgment on "this generation" of Israel.

While this hypothesis explains some of the dynamic visible in the Q document, it takes us only far enough into it to suggest the larger mystery of Q. What was the content of the Q gospel at its earliest stage, before rejection pushed its composers to revise it under the dominant motif of judgment? What was the purpose of the Q community, as seen through the tensions of the Q gospel? What was the historical crisis transpiring around Q, to which its gospel responds? What was the struggle going on among the Q people in their efforts to organize Jesus' words so as to respond in the best way possible to that historical crisis?

The Q gospel we are given by reconstruction is clear from beginning to end that "this generation" of Israel is threatened by destruction. That destruction is imminent, proclaimed as God's judgment. It has become the theme of Q2, which has in turn become the editorial framework and dominant motif of the gospel as a whole. Q proclaims that a time of fiery destruction, symbolized by Sodom, lies ahead. In a series of symbolic statements, John, Jesus, and the Q prophets warn repeatedly of a disaster that seems certain for their generation. Their words and symbols cry out for a concrete point of reference. We do not have to invent one. The history in which Q was composed culminated after its final editing in a cataclysmic event: the Jewish-Roman War, climaxed by the destruction of Jerusalem. If we suppose that a gospel of Jesus' sayings was composed in response to that rising crisis, before it broke into catastrophe, might that hypothetical gospel not look very much like what we are in fact given in Q?

In a Q1 passage Jesus' mission speech to the disciples offers a revelation of the Q community's purpose—and behind it Jesus' own purpose for the movement he founded in Galilee. The explicit purpose for which Jesus commissions the disciples, when he sends them out to the villages of Galilee, is *peace:* "Into whatever house you enter, first say, 'Peace be to this house'" (Luke 10:5; Matt. 10:12)! This proclamation of peace is not an empty greeting but a life-challenging invitation to nonviolent transformation. The way of peace demands a soulful commitment, a choice with one's whole life for or against peace: "And if a child of peace is there, your peace shall rest upon her; but if not, it shall return to you" (Luke 10:6; par. Matt. 10:12).

It is remarkable how little attention has been paid to this given purpose of the disciples' mission, peace, when the context of their mission was a century in which a devastating war would destroy the Jewish nation. Why did Jesus send out the disciples? The speech handed down to us in Q says his purpose was that peace (rather than war) should come to every house the disciples entered. But many of these same houses in Galilee would end up being burned down by Roman legions forty years later, and their inhabitants killed or sold into slavery. Much of "this generation" of Israel would be destroyed by the war with Rome.

The life-determining invitation to peace that Jesus prepared the disciples to share is stated fully in Q's inaugural sermon, which makes up the first Q1 cluster of sayings and is the core of what would become Matthew's Sermon on the Mount and Luke's Sermon on the Plain. Prominent in the inaugural sermon are the sayings on love of enemies, nonviolent resistance to evil, and rejection of retaliation. These radically transforming teachings, designed to turn a nation and a world from destruction, are the substance of the disciples' village-to-village mission of peace — and the Q community's continuation of that mission up to the Jewish-Roman War.

The mission speech in Q is also a revelation of the tensions between Q1 and Q2. As the speech progresses, it emphasizes the collective nature of the repentance demanded of the nation. Entire cities must change in response to the disciples' invitation if the nonviolent alternative to war, the kingdom of God, is to be realized. But the speech at this point begins to veer toward a decidedly negative outlook toward the prospect of peace, as the specter of Sodom's destruction is reasserted in Q:

> "But whatever city you enter that does not welcome you, go out into its streets and say, 'Even the dust of your city that clings to our feet, we wipe off against you; but know this that the reign of God has come near.' I tell you that it shall be more tolerable on that day for Sodom than for that city" (Luke 10:10-12).

It is here that the disheartening experience of the later Q community, preaching peace to a nation turning increasingly toward war, begins to dominate the speech. In a Q2 passage identified by scholars as a secondary interpolation,[42] the one sending out the disciples suddenly proclaims a judgment which assumes the failure of a mission not yet begun:

> "Woe to you, Chorazin! woe to you, Bethsaida! for if the miracles done in you had been done in Tyre and Sidon, they would have repented long ago in sackcloth and ashes. But it shall be more tolerable on the judgment for Tyre and Sidon than for you. And you, Capharnaum, will you be exalted to heaven? *You shall descend to Hades!*" (Matt. 11:20-24; Luke 10:13-15).

Is the meaning of these Q2 woes on the Galilean towns to be found in a heightened sense of the coming of Roman legions? Consider this description by Josephus of the fate of the Galilean village Japha, only a mile and a half from Jesus' home of Nazareth,[43] when it tried to fight Rome in 67 C.E.:

> The soldiers brought up ladders to the wall on every side, and for a short while the Galileans on the battlements tried to fight them off; but they soon abandoned their defences, and at once Titus' men sprang on to the battlements and a moment later were in possession of the town. Those inside the wall, however, rallied to oppose them and a furious struggle broke out. In the narrow streets the men of action fell upon the legionaries; and from the house-tops the women pelted them with anything they could lay their hands on. For six hours they kept up their resistance; but when the fighting men had been expended, the rest of the population were butchered in the open and in the houses, young and old together. For no male was left alive apart from infants in arms, who with the women were sold into slavery. Those who had been slaughtered, either in the town or in the preceding engagement, totalled 15,000, the slaves 2,130.[44]

The slaughter and enslavement of "this generation" that would come in 66-70 is, I believe, the reality conveyed by Q's theme of judgment.

We shall see more of Q in the context of Luke's gospel.

PROPHETIC HOPE IN LUKE

REVIEWING MARK, MATTHEW, AND Q

The Gospel According to Luke offers the possibility, almost always overlooked, for a transforming insight into the historical Jesus' response to the greatest crisis of his time, the threatened destruction of his people. Alone of the synoptic gospels, Luke can serve as a bridge between Jesus' own concern with the question of Israel's survival in the Roman Empire and the later perspectives of the evangelists. We are given sporadic openings in Mark, Matthew, and the Sayings Gospel Q (found within Matthew and Luke) to Jesus' attitude on this question. But each of the gospels, except Luke, has a redactional position which precludes its ever becoming a major bridge of understanding to the most critical question in Jesus' and Israel's life.

Mark's gospel, as we have seen, was written in the late 60s, in the final hour of the Jewish Temple state, which he opposed. Mark saw his own time as one in which Jesus' hope to save his people from disaster was simply too late. Israel was already fighting a full-scale war with Rome. The legions were marching on Jerusalem. As the city-state braced itself for the Romans' terrible onslaught, rebel recruiters were out forcibly drafting Galilean peasants into the final tragedy. Mark's gospel responds powerfully to that eleventh-hour crisis.

Mark uses the heart of Jesus' vision, the paradox of his nonviolent cross, for a historical project different from Jesus' own: the faithful endurance of a remnant community in the midst of a collapsing world. The symbolism of Mark's gospel turns the end of the existing world, through the power of the cross, into the beginning of a new world. But his gospel makes no suggestion that a new Jerusalem might arise within the walls of the old in time to save the latter from destruction by Rome. Mark's new world must be created somewhere beyond a doomed Jerusalem. The gospel's final symbol points to that new world's coming in Galilee, where the Markan community is: "He has risen, he is not here [at Jerusalem]; see the place where they laid him. But go, tell his disciples and Peter that he is going before you to Galilee: there you will see him, as he told you" (Mark 16:6-7).

"There [in Galilee] you will see him" is only the third time in his gospel that Mark has used the future tense of the verb "to see."[45] The other two passages we are already familiar with: "And then they will see *Bar Enasha* coming in clouds with great power and glory" (Mark 13:26). "And you will see *Bar Enasha* seated at the right hand of Power, and coming with the clouds of heaven" (Mark 14:62). In the message to the women at the tomb (16:6-7) the transformed world of this coming Human Being whom they will see is identified with Galilee, not Jerusalem. Mark voices his hope that, faithfully resistant to the violence of the Jewish-Roman War, his Jewish-Christian community will see their Galilean seeds grow into a nonviolent transformation of the earth.

Thus, for Mark's community in the late 60s, it is already too late to match Jesus' nonviolent faith to his specific hope in history: to save Jerusalem, and through it, the Jewish nation. While Jerusalem burns, Jesus' hope of nonviolent transformation must now be shifted to Galilee's remnant community. The challenge and achievement of Mark's gospel was to proclaim good news beyond the total, tragic loss of Jesus' original hope.

As we have also seen, Matthew found himself compelled to explain the historical failure of Jesus' radical hope for his people. Writing a decade or more after the fall of Jerusalem, Matthew saw his task as one of shifting Jesus' vision from its original hope to a divine judgment upon the failure of that hope, a judgment attributed indiscriminately to a faithless Israel. Jesus' failed historical project Matthew adapts into a judgment upon the age of Israel as terminated by God, prior to a new age of the church. Within his scheme of divine providence, Matthew dramatized his interpretation of Jerusalem's fall as Israel's rejection of Jesus and God's rejection of Israel. Thus, in the vision of a Gentile, Christian world, the tragedy in 70 is explained, but Jesus' hope in 30 is eclipsed. In this explanation Matthew has laid the foundation for further historical tragedies. Moreover, Jesus' hope for transformation that breaks into view in the Sermon on the Mount, "Love your enemies and pray for those who persecute you," becomes largely a hidden hope. In the course of the gospel, Jesus' command to love one's enemies is reversed to a final terrifying judgment on his own people. On Matthew's scroll, Jesus' hope for Israel becomes *Bar Enasha's* return in the form of Roman legions in the annihilating judgment of 70.

In its earliest form the Sayings Gospel Q also proposed a hope of non-violent transformation. Jesus' inaugural sermon and mission speech to the disciples raise in Q the transforming alternative of the kingdom of God, a way of total peace. But in proclaiming that alternative, the Q community experienced frustrations which turned its gospel toward a judgment on "this generation." The final editing of Q emphasizes Q2 texts pronouncing judgment upon an unrepentant Israel destined for war with Rome. But we have yet to consider Q prophecies concerning Jerusalem within Luke.

Thus, neither Mark, Matthew, nor even Q in its final redaction can serve as an adequate bridge of understanding to Jesus' specific hope in history, to save the Jewish people from destruction. What, then, is different about Luke?

TO SAVE THE PEOPLE FROM DESTRUCTION

To explore this question of the difference in Luke, I have found the best guide to be Lloyd Gaston's *No Stone on Another,* a neglected exegetical masterpiece published in 1970. Gaston's lack of recognition can be attributed in part to his tightly woven, ingenious argument. It is too scholarly for laypeople, and in its implications, too revolutionary for scholars. In the labyrinth of *No Stone on Another* lies a bridge to the historical Jesus. By citing Gaston, I hope I can suggest the transforming implications of his work.

Scholarly consensus has the gospel of Luke being written about the same time as Matthew, between 70 and 90 C.E.; its companion volume, The Acts of the Apostles, about a decade later.[46] As to its place, "we can say for certain only that Luke was written outside Palestine."[47] Luke dedicates both his gospel and Acts to a Gentile official, Theophilus (Luke 1:1-4; Acts 1:1). Thus, Luke himself is usually assumed to be a Gentile writing for Gentiles.

Understanding Luke, however, requires a reversal of scholarly prejudice, just as with the final editor of Matthew's gospel. To understand the last Matthew editor's handling of the fall of Jerusalem, we have had to recognize him not as a Jewish Christian, but as a Gentile Christian hostile toward Judaism. To understand Luke's handling of the same matter, we shall need to follow a somewhat opposite route: revise the usual characterization of that "Gentile Gospel" at least sufficiently to account for the positive side of its inner contradictions on Jerusalem.

Lloyd Gaston has begun this task for us by identifying "an astonishing fact": that all of the explicit references to the destruction of Jerusalem in the synoptic gospels are to be found in the special material of Luke.[48] Combining these explicit texts with other implicit warnings adds up to a total of eight passages in Luke envisioning Jerusalem's destruction. It has been an unquestioned assumption among scholars that these repeated warnings to the city were not original to Jesus. They were merely the post-70 Luke's prophecies after the event. Gaston, however, has countered this assumption by a detailed, text-by-text analysis. I shall follow that approach here.

Jesus' eight prophecies to Jerusalem derive from two sources. The first source we are already familiar with, the Sayings Gospel Q, from which Luke has drawn three of his prophecies (Luke 11:49-51, 13:34-35, 17:20-37). Q's own reason for proclaiming these prophecies of destruction we have seen. They correspond to the Q community's failure to convert "this generation" to a nonviolent alternative to war with Rome, the kingdom of God. Thus the Q prophets foresaw a judgment of fire. The remaining five prophecies in Luke occur in material unique to that gospel (12:54-56, 13:1-5, 19:41-44, 23:28-31, 21:5-28; the latter interspersed with sayings from Mark), identified by scholars as "Special Luke." From what further source might these Special Luke texts on Jerusalem's destruction have come?

Following Gaston's suggestion, we can relate these sayings to a *Sitz im Leben,* or life situation in the church, which would account for their retention as prophecies of Jesus. As in the case of Q's judgments on "this generation," the Special Luke texts represent a prophetic alternative, but as we shall see, in a more hopeful way. Gaston contends that Luke's warnings of destruction "have a natural *Sitz im Leben,* " the missionary preaching of the church to the inhabitants of Jerusalem. Luke, therefore, "is using an older source in those passages concerning Jerusalem."[49] The Special Lucan prophecies may come specifically from the Jerusalem church, which, before its flight on the eve of war or destruction in 70, was the fount of authority in the Jewish Christian movement.[50]

But before we cross the bridge of these prophecies to the perspective of Jesus, we shall have to recognize a paradox, if not a contradiction, in the larger context: "Luke-Acts is one of the most pro-Jewish and one of the most anti-Jewish writings in the New Testament."[51] In this comment Lloyd Gaston brings together the two major influences on Luke-Acts: 1) the Special Lucan source, expressing the earlier, pro-Jewish traditions of the Palestinian church; 2) Luke himself, writing with a later theological purpose that is anti-Jewish, yet anti-Jewish in such a way that Luke still needs his pro-Jewish source.

In Acts, perhaps because of Jewish challenges to his community, Luke was compelled to explain why a church worshipping a Jewish messiah had itself become a Gentile church. Paul and Barnabas answer this question on Luke's behalf when they tell Jewish opponents in Antioch of Pisidia: "It was necessary that the word of God should be spoken first to you. Since you thrust it from you, and judge yourselves unworthy of eternal life, behold, we turn to the Gentiles" (Acts 13:46). In the final scene of Acts Paul repeats this answer, again to skeptical Jewish opponents, this time in

Rome: "Let it be known to you then that this salvation of God has been sent to the Gentiles; they will listen" (Acts 28:28).

Like Matthew, Luke bases a Gentile mission and church on a Jewish rejection of God's word. Nonetheless, Luke recognizes the counter need to show the church's continuity with Jesus' people:

> Under the dual impact of the fall of Jerusalem and the shift of the church to an almost completely Gentile Christian movement, Luke must deal with some major theological problems. The status of his community as a legitimate people of God is under attack by Jewish neighbours and is questioned in the minds of Christians themselves. Luke overcomes the problem (1) by stressing the continuity of the church with Judaism, by showing its great popularity among Jews and the approval given to it by the Pharisees [in the Acts of the Apostles], and (2) by relegating this period of continuity to a generation of the past.[52]

Luke's nascent Gentile church, proclaiming a Jewish messiah, needs a theological connection with Judaism but not apparently with living Jews. He makes the necessary connection to the past, to an earlier Jewish-Christian church, while holding to the counter theme of Acts, that Jews have rejected the gospel and God has rejected the Jews. Luke therefore adapts into his story the pro-Jewish material of the Jerusalem church, using it in the gospel and the early chapters of Acts to stress Jesus' and the church's past popularity among Jews, before the Jewish rejection occurred.

Luke is known as the gospel in which Jesus journeys toward Jerusalem. This extended journey takes up ten chapters of the gospel: Luke 9:51-19:28. The journey's purpose is stated at its beginning in terms of Luke's theology: that Jesus "be received up" (Luke 9:51), that he be assumed into heaven through his crucifixion at Jerusalem. According to Luke, Jesus goes to Jerusalem to die in predestined fulfillment of the scriptures and God's will. For Luke, that is purpose enough. It is not enough, however, for us to see the historical purpose of Jesus.[53]

The Special Lucan and Q prophecies suggest a more specific reason for Jesus' journey to Jerusalem: to save the city from destruction. The prophecies of Special Luke seem to represent a strand of tradition passed on to Luke from Jewish Christians living in Palestine at the middle of the first century. Because it shared Jesus' special hope and concern for his people, the Palestinian church cited his contingent prophecies for Jerusalem, proclaiming a choice between transformation and annihilation. There was still time for these prophecies to be heeded by the people of Jerusalem. Luke retains the prophecies after 70 C.E. for a different reason: to show that they were not heeded and to base a mission to the Gentiles upon his and the church's interpretation of that failed purpose. Yet his gospel, by including these prophecies from the Palestinian church, preserves through them the original reason for Jesus' journey to Jerusalem. Within this strand of tradition, as in Luke's larger gospel, Jesus goes to Jerusalem out of a willingness to die. But in the Palestinian tradition, he does so specifically to save the life of Israel from destruction by the Roman Empire, proclaiming a way of nonviolence, a way that today might save the lives of all people from destruction.

Within this Special Lucan strand of tradition, there is a memorable saying of Jesus that I take to be a key to his hope that Jerusalem would be saved: "I saw Satan fall like lightning from heaven" (Luke 10:18). I believe that here, in contrast to the post-70 view of Luke, we can see in its transforming power a startling vision that fired Jesus' hope. Because Satan had fallen, Jerusalem need not fall. Jerusalem and Israel could be transformed. Rome could eventually be transformed. The key to this prophetic hope was Jesus' own experience of Satan's fall like lightning from heaven, his certain sense of evil's fall from power.[54]

Satan's fall from heaven is a mythological way of seeing good's victory over evil on earth.[55] It is the other side of the presence of God's kingdom. Satan's fall and the kingdom's presence express Jesus' hope for nonviolent change. Satan, or evil, is not in control of the earth. Caesar is not in control. The Roman legions are not in control. The Temple authorities are not in control. Multinational corporations are not in control. The nuclear powers are not in control. God alone is in control, to the extent that we realize, as Jesus did, the truth of God's kingdom — a nonviolent kingdom of infinite power. Jesus realized that truth in his evil-shattering vision of Satan's fall like lightning, then in his living out that vision and the presence of the kingdom in response to his people's crisis of violence. Because Satan had fallen, Jerusalem did not have to fall, however desperate the situation. The kingdom of God was at hand, is at hand. Its power is no farther away than your and my hands. Gandhi realized the same transforming truth in his doctrine of *satyagraha,* or truth-force. Satan's fall, the kingdom of God, and *satyagraha* are all ways into an infinite power of change that is always present, yet seldom realized. This Nonviolent God of Love is the forgotten factor in every apparently hopeless conflict.

As Jesus journeys toward Jerusalem, however, tensions appear in Luke's text. We shall try to understand the causes of these tensions as we reflect now upon the eight prophetic warnings to Jerusalem found in Luke, all of them derived from either Q or an early strand of Special Luke. I believe we are addressed by these prophecies, in humanity's ultimate crisis, more profoundly than were those who first heard them. The purpose, then, of this reflection will be to make our own journey into Jerusalem. Even more so than Jesus and his people, we are faced by the question of Jerusalem: transformation or an inconceivable future.

"UNLESS YOU REPENT"

Jesus' first prophetic warning in Luke draws upon the Q text which Matthew used after the woes against the scribes and Pharisees to begin his explanation of the destruction of Jerusalem. Following the same sequence (but placed at a less climactic point in his gospel), Luke puts this saying after his own woes against the Pharisees and lawyers:

> "Therefore also the Wisdom of God said, 'I will send them prophets and apostles, some of whom they will kill and persecute,' that the blood of all the prophets, shed from the foundation of the world, may be required of this generation, from the blood of Abel to the blood of Zechariah, who perished between the altar and the sanctuary. Yes, I tell you, it shall be required of this generation" (Luke 11:49-51).

What is remarkable about this first of Luke's eight prophetic warnings is that, as in Matthew's use of it, it seems to have closed the door to repentance. What "shall be required of this generation" has already been determined. But unlike Matthew, Luke's gospel will reopen the door to repentance in subsequent warnings. Repentance will be seen as the alternative to destruction. There is, then, apparently a struggle going on within the text of Luke as to whether or not repentance — and with it, the salvation of Jerusalem is possible. From the standpoint of the final writer editor, whose theology emphasizes God's foreknowledge and determination of events, the question would have been: How could God intend a repentance that did not in fact come to pass?

Yet the tension within this particular text exists at a level deeper than the theology of Luke, who is simply confirming by his use here the meaning of a Q text from the 50s which is itself pessimistic on repentance. Judging from its introduction, "Therefore also the Wisdom of God said," Gaston believes the saying is clearly not from Jesus but from an early Christian prophet: "Jesus spoke in his own name, but the Christian prophets transmitted words of the Lord, or in this case of his attribute of wisdom."[56]

With its emphasis on judgment rather than repentance, this saying reveals a growing discouragement in the Q community and the larger Palestinian church. Its prophets were frustrated at the lack of response in Israel to their proclamation of peace, while war clouds gathered. The saying gives us an insight into the half-faithful, half-desperate attitude of Jewish Christian prophets in the latter days when their nation's conflict with Rome deepened.

Josephus tells the story of such a prophet, who was killed by the war he failed to prevent. Josephus' story begins four years before the war, at the Feast of Tabernacles in October 62:

> One Jeshua, son of Ananias, a very ordinary yokel, came to the feast at which every Jew is expected to set up a tabernacle for God. As he stood in the Temple he suddenly began to shout: "A voice from the east, a voice from the west, a voice from the four winds, a voice against Jerusalem and the Sanctuary, a voice against bridegrooms and brides,

a voice against the whole people." Day and night he uttered this cry as he went through all the streets. Some of the more prominent citizens, very annoyed at these ominous words, laid hold of the fellow and beat him savagely. Without saying a word in his own defence or for the private information of his persecutors, he persisted in shouting the same warning as before. The Jewish authorities, rightly concluding that some supernatural force was responsible for the man's behavior, took him before the Roman procurator. There, though scourged till his flesh hung in ribbons, he neither begged for mercy nor shed a tear, but lowering his voice to the most mournful of tones answered every blow with "Woe to Jerusalem!" When Albinus — for that was the procurator's name — demanded to know who he was, where he came from and why he uttered such cries, he made no reply whatever to the questions but endlessly repeated his lament over the City, till Albinus decided that he was a madman and released him. All the time till the war broke out he never approached another citizen or was seen in conversation, but daily as if he had learnt a prayer by heart he recited his lament: "Woe to Jerusalem!" Those who daily cursed him he never cursed; those who gave him food he never thanked: his only response to anyone was that dismal foreboding. His voice was heard most of all at the feasts. For seven years and five months he went on ceaselessly, his voice as strong as ever and his vigour unabated, till during the siege after seeing the fulfilment of his foreboding he was silenced. He was going round on the wall uttering his piercing cry: "Woe again to the City, the people, and the Sanctuary!" and as he added a last word: "Woe to me also!" a stone shot from an engine struck him, killing him instantly. Thus he uttered those same forebodings to the very end.[57]

The strange prophet in Josephus's story may not be a follower of Jesus, but he is engaged in a similar project. His prophecy is strikingly similar to what we have already seen in Q, for example: "Woe to you, Chorazin! woe to you, Bethsaida! for if the mighty works done in you had been done in Tyre and Sidon, they would have repented long ago, sitting in sackcloth and ashes. But it shall be more tolerable in the judgment for Tyre and Sidon than for you" (Luke 10:13-14). Jeshua's prophetic woes to Jerusalem, and the Q prophets' woes to Chorazin and Bethsaida, anticipate the same historical judgment: Roman legions, flying their eagle standards, thundering down from Syria upon the Galilean towns, and, eventually, Jerusalem. This is "the judgment" in which Tyre and Sidon, pagan cities not involved in the Jewish uprising, would fare better. Unless the Jewish nation turned ("repented") to peace, all would be destroyed, according to Jeshua and Q. But as the days passed for Jeshua, Q, and their nation, and as their woe sayings were ignored in Jerusalem and Galilee alike, their pessimism deepened. Repentance seemed hopeless. And so they delivered their judgments.

"The blood of all the prophets" (some of whom, like Jeshua, were scourged by the empire at the urging of those they sought to save from the empire) "shall be required of this generation" (Luke 11:50-51). Josephus's story helps us to understand the anguish of the prophets behind the kind of judgment we find in Luke 11:49-51.

The second prophetic warning is from Special Luke.[58] It is more likely than the first to have come originally from Jesus. It uses the people's keen sense of the weather to question their failure to understand their "present time":

> He also said to the multitudes, "When you see a cloud rising in the west, you say at once, 'A shower is coming'; and so it happens. And when you see the south wind blowing, you say, 'There will be scorching heat'; and it happens. You hypocrites! You know how to interpret the appearance of the earth and sky; but why do you not know how to interpret the present time?" (Luke 12:54-56).

G. B. Caird, commenting on this text, writes: "When a small cloud appeared over the Mediterranean, or when the wind veered round to the south, the weatherwise Israelites knew how to draw the proper conclusion; but when the storm clouds were racing before high winds on the political horizon, they remained unconcerned."[59]

Does this sound at all familiar in a modern nation that daily plans its children's activities by listening to weather forecasts and prepares for their future by complacently stockpiling thousands of nuclear weapons? Do we interpret the present time of annihilation any more truthfully than those whom Jesus challenged in his nation?

Repentance is the essence of Luke's third prophetic warning. Jesus is confronted by a group of people who are outraged at a massacre by Pilate in Jerusalem of Galilean Jews. They want Jesus to lash out against the Roman governor. Instead, he tells them to repent of their violent attitude toward Pilate:

> There were some present at that very time who told him of the Galileans whose blood Pilate had mingled with their sacrifices. And he answered them, "Do you think that these Galileans were worse sinners than all the other Galileans, because they suffered thus? I tell you, No; but unless you repent you will all likewise perish. Or those eighteen upon whom the tower in Siloam fell and killed them, do you think that they were worse offenders than all the others who dwelt in Jerusalem? I tell you, No; but unless you repent you will all likewise perish" (Luke 13:1-5).

We do not have the specific historical circumstances for "the Galileans whose blood Pilate had mingled with their sacrifices" (thus a massacre presumably in the Temple or its vicinity) or for the "eighteen upon whom the tower in Siloam fell and killed them." However, this Special Lucan passage is the third segment in a unit of four, all of which have the same general theme of warning Israel of imminent disaster: 1) the need to interpret the time instead of just the weather (12:54-56), which we have just seen; 2) the little parable on settling with an adversary (an allusion to Rome), rather than allowing a conflict to go to a Roman court (war) and disaster (12:57-59); 3) this passage on the urgency of repentance to avoid total destruction; and 4) the parable of the fig tree (13:6-9), in which Israel, the fig tree, is symbolically warned that it must soon bear fruit or be cut down. In this context repentance means a turning from hatred of the enemy, Pilate and Rome, before the nation perishes: "Unless you repent, you will all likewise perish."

Pilate's killing of the Galileans may have been his reaction to an incipient uprising at Passover, when Jerusalem swelled with pilgrims and anti-Roman sentiment, a first strike carried out when the Galileans went up to the Temple to offer sacrifice. Alternatively, commentators have suggested that the basis for the question to Jesus could have been an incident described by Josephus: Pilate's violent repression of a protest against his use of the Temple fund, "Corban," to build an aqueduct to Jerusalem.[60] When a large crowd shouted their disapproval of this misappropriation to Pilate, his soldiers clubbed many of them to death.[61] Similarly, the eighteen deaths at the Siloam tower, located by a reservoir connected to this aqueduct, may have been caused by a violent clash with Pilate's troops. Both literary and historical contexts strongly support Gaston's reading of the text: "Unless you repent as a nation, you will be massacred by Roman soldiers or you will be crushed under the falling walls of Jerusalem."[62]

Jesus is speaking collectively to his nation: "Unless you repent [from violence], you will *all* likewise perish." Unless the nation repents by putting away its sword, it will perish by Rome's sword. There is an echo here consistent with Jesus' admonition in Matthew to the disciple who used his sword in Jesus' defense, cutting off the ear of the high priest's slave: "Put your sword back into its place; for all who take the sword will perish by the sword" (Matt. 26:52).

What does repentance from a nation's violence mean? To begin with, we know that the rabbinic word for repentance is *teshuvah,* "turning," a turning from sin to God,[63] as derived from the biblical verb *shuv,* "to return."[64] "Its original meaning is a returning to God from *exile,* i.e., from that place of alienation/separation."[65] Thus, *teshuvah* means returning to the path or way we have been given by the Creator, "the path at return from exile, from Babylon (Babylon = the empires of this world)."[66] Our violence has put us in exile in Babylon, the empire of violence. *Teshuvah* means re-turning from the empire of violence to the nonviolent path of our Creator.

In considering a *teshuvah* or turning from violence as proclaimed by this text, we should remember that we are reading these prophetic warnings in Luke in four different historical contexts, three in the first century and one in the twentieth. Let us imagine we are viewing these four situations in history through a telescope, refocusing the telescope as we turn to each so as to distinguish its respective importance. We see, first, the situation of Luke's own post-70 gospel. There, in a Gentile church after the fall of Jerusalem, the prophecies are seen as predictions fulfilled upon another people. Their purpose, in the post-70 Lucan editor's context, is to help explain why the fires of Rome have already consumed Jerusalem. Refocusing our telescope, we see an earlier image, the Palestinian church in the 50s and 60s. From Galilee to Jerusalem, Jewish Christian prophets are warning their people that disaster lies ahead. As the years pass and time runs out for the nation, the Palestinian church's warnings deepen in desperation and finally become judgments. We turn the telescope next to the late 20s, focusing on Jesus' ministry. Jesus proclaims his prophecies to the nation urgently but with a profound hope for change. Satan has fallen from heaven. The kingdom of God is at hand. The power of transformation is present, but it must be chosen. There must be a collective turning from violence to nonviolence. "Unless you repent, you will all likewise perish." Finally, since the fourth historical context is so removed in time from the first three, we may imagine our fourth image as seeming to appear from the wrong end of the telescope. As we concentrate our viewing, we realize that to see our own nuclear age clearly we must also focus upon it from the right end. We see the question. In a situation that is globally analogous to the looming destruction of Jerusalem, we, too, but in a more critical context, are asked to turn. "Unless you repent, you will all likewise perish."

As important as are the first three situations for our understanding of *teshuvah,* it is the fourth in which we shall make our own decision to repent or perish, to turn away from violence and toward our Nonviolent Creator or to be totally destroyed.

TESHUVAH *AT BANGOR*

On overcast nights when Shelley and I have walked our dogs, we have seen an orange glow in the clouds over Naval Submarine Base Bangor, our next-door neighbor. Straining on their leashes, sniffing busily in the bushes, our dogs are a tug of life. The glowing clouds are a sign of death. Reflected off the clouds are the high-intensity security lights for the nuclear weapons entombed in bunkers at the center of the Trident submarine base. As our dogs frolic and bark in the darkness, we can see in the radiant clouds overhead a sign of the end of all life.

I once stood in front of the huge concrete bunkers at the center of the Trident base praying for God's forgiveness for our having created the power of evil stored inside them. It had taken a friend, John Clark, and me twenty-eight hours, struggling through the dense foliage of the base and climbing high concertina-wire fences, before we arrived inside Strategic Weapons Facility Pacific (SWFPAC). It was a journey through our illusions to the end of the world. From the Kitsap County roads ringing the Trident base, looking inside the perimeter fence, one sees a serene forest—with an occasional deer wandering at the edge of that government game preserve. What lies at the center of the forest, shielded by evergreens, is our own inconceivable evil. SWFPAC is a massive wasteland of row after row of bunkers housing thermonuclear warheads and Trident missile propellants, a desolation hidden from the outside world by hundreds of acres of rain forest. To see that evil, John and I had to work our way foot by foot through untamed Northwest rain scrub. When we reached SWFPAC, we used kitchen stepping stools and rug remnants to climb over the twelve-foot-high double security fences. We then walked alone and unimpeded to the first nuclear weapons bunker—to pray. It was like a tomb: huge sliding concrete slabs shut in front of us, beneath a small mountain of earth that formed a canopy. We stood in silence for several minutes on the concrete entry, joined hands, and said aloud the Lord's Prayer and the Hail Mary. We continued our nuclear Stations of the Cross in front of five more bunkers before we were arrested by Marine security guards.

Praying in front of those tombs of humankind was, for me, the same experience as praying at another time in front of the ovens at the Dachau concentration camp. Dachau even looked and felt like SWFPAC: a massive white wasteland, devoid of vegetation within its fences. Its bleak white emptiness was broken by rows not of bunkers but of barracks to house those not yet sent to the ovens at the far corner of the compound. I have no words to describe the ovens. At Dachau's ovens and SWFPAC's bunkers, I was praying at the end of the world, asking God's deliverance of us all from the civilization of death concentrated in those mechanisms of mass murder.

Yet it was at these terrible places of rock-bottom despair that I experienced the deepest hope for *teshuvah,* given in a darkness where all possibility of life-giving change seemed stripped away from my heart and imagination. I knew then the truth that in God alone lies our hope of turning from the inconceivably evil choices we have made to destroy the earth and all its creatures. If we act in faith, resisting that evil to the point of experiencing a powerless despair at our own efforts to turn from it, I believe God will turn us from death to life in more profound ways than we can imagine. At Dachau and SWFPAC, by experiencing the void, we recognize its presence in ourselves. In resisting powers of death to that point of ultimate darkness and despair where we stand before our own inconceivable evil, we realize that God alone can give that new world we are seeking. That moment of turning in darkness is both our hope in God and God's hope in us. It is *teshuvah.*

Teshuvah is our wholehearted turning to God. It is impossible for us to understand the prophets, and Jesus in particular, without probing the depths of *teshuvah:* Unless you repent, unless you turn and re-turn, you will all likewise perish. On the other hand, if we turn deeply enough to see and feel Dachau's ovens and SWFPAC's bunkers, we are on the edge of transformation. At that point, we have no illusions about any nation or anyone. The only way to turn is to re-turn to our Creator. Thus, when Jesus told his people that the kingdom of God is at hand, he made the breakthrough to that transforming reality contingent upon *teshuvah,* turning to God with one's whole being.

Perhaps the greatest obstacle to *teshuvah* is our belief in the illusion of our own light. In the age of Auschwitz and Trident, to ignore the darkness is to surrender to its forces. Walking more deeply into our darkness is our only hope. We have to struggle through the forest shielding our evil creations. Seeing our machines of annihilation for what they are, and ourselves as their hidden creators, makes it finally possible for us to turn, to re-turn from our exile in a world of violence. A worldly optimism is the enemy of world transformation. The world we have chosen to live in, as exiles from our Creator, is one in which Trident submarines protect an economic system that results in the starvation of millions of people. The threat of nuclear omnicide tomorrow becomes necessary to protect economic genocide today. To have an optimistic vision of that world is to look up from the darkness to the radiant glow over the Trident base and to say, "How beautiful," just as Jesus' disciples said, "What wonderful stones and what wonderful buildings," while forgetting the poor who had paid in sweat and blood for the system. The reality we have created beneath the clouds is not beautiful. Not to see heaven in our nuclear clouds but to acknowledge instead the immense evil on the face of the earth, which is beyond our control alone, is to begin a real turning toward God, our *teshuvah.*

What will it take for us to experience real *teshuvah* in the face of Trident?

We might listen first to a voice from the Holocaust. Before we choose to turn, we have to know in our depths the despair and horror of that from which we turn. We might listen to Dr. Samuel Pisar, a world-renowned lawyer and one of the youngest survivors of Auschwitz. In June 1981, six-thousand Jews gathered in Jerusalem at the International Holocaust Survivors Conference. Dr. Pisar addressed the Holocaust Conference and the Israeli Knesset (Parliament), using his experience of Auschwitz as the basis for his warning of the holocaust still to come:

> To us, the Holocaust is not only an indelible memory of horror; it is a permanent warning. The fear, the despair, the mounting anger at the root of simmering international issues that are debated so bloodlessly and impersonally by diplomats, economists and politicians, and that endanger what remains of liberty and of peace—we feel them in our bones.
>
> For we have seen the end of creation. In the shadow of permanently flaming gas chambers, where Eichmann's reality eclipsed Dante's

vision of hell, we have witnessed a pilot project for the destruction of humanity, the death rattle of the entire species on the eve of the atomic age, of thermonuclear proliferation—the final solution. . . . We know that the unthinkable is indeed possible.[67]

Samuel Pisar is telling us that just as the unthinkable evil of Auschwitz was indeed possible, so too is the unthinkable evil possible which we have already created in nuclear weapons. It is reflected in the clouds over the Trident base. The next step in initiating the end of life itself is equally possible through a Trident first strike. Our willful optimism about ultimate evil when it involves our own nation makes that evil more possible, more likely. We cannot turn to God in our depths so long as we do not recognize that there is darkness in our nation.

The question of how far God can or will go in preserving us from the final consequences of our own evil links the death camps with our preparations for nuclear omnicide. How is it possible to turn to God if the only God we want is one that will save us from our own choices? We cannot cooperate massively with Trident and other nuclear weapons and then expect God's intervention to prevent our being burned by the evil we have chosen. To continue doing evil and then expect God to save us from its consequences is to mold the Creator in our own image.

Perhaps faith begins in our own darkness at the end of the world. Darkness acknowledged is the beginning of our *teshuvah,* our turning to God in a new possibility. Our time of the end can then become a time of beginning.

Martin Buber is a modern prophet who knew that turning in darkness is the condition for the coming of the kingdom. In the deepening night of the early 1940s, Buber wrote in his classic, *For the Sake of Heaven:*

An hour dawns in which the redemption of the world is near; all that is needed is that we grasp this hour. But it cannot be grasped otherwise than by virtue of that entire turning of the human being from the way of man to the way of God, which we call *teshuvah.*[68]

To grasp this hour after Auschwitz is to acknowledge first that history is now totally vulnerable to the most terrible evil we can conceive. Nothing we can choose — and are choosing — is ruled out. The evil we choose is the evil we get, with all its consequences. Unless we turn, we shall all likewise perish. If we choose to live by Trident, we and our children will die by Trident. We cannot expect God to save us from our choices. The God of Auschwitz and Trident respects human freedom in a terrifying way.

But to grasp this hour as redemptive is to turn, as Buber says, with that entire turning of the human being to God which is our redemption. We can turn to God in a night of death which is within and beyond us. To stand before the nuclear bunkers of SWFPAC is to stand before the death of life itself. The reality of those bunkers crushes all illusions of power. As much as we can and must act for the sake of life, we are in the end powerless before our own evil creations. The necessity and paradox of nonviolent action is that we cannot turn deeply until we have acted to the point of realizing our own powerlessness.

Our own ultimate evil is now poised for realization beneath the oceans and at military sites across the globe. It can be released at any moment. Through a miracle of grace, our evil has been held in check year after year. The moment in which you are reading this is a miracle of grace: Life continues. But we cannot expect miracles of mercy to forestall judgment forever. We shall get what we have chosen.

Unless we turn deeply, we, like our sisters and brothers in first-century Jerusalem, shall all likewise perish—all around the earth.

MORE CONTINGENT PROPHECIES

Luke's fourth prophetic warning of the destruction of Jerusalem is Jesus' lament over the city that is taken from the Sayings Gospel Q and is thus found also in Matthew:

"O Jerusalem, Jerusalem, killing the prophets and stoning those who are sent to you! How often would I have gathered your children together as a hen gathers her brood under her wings, and you would not! Behold, your house is forsaken. And I tell you, you will not see me until you say, 'Blessed is he who comes in the name of the Lord!' " (Luke 13:34–35).

The introduction to this passage, "O Jerusalem, Jerusalem, killing the prophets and stoning those who are sent to you," creates a context for both Jesus and for the Jewish-Christian prophets following him who gave similar warnings up to the eve of the Jewish-Roman War.

The "I" in the text, who has longed "to gather your [Jerusalem's] children" under her wings, is God in the image of a mother hen gathering her chicks, as professed by Jesus and the prophets. This Mother God who longs to protect her children, the people of Jerusalem, from their enemies can do so only through their acceptance of her wings of prophecy. In terms of both the domestic and political experience of Palestinian Jews, for a prophet to evoke the image of a hen gathering her chicks under her wings was to suggest also a second image. Implicit in the prophecy is the cause of the mother hen's concern, circling overhead in the sky, an eagle ready to attack—the Roman eagle. Not to accept the mother hen's prophetic wings is to become prey to the imperial eagle's talons.[69]

The next sentence, "Behold, your house is forsaken," indicates that the "house" of the Temple—or more generally, Jerusalem—has now been forsaken by God's protective wings because Jerusalem has rejected her prophets. That divine presence will not return until Jerusalem turns, by accepting the warnings of Jesus and the Palestinian Christian prophets: "You will not see me *until* you say, 'Blessed is he who comes in the name of the Lord!' " Thus is expressed the hope that Jerusalem will see God through the people's having blessed the prophet of nonviolence, who comes in God's name.

This hope is seen, again, in three different perspectives.

The first is the perspective of Jesus' ministry, in which the hope of nonviolent transformation through a divine love of enemies is offered as the alternative to Jerusalem's destruction.

The second perspective is that of the Q community prophets, who in a time of deepening national crisis (and their own rejection) express the hope that Jerusalem will still turn in time to avoid destruction.

The final perspective is that of the post-70 editor, Luke, who contravenes Jesus' prophetic hope for Jerusalem as a prediction fulfilled in Jerusalem's destruction. Luke therefore relates the "until you say" of this text specifically to Jesus' own entry into Jerusalem, when he is indeed blessed as one "coming in the name of the Lord" (Luke 19:38) — only to be rejected then by the people in Luke's passion narrative. Luke thus explains to the gospel's readers the destruction of Jerusalem.

In addition to the first-century shifts of interpretation, we should note subsequent chapters in the history of these prophetic texts. From beginning to end, the sequence runs:

What originated with Jesus as a deeply hopeful contingent prophecy to his own people . . .

became, in the 50s and 60s, the Palestinian church's discouraged but still-prophetic woes to its nation on the verge of war. . .

became, after 70, the Lucan editor's and Gentile church's fulfilled prediction and explanation of *another* people's defeat. . .

became, in succeeding centuries, the established Christian church's justification for its violently anti-Semitic canon laws[70]. . .

became, in the Third Reich, a basis for Hitler's extermination policy.

Jesus' contingent prophecy, with its hope for transformation, has been recycled into prediction, fulfillment, explanation, justification, persecution, and attempted extermination. In the hands of militarist preachers these same texts are now used as deterministic predictions of nuclear war so as to justify our own preparations for omnicide.

At the beginning of this chapter we saw two of the four remaining prophetic warnings of the destruction of Jerusalem: Jesus' weeping over the city (Luke 19:41-44); his final words to the women of Jerusalem (Luke 23:28-31). Both texts are from Special Luke.

Gaston identifies Jesus' weeping over Jerusalem in a way which helps us see more deeply the redemptive nature of prophecy: "The whole scene of Jesus weeping over Jerusalem could have come straight from the pages of Jeremiah."[71] Like Jeremiah's prophetic warnings six centuries earlier that Jerusalem would be destroyed by the Babylonians, Jesus' prophecies have a conditional nature, contingent upon whether or not the people turn. In the bible's classic statement of contingent prophecy, Yahweh had said to Jeremiah, "If at any time I declare concerning a nation or a kingdom, that I will pluck up and break down and destroy it, and if that nation, concerning which I have spoken, turns from its evil, I will repent of the evil that I intended to do to it" (Jer. 18:7-8). In this prophetic tradition, Yahweh too turns and repents—when a nation turns from its evil. In this way a prophecy is fulfilled most profoundly when its threat does *not* come to pass. When a nation turns from violence and injustice, God turns from the dire future foreseen for that nation by the prophet. The equally bold way in which the *Jerusalem Bible* translates this phrase rendered by the *Revised Standard Version* as "I [Yahweh] will repent of the evil" is "I [Yahweh] then change my mind about the evil."

When Jesus weeps over Jerusalem, the condition for "changing the mind of Yahweh" from allowing the city's destruction by Rome is for Jerusalem "to know the things that make for peace" (Luke 19:42) in Jesus' proclamation of the nonviolent kingdom of God and the New Humanity. The same condition for changing a future seen prophetically is evident in the words to "the daughters of Jerusalem," when Jesus uses his own execution by Rome as a prophet of nonviolence to warn of Rome's response to a violent revolt: "For if they do this when the wood is green, what will happen when it is dry" (Luke 23:31)?

These contingent prophecies of Jesus are later given the same shifting shades of meaning as the other texts in Luke which we have considered. They are used by the Palestinian church of the 50s as prophetic threats more and more apt to overtake an unresponsive Israel; finally, by the post-70 editor of Luke, as predictions fulfilled already upon those he saw as a superseded people, in the fall of Jerusalem.

We are left with two contingent prophecies of Jerusalem's destruction still to consider, Luke 17:20-37 and 21:5-28, which comprise most of Luke's divided version of the eschatological discourse.[72] Luke 17:20-37 (a Q passage with a few additions from Luke) presents Jesus' statement of the choice facing his generation, no different from the choice facing ours: a choice between nonviolence and nonexistence, between a nonviolent kingdom (or world) of God and a violence that will destroy Jerusalem (the world). This passage is both a contingent prophecy of Jerusalem's destruction and a statement of the transforming alternative to that destruction. It need not happen.

The alternative is given first. The context for it has been created by a question to Jesus: When is the kingdom of God coming (17:20)? The "kingdom of God" means the religious, political, and social liberation of the

Jewish people from the Roman Empire through the power of Yahweh. The question of the kingdom of God is *the* question of Jesus' ministry. It is the question that pervades the gospel of Luke from its opening scenes, when the prophetess Anna speaks of the child Jesus "to all who were looking for the redemption of Jerusalem" (2:38), to its closing scenes when the disciples after Jesus' death are still puzzling over the question of national liberation: "But we had hoped that he was the one to redeem Israel" (24:21).

When Jesus is asked when the kingdom of God is coming, he is therefore being challenged as a prophet to present his own revolutionary vision to the people: When does he envision the people being liberated from Rome by Yahweh? Jesus' answer, which serves to introduce his prophecy of destruction, transforms the question: "The kingdom of God is not coming with signs to be observed; nor will they say, 'Lo, here it is!' or 'There!' for behold, the kingdom of God is within your power" (17:20-21).

Josephus helps us to understand the history behind the "signs to be observed." He tells of an incident in the 50s when revolutionary prophets had led a large number of the people "out into the desert on the pretence that there God would show them signs of approaching freedom." However, the Roman procurator, Felix, "regarding this as the first stage of revolt, sent cavalry and heavy infantry who cut the mob to pieces."[73]

The particular prophet of "signs to be observed" whom the Palestinian church of the late 50s remembered most was "the Egyptian," a revolutionary leader for whom Paul was mistaken in the Acts of the Apostles (21:38). Josephus, with undisguised prejudice, describes in *The Jewish War* the Egyptian's brief but turbulent revolutionary movement, which took place about 56 C.E.

> Arriving in the country [from Egypt] this man, a fraud who posed as a seer, collected about 30,000 dupes, led them round from the desert to the Mount of Olives, and from there was ready to force an entry into Jerusalem, overwhelm the Roman garrison, and seize supreme power with his fellow-raiders as bodyguard.[74]

In a parallel account in his *Antiquities*, Josephus includes the sign the Egyptian claimed he would show the people in the course of liberating Jerusalem. It would be a sign like Joshua's at the battle of Jericho. At the Egyptian's command, the walls of Jerusalem would fall down so that his followers could enter and seize the city. But before any such sign could be attempted, Felix met the Egyptian's people's army with Roman cavalry and infantry, killing and capturing hundreds and putting the rest to flight, including the Egyptian.[75]

What is being presented in these accounts is not a series of lunatic leaders, as Josephus tends to caricature them, but what Richard Horsley and John Hanson call "action prophets," who "led movements of peasants in active anticipation of divine acts of deliverance."[76] This prophetic method of revolution drew on powerful symbols from Israel's past. In first-century Palestine prophetic leaders gained popular support through signs taken from the exodus and the conquest, just as today United States politicians propagandize in their context through signs suggesting images of the American Revolution. In the struggle against Rome, sign propaganda continued as an important means of power over the people right through to the final events of the war. In one of those events Josephus describes the Roman massacre of thousands of Jewish women and children, acting in obedience to another prophet, "who that very day had declared to the people in the City that God commanded them to go up to the Temple to receive the signs of their deliverance." This prophet and others had been ordered by the provisional revolutionary government to stem the tide of deserters in the final hour of the war by creating hopes of deliverance in the people.[77]

Action prophets, basing their revolutionary movements on promises of signs to the people, were already active in Jesus' time. Josephus gives the example of a Samaritan prophet, during the rule of Pontius Pilate, whose sign of liberating his people was to lead them up the sacred Mount Gerizim, in order to find holy vessels left there by Moses. Instead, the armed crowd was attacked and overwhelmed at the foot of the mountain by Pilate's troops.[78]

When Jesus says, then, that "the kingdom of God is not coming with signs to be observed; nor will they say 'Lo, here it is!' or 'There!' " (Luke 17:20b-21a), he is rejecting the specific way in which popular prophets led masses of the people to their deaths by Roman soldiers. The reference to such leaders becomes more specific a moment later in the text when he warns again, "And they will say to you, 'Lo, there!' or 'Lo, here!' Do not go, do not follow them" (Luke 17:23). Those who did follow them perished needlessly in terrible slaughters by Rome.

This twofold rejection of prophetic power-seeking through signs is the frame for Jesus' alternative vision of revolution: "For behold, the kingdom of God is within your power" (Luke 17:21b).

The alternative to a revolution promising seductive signs of a liberating future is an already transforming present. To follow prophets seeking signs of liberation from Rome was a trap. To look to a future revolution for hope in the present was an illusion. The present held its own nonviolent transformation: "For behold, the kingdom of God is within your power." Or as was said once by Jacques Maritain, the means are "in a sense the end in process of becoming."[79] The means, for Jesus, is God. God's kingdom is not only the end. God's kingdom is the means, present and waiting: "For behold, the kingdom of God is within your power." The kingdom of God, the nonviolent coming of God, is truly at hand. But what kind of kingdom is it that is within our power? Ordinary kingdoms are not. But if we recall here Q's Inaugural Sermon and Luke's Sermon on the Plain, the specific kingdom Jesus is talking about is one in which the ruler is a parent who "showers kindness on the ungrateful and the evil." The power in this kingdom is love, especially love of enemies: "But I tell you who listen, Love your enemies, do good to those who hate you, bless those who curse you, pray for those who mistreat you. . . . If you love those who love you, what credit is that to you? For even the sinners love those who love them. . . . Instead, love your enemies, and do good, and lend, expecting nothing back; and your reward will be great, and you will be children of the Most High, who showers kindness on the ungrateful and the evil" (Luke 6:27, 32, 35). Perhaps that is what puts this strange kingdom within our power, because its power is love, God's love for us and for our enemies, an indiscriminate love showered like rainfall on all of creation. The kingdom of God is within our power because we can choose to accept God's transforming love for our enemy—no matter who that enemy is, or what he or she may have done to us. God's love for our enemy is the kingdom within our power, once we affirm that divine power of enemy love, *agape*, and begin to experience it. Through our enemy we meet the heart of God's love and the possibility of salvation from violence.

SAVED BY OUR ENEMIES

How can I convey the mystery of relationships with the enemies we have known at Ground Zero? It is those we felt were enemies who have often redeemed us from our own prejudice and fear toward them, our enemies who have opened us to a truth or love we had little or no sense of, our enemies who have won us over and become sources of our hope.

In December 1977, when nine of us bought the little farmhouse on 3.8 acres of land alongside the Trident base and named it "Ground Zero Center for Nonviolent Action," our new neighbors were not pleased. Soon after Ground Zero was born, I walked up and down Clear Creek Road knocking on doors to meet the neighbors. The reaction was mixed. The few supportive residents were fearful and isolated, saying (in each case) they knew no one else in Kitsap County who would share our concerns. The Navy, they said, was in total control of the county: Its shipyard and two bases dominated the economy and politics. The more hostile residents were more secure in their convictions. One man said he would shoot me if I didn't leave his driveway immediately. A woman spoke with emphasis and a chilling stare, "You don't understand. You don't belong here," and shut her door. As I made my way from house to house, I became aware that those I had already visited were using a CB radio to warn their neighbors of the coming protester.

After days of such door-to-door encounters, while sleeping on the Ground Zero floor at night, I had the feeling the house might be burned down at any time and the resident shot with impunity. This was an anticipation of things to come. Three years later Ground Zero's geodesic dome would in fact be burned down in the middle of the night by unidentified arsonists, who would also use heavy tools to smash a Buddha statue sitting inside. No one would shoot us, although Coast Guard members would come close to it while boarding our boats blockading the first Trident submarine, the U.S.S. Ohio.

I recall these incidents to convey a sense of the atmosphere around Ground Zero in its first years: one of alienation. We felt ourselves aliens, born of a separate species called protester, in a Navy county that wanted us out. Our pockets of support, such as Clear Creek farm owners Gerry and Dorothy Petersen (who hosted Live Without Trident rallies on their farm, attended mainly by people from outside the county), were themselves besieged by the Navy. One-third of the Petersens' farm was about to be bulldozed to make way for a freeway leading onto the Trident base. The county consensus seemed to be that "if anything should happen to them" (meaning us), it would be our own fault for having provoked violence by our resistance to Trident. And in a sense they were right. Resisting Trident in Kitsap County was like trying to stop a war in progress. It was a context in which the survival of Ground Zero's work, and perhaps members, depended on the toleration and mercy of those whose values we questioned. Like it or not, we could only be saved by our enemies. And we were.

A deputy sheriff we met in those days went by the name Dusty. Dusty Wiley arrested us frequently for passing out leaflets in front of the Trident base, under a variety of charges, usually blocking traffic. He put real feeling into his arrests. Dusty seemed to feel a special obligation to rid Clear Creek Road of Ground Zero leafleters (who are still there, once a week, twelve years later).

Dusty testified against us in many trials challenging our right to leaflet. While taking us to jail or sitting with us in the courthouse, he and Ground Zero folks got to know one another. He arrested us in other contexts as well — in front of trains carrying nuclear weapons and Trident missile propellants. As the years passed, Dusty mellowed in our conversations. He also smiled more, as we waited together for trials to begin — a gentle, disarming smile.

One day Ground Zero member Karol Schulkin was raking leaves in her front yard. Dusty, true to his name, was in a swirl of dust nearby, directing traffic to assist a road crew. A road worker, passing the time with Dusty, gestured at the bumper sticker on the car in Karol's driveway, "CREATE PEACE."

"What do you think that means?" he asked.

"Oh, those are the Ground Zero people," Dusty said, "They're protesting the Trident base. You know, peace isn't just going to happen. You have to create peace. You have to work at it."

Dusty did work at it. As did others in the Kitsap County Sheriff's Department, where we began to experience respect and trust, even as our arrest and jail records lengthened. Sheriff Pat Jones said that Ground Zero people always did what we said we were going to do. He didn't agree with us, but he trusted us to do what we said. And we in turn trusted him and his officers.

Another apparent enemy of ours who worked at peace was the head of the Trident base security police, John Easterbrooks. What I thought was my first encounter with John took place after I had been arrested for an act of civil disobedience at the base. While I was being held for questioning, John came into the room and said, "How is Tom Met?" I asked how John knew the name of Tom Met, a U.S. Marine Corps friend who, in Honolulu ten years earlier, had become a conscientious objector in the middle of the Vietnam War. Tom subsequently served two years in a Marine brig. John said he had been the security officer at Kaneohe Marine Base when Tom had turned himself in, after making public his resistance to the war. I had also been there, as one of Tom's supporters. Now John had become head of the civilian security police at Naval Sub Base Bangor. We were once again literally on opposite sides of the fence.

Over the next decade John would supervise the arrests of hundreds of people resisting Trident. And we would talk periodically. We disagreed on Trident. We respected each other and, despite disagreements, agreed that nonviolence could grow on both sides of the fence. John said he trained his security police to be nonviolent in making arrests.

As a result of one of those arrests, Shelley was sentenced to three months in jail. When our son, Tom, and I returned home after witnessing the sentencing, the phone was ringing with a call from John. After inquiring about Shelley, he asked how he could buy a copy of my book, *Lightning East to West*. He had looked for the book without success. I told him I would get him a copy.

When John and I met so I could give him the book, it was at the base gate in front of our house. John walked from his security truck across the government property line to where I stood. Had we reversed the process, I would have been subject to six months in jail for trespass, for which he had already arrested me several times.

John asked if I would please inscribe the book. He said it was for his commanding officer, on the occasion of his leaving the Trident base for another command. This was to be his farewell present. John added he would now have to "break in" a new commanding officer to the attitude of mutual respect that existed between Ground Zero and Trident base personnel. It was always hard for a new commanding officer to understand that.

I believe John and other security officers we have known at the Trident base have respected Ground Zero people even to the point of saving our lives. We could have been shot, for example, for climbing over the SWFPAC double fences to pray at the nuclear weapons bunkers (after telling the base we were going to do it). By such an action we were pushing beyond all limits the consciences of security people whose beliefs differed radically from ours. In their response to that high-risk action, they were resilient to the point of trusting us to do exactly what we said we would do: pray. They must have prayed also, in making their decision to trust us. In terms of resisting social pressures for violence, theirs was the real nonviolence.

In the campaign to stop Trident, the greatest strain on a mutual trust with our opponents occurred on July 27, 1984, when the White Train came to Bangor. It was met by chaos. Running in front of the moving train, struggling with sheriff's deputies and railroad security guards in front of it, jumping on the train, yelling and cursing at police were all elements of our demonstration's chaos. What had happened in the days before the White Train arrived at Bangor is that the haste to reach consensus had prevented a real consensus between Ground Zero and other groups with different philosophies of action. The result was chaos on the tracks.

In evaluating the July '84 White Train action, Ground Zero members agreed that the Kitsap County sheriff and deputies together with the railroad security guards were the one group of people whose response to the stress of the situation had been nonviolent. We had risked their lives in front of a train. They had saved ours. Shelley recalled a friend of ours—caught up by the combined horror of the train, the thought of his daughter being killed in the future by nuclear weapons, and the spirit of chaos in the demonstration—losing control of himself and trying to throw his body under the wheels of the train. Security guards stopped him and sat on him until the train passed.

After the train had entered the base, thirty-one of us who had been arrested were taken to a police station for booking. We were given an unintended lesson in nonviolence by the sheriff and his deputies. Although we had risked their lives, they in turn were disciplined, polite, and good-humored. I was astounded by their patience and forgiveness.

That night, after our group had been booked and released until trial, Shelley and I sat in silence in our house by the tracks, trying to absorb it all. The phone rang. It was a reporter, asking what I thought of the day's events. I said I thought the police had been more nonviolent than we were. Our putting their lives in jeopardy had been wrong. The reporter's article on my statements in a Seattle paper the next day raised a storm of anger in the peace movement: Why had I said such things? How was it possible for police protecting a cargo of nuclear weapons to be more nonviolent than those resisting it, no matter how undisciplined they were?

When our next *Ground Zero* newspaper was published, with Shelley's and my criticisms of the train action, the controversy intensified. In her article Shelley said that in our actions we had to be very clear about who we are. She enumerated the bedrock beliefs of the Trident campaign as an experiment in nonviolence: a recognition of our own complicity in violence, making decisions together, openness, trust, mutual conversion, long-term patience, and a nonviolent discipline. I wrote that what I felt on the tracks July 27, during our struggle for the victory of stopping the train, is that we *became* the White Train. But we could not stop the White Train by being the White Train.

Some of our friends refused to distribute this issue of *Ground Zero*. Others were dismayed that Ground Zero was dividing the peace movement by its continuing critique of the train action.

Three of us, Ellen Stepleton, George Greenwald, and I, went to jail voluntarily for the July '84 action. Although once again, as in previous actions, we believed the train itself was criminal, we nevertheless pled guilty this time to blocking it so as to accept responsibility for the violence at the tracks. At our sentencing we were startled to hear the county prosecutor in our case, Russ Hauge, argue on our behalf against the judge's putting us in jail. Although confused by the prosecutor's position, the judge gave us sentences ranging from two weeks to the maximum of three months in Kitsap County Jail.

We were visited in jail by Russ Hauge. He told us that he was resigning his job as assistant prosecutor because he wished to join a private law firm. Russ then began to study international law and gave talks affirming the right and responsibility of United States citizens to block the deployment of nuclear weapons. Russ would also become a defense attorney in the June 1985 trial for the next White Train.

In preparation for that next train the Puget Sound Agape Community (made up of Ground Zero and the Seattle Agape Community) held a series of meetings with the Kitsap County sheriffs and Burlington Northern Railroad security guards. We proposed an act of mutual trust to the police representatives, as a way of stopping the train together and without threatening people's lives. The people doing civil disobedience would go out on the tracks early, before the train came, so as to avoid struggling with police to get in front of the train. Our risk was that of telling the police our plans and of possibly being removed by them before the train's arrival. In turn, we asked the Kitsap County sheriffs to risk leaving our people on the tracks until the train came, in spite of pressures to arrest us immediately. Sheriff Pat Jones and Undersheriff Chuck Wheeler, who disagreed as usual with our blocking the train, agreed to our proposed mutual trust on the grounds that it was the safest way for their deputies to arrest people. Finally, the sheriffs, Ground Zero, and Seattle Agape asked Burlington Northern Railroad to risk stopping the train (over government pressures to keep it going), in the faith that our more careful preparations for this train and our mutual trust would avoid the chaos of July 27.

While the railroad representatives refused to give a definite response, they did reveal to us why the July '84 train had kept going, at the risk of running over people: We had helped to keep the train moving into the Bangor base. How had we done that? By breaking our own nonviolent discipline and rushing the train. The Burlington Northern people in the train's engine were afraid of how the heavily armed Department of Energy guards in the turret cars behind them were reacting to the crowd of several hundred people, some of whom were rushing a train which held nuclear weapons. The Burlington Northern people decided that pushing the train through people on the tracks was less of a risk than that of their being fired upon from the turret cars if the White Train were stopped in the midst of such a crowd. The rush from the vigil line had helped to keep the train going.

An interlocking act of mutual trust did stop the next White Train to Bangor on February 22, 1985. The twenty people who had decided through nonviolence training to block the train went on the tracks early. The police warned them that they were disobeying the law—and left them there. The White Train rolled in slowly, bell clanging, engine covered with security guards, and ground to a halt. The vigil line held its ground and sang round after round of "Love, love, love, love, people we are made for love; love each other as ourselves, for we are one." Carolyn Grissom, representing Puget Sound Agape Community, walked side by side with a Burlington Northern representative to the engine where she gave the railway employees a loaf of bread and a statement affirming their questions of conscience. The arrests of those on the tracks were carried out deliberately and peacefully, one by one, by the sheriff's deputies as the train waited. Through a combined act of trust all of us, police and protesters alike, had stopped the train together—for a few minutes. In those minutes of mutual faith and love, despite the presence of two hundred hydrogen bombs, the kingdom of God was at hand. Love had stopped the train.

The community of opponents, who by acting together stopped the February '85 White Train, has had an enduring impact. Its underlying threat to government control was recognized immediately by Russ Hauge's former employer, the Kitsap County Prosecutor, who filed conspiracy charges against our four representatives who had met with the police authorities beforehand. This government response led to the recognition of a still larger community, that of the tracks campaign and the sanctuary movement for Central American refugees, both now faced with conspiracy charges. We joined hands in holding a "Conspiracy of the Spirit Forum" at University Baptist Church in Seattle at the conclusion of the June 1985 White Train trial, with speakers from both movements, including expert witnesses from our trial: Robert McAfee Brown on the theology of the two movements, Daniel Ellsberg on their political significance, and Richard Falk on their international law dimensions.

The witnesses whom the government called to prove the train conspiracy, and to convict those on the tracks of trespass, gave their most effective testimony for the defense. The sheriffs told judge and jury how openly we had shared our plans with them. To conspire, from its Latin derivation, *conspirare*, means "to breathe together." In that root sense, we had indeed been conspiring with the sheriffs, in a spirit deeper than our differences; sheriffs and defendants continued to breathe in one spirit in the courtroom. Judge W. Daniel Phillips deemed that not a crime and dismissed the conspiracy charges. The six-person, Kitsap County jury then found those who had acknowledged that they were on the tracks not guilty of trespass. At the "Conspiracy of the Spirit Forum," juror Suzanne Smith told the crowd celebrating the verdict that her life had been changed by the trial. Former Pentagon strategist Daniel Ellsberg said that the impact of this trial would be felt in Washington.

At the time I thought Ellsberg was exaggerating the trial's importance. And he was, in the sense of lifting one train-stopping action and trial out of the context of a tracks campaign involving many actions and trials across the country (as described in Chapter 3). It was the cumulative impact of this extended community and campaign along the tracks that in fact stopped the White Train, which ceased coming to Bangor as of the February 22, 1985, train. In a secret memorandum written August 6, 1985 (fortieth anniversary of the Hiroshima Bomb), and declassified in 1990 under the Freedom of Information Act, the Department of Energy's director of nuclear weapons transportation spelled out the reason why the train would stop running: "IN VIEW OF THE GROWING ANTI-NUCLEAR MOVEMENT IN THE UNITED STATES, WITH ITS APPARENT FOCUS ON THE WHITE DEATH TRAIN, THE DEPARTMENT OF ENERGY IS IMPLEMENTING ALTERNATE METHODS OF DELIVERY OF WARHEADS" (capitals in original).[80]

But I think Daniel Ellsberg was right in his intuition that the June '85 trial verdict, and the deepening "conspiracy" across all differences that it confirmed, would be decisive factors in a government decision to stop sending the train. The secret DOE memorandum followed the trial by six weeks. The "anti-nuclear movement," as it noted, was indeed "growing." People who were supposed to be enemies, or at least in opposing camps—sheriffs, Trident resisters, railroad security guards, a former prosecutor, Kitsap County jurors unswayed by Navy pressures—were now all breathing together in transforming ways, which the government acknowledged in its decision to stop the train. The kingdom of God was not only at hand. It was getting out of hand. The White Train, and the growing community it inspired, had to stop.

But we have discovered that this community which transcends differences—a community in which Dusty Wiley, John Easterbrooks, Pat Jones, Chuck Wheeler, and all Ground Zero's opponents over the years, touch our lives in extraordinary ways—is a community which endures beyond encounters with the White Train or the Trident submarine.

Not long ago, while my mother and I were eating lunch at a pancake house in Seattle, four men in suits stopped by our table and asked if I remembered them. I did. They were federal marshals who had accompanied me several times to prison. One of them had taken me handcuffed in a commercial airliner from Seattle to Los Angeles. At the time he had expressed concerns about my impending confinement in Los Angeles County Jail (en route to a federal prison), a particularly difficult jail. He had spoken more as a friend than as a guard. In the pancake house the marshals and I smiled in mutual recognition of a few past experiences that no one else had shared. They asked what I was doing these days, since they hadn't seen me in court. I said I had been up in Canada, writing a book. As they left our table the marshals shook hands with me and said they would like to read my book. I hope they do. They are in it. And in ways that inspire gratitude, they helped live it.

"The kingdom of God is within your power: Love your enemies."

"THE DAYS ARE COMING"

In the historical alternatives we and Jerusalem are given, not to realize the presence of the kingdom of God through our enemies is to choose death. We begin to choose death as soon as we place the kingdom of God at a distance and yearn for the means of getting there, as every violent revolution has done. Set at a distance, the kingdom as end will justify any means on earth, beginning with the killing of our enemies, those same enemies who right now represent the possibility of God's kingdom. To kill our enemies is to kill the presence of the kingdom.

It is the second possibility of Jesus' prophetic vision, death and destruction, which gains power in history when we overlook our first option, the nonviolent one within our power, the kingdom of God's love of enemies:

> And he said to the disciples, "The days are coming when you will desire to see one of the days of *Bar Enasha*, and you will not see it. And they will say to you, 'Lo, there!' or 'Lo, here!' Do not go, do not follow them. For as lightning flashes and lights up the sky from one side to the other, so will *Bar Enasha* be in his day" (Luke 17:22-24).

As with the others we have examined, this prophecy has three variant contexts besides the one in which we are reading it: 1) its original context during Jesus' ministry; 2) its context, then, in the Palestinian church's preaching to its own Jewish nation; and 3) the context of Luke's post-70 Gentile gospel.

In the first, Jesus is preaching against the illusory logic of violence pursued by revolutionary prophets and messiahs, warning that it will lead to the destruction of the nation, just as such logic had led to the destruction of Sepphoris. In 4 B.C.E., about the time of Jesus' birth, there had been "a mass movement among Galilean peasants from villages around Sepphoris [such as Nazareth]. . . . [They had taken] common action under the leadership of a popular figure they recognized as king,"[81] Judas *Bar Hezekiah* (Son of the bandit leader Hezekiah, murdered by Herod), seeking the messianic kingdom by assaulting the royal palace at Sepphoris. Rome had retaliated by sending its legions to burn Sepphoris and enslave its survivors, as it would do also at Jerusalem. The disciples will become willing instruments and victims of that same logic of attack, retaliation, and annihilation if they follow those who claim they can hasten the day of national liberation. The "day of *Bar Enasha*" the disciples desire to see, the day of Israel's liberation, will, for those who "follow them" (as for those who followed *Bar Hezekiah*), turn out to be instead a day of lightning judgment on the nation, as had occurred at Sepphoris. But do not go, do not follow the prophets and messiahs of violence, Jesus says. The day you desire to see can already be experienced now in our nonviolent movement.

Jesus told the disciples that what they sought was already there, if they could and would only realize it. The kingdom of God is in your midst, within your power, in the midst of a nonviolent community struggling for the same reality as end, God's kingdom. Its immediate presence in the community did not mean any less struggle for a deeper, wider realization of God's kingdom for Israel. On the contrary, to see the kingdom on the way, in the way itself, would deepen the struggle for its total achievement for the people. The key to the kingdom as end was to see it first as the means, as a present reality — as in the kingdom of God given to us at Ground Zero, in the discovery of a new community with our opponents who sent us to jail. The means is the end in the process of becoming. The means is love of enemies; the means is compassion; the means is healing.

When the disciples heal the sick, Jesus says the kingdom of God "has come near" those healed (Luke 10:9). When Jesus casts out demons from the people, he says the kingdom of God "has come upon them" (Luke 11:20). To see fully the possibilities of these exploratory actions by a divinely inspired nonviolent movement, a movement of the Spirit, is also to see the end, as Jesus did: "I saw Satan fall like lightning from heaven" (Luke 10:18). But to follow armed prophets, who promise divine signs of victory over Rome, will lead to a day not of liberation but of lightning judgment.

In the middle of the first century the Palestinian church is proclaiming this same contingent prophecy of destruction or transformation to its nation; at the same time, hostility to Rome is deepening and revolutionary movements are increasing. But in warning its own people of the consequences of these developments, as Jesus did, the church has also revised Jesus' prophecy by making him, rather than Yahweh, the source of a future judgment on the nation: "For as lightning flashes and lights up the sky from one side to the other, so will *Bar Enasha* [Jesus] be in his day [of judgment]."

Jesus himself has explicitly refused the office of judge: "Man, who made me a judge or divider over you?" (Luke 12:14). He counseled others to do the same: "Judge not, and you will not be judged" (Luke 6:37). In identifying Jesus, the embodiment of the New Humanity, as the judge he refused to be in his lifetime, the church has taken a critical first step toward assuming that divine power itself.

After the fall of Jerusalem, Luke, in interpreting Q, takes a further step down the road of judgment. In his gospel he uses this prophecy warning one's own nation of danger (coming from Jesus and the Palestinian church to their own people, Israel) as a fulfilled prediction of the inevitable destruction to be visited upon another people (coming from the Gentile church over against the defeated Jewish people). The transition between these two radically different perspectives has occurred first simply by changes of history and community. Luke is writing not only after the event, but also outside the people who experienced it. To these profound changes of context Luke adds his distinctive theological perspective, which tends to emphasize divine foreknowledge and predestined human actions. So, into this Sayings Gospel passage, immediately after *Bar Enasha*'s lightning judgment on Jerusalem, he inserts the following: "But first he must suffer many things and be rejected by this generation" (Luke 17:25).[82] The force of this Lucan comment derives from two independent insights of Jesus: to take on suffering rather than inflict violence is the Human Being's calling; to reject a contingent prophecy is to invite destruction. Luke, however, has combined the two so that they have become the predetermined steps in a divine plan: "But *first* he *must* suffer many things and [*must*] be rejected by this generation [before its destruction]." The contingent and simultaneous alternatives of Jesus' prophecy have now become the necessary, successive steps in a "salvation plan" that includes another people's destruction.

JESUS' TRIDENT PROPHECY

Our larger passage (Luke 17:20-37) continues with another prophecy by Jesus to Jerusalem, this one based on the stories of Noah and Lot. I shall use here Robert Tannehill's arrangement and translation of the text,[83] which brings home the rhetorical power of the prophecy:

> "As it was in the days of Noah,
> So will it be in the days of *Bar Enasha*.
>   They were eating,
>   They were drinking,
>   They were marrying,
>   They were being given in marriage,
>   Until the day when Noah entered the ark
>   and the flood came and destroyed them all.
> Likewise as it was in the days of Lot—
>   They were eating,
>   They were drinking,
>   They were buying,
>   They were selling,
>   They were planting,
>   They were building,

> But on the day when Lot went out from Sodom
> fire and brimstone
> rained from heaven and destroyed them all.
> —So will it be on the day when *Bar Enasha* is
> revealed" (Luke 17:26-30).

We are dealing with another contingent prophecy of the violent judgment to come—a judgment related by Luke to the coming *Bar Enasha*, Jesus.

In the period before Jerusalem's catastrophe there were, as we have just seen, revolutionary movements led by prophets and messiahs claiming a definitive way to God's kingdom. These leaders appealed to the people with elusive signs of God's favor as they struggled against the established violence of the high-priestly power structure and the Roman Empire. Jesus warned against following such prophets of violence: "Do not go, do not follow them." In that direction lay disaster.

But at least equally disastrous was the way of complacent acceptance of the power structure exploiting the peasant population, controlled by Rome and the Temple aristocracy. It is this second side of the destruction overtaking Jerusalem, the side of comfort and profit, that Jesus alludes to in his poetic parallels to the days of Noah and Lot. Who, in the analogous "days" (meaning period) before Jerusalem's destruction, were those so complacently "eating, drinking, buying, selling, planting, and building"? We know that Jewish peasants of the first century, squeezed by absentee landowners and imperial taxes, found it increasingly difficult to "eat, drink, buy, sell, plant, and build," just as third-world peasants find it increasingly hard to sustain themselves today. Those whom Jesus is characterizing as so comfortably carrying on these activities before disaster strikes can only be the profiteers.

As Tannehill suggests (but without reference to the social background), this text's poetic ticking off of "the rhythms of ordinary life" (ordinary to the privileged) makes us aware of their limits. Our heightened consciousness of these comfortable rhythms alerts us to their coming disruption. The rhythms of eating, drinking, buying, selling, planting, and building by the privileged become, in this prophetic poetry, "like the ticking of an alarm clock—we anticipate the alarm."[84] When that decisive moment comes, with the outbreak of a violent revolution and imperial counter-violence, it will "destroy them all." The urgent hope within these prophetic lines is to awaken the people to an alternative way out before the fatal event occurs.

There is also a deeper meaning in this text to which I have been alerted by John Pairman Brown:

> Jesus in part, following prophecy, uses the symbolism of the end of the planetary environment as symbol of the end of the autonomous city-state in the form of Jerusalem. But the form of that symbolism,

fire and flood, goes back to a true global catastrophe, the explosion of Thera.[85]

In about 1470 B.C.E. the volcanic island of Thera exploded in the Eastern Mediterranean. The force of Thera's explosion has been estimated as more powerful than that of Krakatoa in 1883. The Krakatoa explosion created huge tidal waves (*tsunamis*) that devastated the coasts of Java and Sumatra. The size of a tidal wave depends on the mass of the trench that a volcano scoops out of its sea-bed; the wave's velocity depends on how deep the ocean is between the wave's source and its point of impact. Thera displaced a land mass almost four times greater than that of Krakatoa. Unlike the Sunda Strait, which is only 50 to 150 meters deep around Krakatoa, the Mediterranean Sea between Thera and the island of Crete averages one thousand meters deep. The tidal waves created by Thera's land displacement may have been over two hundred meters high. Due to the Mediterranean's depths, these mammoth waves would have achieved immense velocities before they crashed over the unprotected coastline of Crete only 120 kilometers away, rolling far inland.

Beneath these waters that smashed and flooded Crete was the "first civilization of Europe," "also one of the most accomplished and inventive that the world has ever known,"[86] that of Minoan Crete. In the fifteenth century B.C.E. Crete was the center of a great empire. Its sea-power controlled the trade among Europe, Asia, and Africa. Minoan civilization had come to dominate the Greek islands and the Aegean Sea, with bases and settlements extending in a northern arc from Crete. Almost precisely in the center of Minoan colonization and influence was the island of Thera with its own Minoan settlement. Thera's thunderous blast, heard from one end of the Mediterranean to the other, sent earthquakes, electrical storms, torrential rain, huge tidal waves, and ash fallout with the density of an impenetrable night over this entire civilization, destroying it beyond any possible recovery.

Scholars have only begun to assess the further impact Thera's eruption had upon Mediterranean religion and culture before the time of Jesus. It is in the twentieth century that Minoan civilization has been rediscovered, together with the accumulating evidence from science and archaeology of its total destruction almost overnight by the eruption of Thera.[87]

John Pairman Brown suggests some of Thera's influence upon Hebraic thought:

The recession-phase of the tsunami is suggested by "Then the channels of the sea were seen, and the foundations of the world were laid bare" (Ps. 18:15 = 2 Sam. 22:16); the tidal wave by "the floods stood up in a heap" (Exod. 15:8); the actual explosion by the plague of darkness, and the pillar of fire and cloud.[88]

In terms of Jesus' symbolic points of reference, "the stories of Noah and Lot received final form a little before Amos"[89] in the ninth century B.C.E., reflecting the earlier calamity of Thera and Crete. Amos himself traces the dispersion of Minoan survivors to Palestine, identifying the Philistines as having come from "Caphtor" (Crete) (Amos 9:7).[90] The setting given for Sodom's and Gomorrah's destruction in the Sayings Gospel Q, as in Genesis, "all the region about the Jordan," is theology, not literal geography. The event whose fragmentary memories have been absorbed into Genesis's theological story could well have occurred at Thera and Crete.[91]

The images of Thera and the dying echoes of Minoan civilization, therefore, may become present to us in Jesus' rhythmic recitations of the days of Noah and Lot. In the days before fire and brimstone rained from heaven and destroyed them all, in the days before the flood came and destroyed them all, there was a great empire where

> They were eating,
>> They were drinking,
>>> They were buying,
>>>> They were selling,
>>>>> They were planting,
>>>>> They were building . . .

And so it is now, Jesus says, when a human eruption of comparable force builds up within the city of Jerusalem, threatening an explosion with Rome that will likewise annihilate the world. Unless you repent, unless you turn from your own volcanic violence, you will all likewise perish.

Beneath these symbols of total violence destroying earlier worlds lies an extraordinary connection with the possible end of our own world. The connection is revealed by the way in which later Greek mythology and literature symbolized Thera's destruction of Crete. For example, the memories of Thera's explosion inspired a tradition found in the Orphic *Argonautica* that the sea-god Poseidon struck Crete with his trident, and thus "scattered it" so that Crete became "islands in the boundless ocean," its survivors widely dispersed.[92] Again, Pindar has one of his characters speak similarly of Crete's destruction: "I tremble at the heavy-sounding [volcanic] war between Zeus and Poseidon. Once with thunderbolt and trident they sent a land and a whole fighting force down to Tartarus [in the underworld]."[93]

In Greek thought, the violence from the sea which annihilated Minoan civilization — that same violence whose Jewish images Jesus uses in turn to warn Jerusalem of its destruction — involved the trident. It was the trident, the three-pronged spear of the sea-god Poseidon, which the Greeks identified as having plunged that earlier civilization into the depths. In an uncanny parallel, our missile-firing submarines have been named Trident and Poseidon by the U.S. Navy. They, too, threaten to erupt from the sea, but if they do, their radioactive fire and ash will leave the earth a wasteland. In Luke 17:26-30, so as to warn Jerusalem of total destruction, Jesus has drawn upon Hebraic symbols alluding to the same explosive violence from the sea, Thera, whose Greek symbols the U.S. Navy has drawn upon with pride to name its most destructive weapons systems: Trident and Poseidon. The catastrophe Jesus has used to warn of the consequences of a growing violence, our naval high command has used to glorify the threat of a far greater violence. Should the Navy's tragic ignorance of the fatal event behind the names it has chosen for its ultimate weapons be understood rather as a prophetic irony for us all? The choice raised by this irony corresponds to the prophetic choice offered in Luke's text. Between the volcanic trident of Thera and our own nuclear Trident lies the connecting prophecy of Jesus: Unless you repent, unless you turn from your own Trident, you will all likewise perish, just as surely as they did beneath that ancient trident's fire and flood.

After what we may call Jesus' Trident prophecy, Luke's text makes a series of references to the threatened destruction of Jerusalem:

> "On that day, let him who is on the housetop, with his goods in the house, not come down to take them away; and likewise let her who is in the field not turn back. Remember Lot's wife. Whoever seeks to gain one's life will lose it, but whoever loses one's life will preserve it. I tell you, in that night there will be two in one bed; one will be taken and the other left. There will be two women grinding together; one will be taken and the other left." And they said to him, "Where, Lord?" He said to them, "Where the body is, there the eagles will be gathered together" (Luke 17:31-37).

Apocalyptic interpreters of this passage have identified "that day" as the day of Jesus' return at the end of the world. However, those on the house-tops and in the fields who are encouraged here to make their escape without hesitation would have a hard time fleeing the end of the world. The images are prophetic, in relation to a specific historical event: the coming Roman attack on Jerusalem.

The Roman connection is reconfirmed by Jesus' response to the question, "Where, Lord?" in a saying that we are familiar with from Matthew: "Where the body is, there the eagles will be gathered together" (Luke 17:37). In a description in *The Jewish War* of Vespasian's marching army, Josephus shows Rome's symbolic identity with the eagle: "And behind [the Roman generals and officials came] the standards surrounding the eagle, which is at the head of every legion, as the king of birds and most fearless of all: this they regard as the symbol of empire and portent of victory, no matter who opposes them."[94] But an empire's eagle is an occupied people's vulture. To Palestinian Jews the eagle was identified with the vulture as a bird that fed on carrion. In this first Lucan eschatological discourse (17:20-37) the eagles-vultures of the Roman legions, feeding on the dead body of Jerusalem, make up Jesus' final, all-encompassing image. There, Jesus says, lies the fate of Jerusalem and the world—in a stinking carcass being torn up by birds of prey—unless you turn from violence.

As a United States citizen I am compelled here to draw our attention to the fact that the Roman legions' deadly symbol corresponds to the official seal of the United States. In both cases an empire has chosen the eagle, a bird of grace and power, as its symbol. However, is the modern eagle, like its Roman predecessor, viewed by the multitudes beneath it as a vulture instead?

TOWARD A NEW JERUSALEM

We come now to the eighth and final contingent prophecy of Jerusalem's destruction from the gospel of Luke, the climactic, eschatological discourse of Luke 21:5-28,[95] a text in which the editor has brought together the prophetic perspectives of Special Luke and Mark.

The instruction to the discourse, Luke 21:5-7, is important for its major difference from its parallels, Mark 13:1-4 and Matthew 24:1-3. The discourse is introduced once again by Jesus' "no-stone" prophecy: "As for these things which you see, the days will come when there shall not be left here one stone upon another that will not be thrown down" (Luke 21:6). However, the expression of awe before the Temple to which Jesus is responding, and the next question, "Teacher, when will this be, and what will be the sign when this is about to take place?" both come not from the disciples as in Mark and Matthew, but from the people of Jerusalem. Gaston notes that the form of address in the question to Jesus, *"Teacher . . . ?"* rules out the disciples as questioners. The address *didaskale,* "teacher," is used eleven times in Luke, but always by the people, never by the disciples.[96]

Luke's eschatological discourse, therefore, is directed not exclusively to the disciples (implying the church) but rather to the people of Jerusalem. Luke has retained not only the Palestinian church's proclamation of Jesus' prophecies on Jerusalem, but also the audience for which they were originally intended, the endangered people of that city-state. The significance of that audience will become more apparent as we consider the words addressed to them.

After four verses that Luke has edited from Mark as a preamble (Luke 21:8-11), the main body of the eschatological discourse falls into three sections: 1) a time of testimony (Luke 21:12-19); 2) the desolation of Jerusalem (Luke 21:20-24); and 3) redemption (Luke 21:25-28). Each of these sections draws its material from both Special Luke and Mark. I shall set down here the preamble and the three sections so that, as we follow the discourse, we can see together Special Luke, Mark, and their present context in Luke. The verses from Special Luke are in the left column, those from Mark in the right column.[97]

Eschatological Discourse: Luke 21:8-28

Special Luke	*Mark*

Mark

Preamble

8) And he said, "Take heed that you are not led astray; for many will come in my name, saying 'I am he!' and 'The time is at hand!' Do not go after them.

9) And when you hear of wars and tumults, do not be terrified; for this must first take place, but the end will not be at once."

10) Then he said to them, "Nation will rise against nation, and kingdom against kingdom;

11a) there will be great earthquakes, and in various places famines and pestilences; (from Mark 13:5-8)

11b) and there will be terrors and great signs from heaven.

A Time of Testimony

12) But before all this they will lay their hands on you and persecute you, delivering you up to the synagogues and prisons, and you will be brought before kings and governors for my name's sake.

13) This will be a time for you to bear testimony. (from Mark 13:9)

14) Settle it therefore in your minds, not to meditate beforehand how to answer;

15) for I will give you a mouth and wisdom, which none of your adversaries will be able to withstand or contradict.

16) You will be delivered up even by parents and brothers and kinsmen and friends, and some of you they will put to death;

17) you will be hated by all for my name's sake. (from Mark 13:12-13)

18) But not a hair of your head will perish.

19) By your endurance you will gain your lives.

The Desolation of Jerusalem

20) But when you see Jerusalem surrounded by armies, then know that its desolation has come near.

21a) Then let those who are in Judea flee to the mountains, (from Mark 13:14)

21b) and let those who are inside the city depart, and let not those who are out in the country enter it;

22) for these are days of vindication, to fulfil all that is written.

23a) Alas for those who are with child and for those who give suck in those days! (from Mark 13:17)

23b) For great distress shall be upon the earth and wrath upon this people;

24) they will fall by the edge of the sword, and be led captive among all nations; and Jerusalem will be trodden down by the Gentiles, until the times of the Gentiles are fulfilled.

Redemption

25) And there will be signs in sun and moon and stars, and upon the earth distress of nations in perplexity at the roaring of the sea and the waves,

26a) people fainting with fear and with foreboding of what is coming on the world;

26b) for the powers of the heavens will be shaken.

27) And then they will see *Bar Enasha* coming in a cloud with power and great glory. (from Mark 13:25-26)

28) Now when these things begin to take place, look up and raise your heads, because your redemption is drawing near."

Let us begin by considering section one of the eschatological discourse, a synthesis of Special Luke and Mark that I have titled "A Time of Testimony" (Luke 21:12-19). In reading this text we should keep in mind the larger context in Luke, whose gospel has shown the people's support of Jesus in passage after passage, both before and after his arrival in Jerusalem. Gaston specifies a total of sixty-four places in Luke where the "people" (*laos*) or the "multitude" (*ochlos*) of Israel are identified as being in sympathy with Jesus or the gospel. Of these, forty-four are from the Special Lucan material, while twenty are either taken from Mark or are additions to Mark.[98] Luke and his sources testify to a massive response in Israel, both outside and inside Jerusalem, to the movement of the prophet Jesus. This immense popular support is what saves Jesus initially, during his teaching on the Temple Mount, from the plots of the Temple aristocracy. Although they "sought to destroy him," "they did not find anything they could do, *for all the people hung upon his words*" (Luke 19:47-48).

Thus, when Jesus addresses the people of Jerusalem in the discourse of Luke 21:5-28, we are aware, by the evidence of Luke's sources, that Jesus is speaking to an extremely large, supportive audience. This discourse is in fact preceded and concluded by two passages which emphasize the popular support for Jesus (Luke 19:47-48 and 21:37-38). During these days of preaching on the Temple Mount, Jesus is at the height of a prophetic ministry that has gained masses of followers all the way from Galilee to Jerusalem. First of all are his intimate disciples, Galilean men who have walked away from their jobs fishing and collecting taxes and Galilean women led by Mary Magdalene who, in the discovery of their new freedom in the kingdom of God, would remain Jesus' most faithful followers through his terrifying death and resurrection.[99] In addition to the disciples, Jesus is surrounded by the "people," the "multitude," especially farmers forced by taxes and debt to become day laborers. The "people" are made up of the destitute and starving who have been drawn to Jesus on his prophetic journey to Jerusalem. At his destination, the "people" are also the poor masses of the capital itself. Joachim Jeremias reminds us that "Jerusalem in the time of Jesus was already a centre for mendicancy" and that "a large section of the population [of Jerusalem] lived chiefly or entirely on charity or relief."[100] These poorest of Jerusalem residents would also have responded to the advent of the Galilean prophet who proclaimed their present and future "blessed" (Luke 6:20-26). These are the "people," destitute and suffering people, whom Jesus addresses day after day on the Temple Mount. These are the people who "hung upon" his words (19:48), a massive gathering of the nation's socially disinherited. Was the Temple aristocracy mistaken to have "feared the people" (Luke 22:2) who formed this movement and to have seen in Jesus the threat of a coming revolution?

Within this socially and politically explosive context, what, then, does Jesus say to the people?

He says, first of all, that persecution, arrest, and imprisonment will all come upon this mass movement if it continues: "They will lay their hands on you and persecute you, delivering you up to the synagogues [which also served as courts] and prisons, and you will be brought before kings and governors for my name's sake" (21:12). But the people's crisis will in fact be a divinely given opportunity: "This will be a time for you to bear testimony" (21:13)—literally so, testifying in courtrooms before judges representing the Roman Empire, who will decide the people's fate. These trials "before kings and governors" will allow them to experience and convey the transforming power of truth: "Settle it therefore in your minds not to meditate beforehand how to answer; for I will give you a mouth and wisdom, which none of your adversaries will be able to withstand or contradict" (21:14-15). Or as it is put in a parallel text in Luke, "the Holy Spirit will teach you in that very hour what you ought to say" (Luke 12:12). Jesus is here anticipating by nineteen centuries Gandhi's definition of nonviolence as a transforming "truth-force," *satyagraha*. Nor is he any less visionary than Gandhi concerning the power of truth in the dispossessed to prevail over politically more powerful opponents: "a mouth and wisdom which none of your adversaries will be able to withstand or contradict" (21:15). The text seems to suggest that by holding on to this force of truth, the people will transform their situation: "By your endurance you will gain your lives" (21:19). The "you" here is, once again, not just a simple plural but encompasses the disinherited from Galilee to Jerusalem. What the saying seems to indicate in the life situation of the Palestinian church is that if these steps of nonviolent transformation are carried out collectively by the people, Jerusalem and the nation will not be destroyed: "By your endurance you [the people] will gain your lives," not lose them in a violent struggle with the eagle-vultures of Rome.

What we are given in this "time of testimony" text from Luke is a contingent prophecy, from Jesus to the people, of the alternative to Jerusalem's destruction: a transforming nonviolent movement that will turn Jerusalem and the nation around.

TOWARD A NEW WASHINGTON

In the final year of his life Martin Luther King, like the Galilean prophet he followed, envisioned a nonviolent movement of poor people from across the land gathering in their nation's capital. Unlike the earlier March on Washington, the Poor People's Campaign would not go home until its demands were met. The basic idea was as simple as the kingdom of God. As King put it, "There are millions of poor people in this country who have very little, or even nothing, to lose. If they can be helped to take action together, they will do so with a freedom and a power that will be a new and unsettling force in our complacent national life.[101] King sought to transform the despair of the poor that smoldered behind urban riots into the hope of massive nonviolent civil disobedience. The purpose was to confront the nation's conscience dramatically with the injustice in its midst: "We've got to find a method that will disrupt our cities if necessary, create the crisis that will force the nation to look at the situation, dramatize it, and yet at the same time not destroy life or property. . . . I see that as massive civil disobedience."[102] To create that crisis of conscience, King and the Southern Christian Leadership Conference decided to recruit thousands of the poorest citizens from various urban and rural areas to join in a "sustained, massive, direct-action movement in Washington."[103] This "nonviolent army," this "freedom church of the poor," would remain in the nation's capital "until the legislative and executive branches of the government take serious and adequate action on jobs and income."[104] To achieve justice for the poor on a still wider scale, it would be necessary to disrupt also the violence being exported from the United States to Vietnam and other countries. From Washington, King said, the Poor People's Campaign "would call the peace movement in, and let them go on the other side of the Potomac and try to close down the Pentagon, if that can be done."[105] The next stage of the nonviolent movement would be international. United States citizens in particular "must help their nation repent of her modern economic imperialism."[106]

Martin Luther King's ultimate purpose through the Poor People's Campaign was to begin "to planetize our movement for social justice."[107] The campaign to Washington reflected an earlier journey to Jerusalem that had sought, on its way and at its end, the kingdom of God. Both prophets knew from the beginning that to choose the journey was to choose his own death. The conspiracy to kill King, like the conspiracy to kill Jesus, came from established power in response to a people-transforming journey. In King's case the execution was carried out before the journey began, a relatively easy task for the conspirators given the size of the intelligence network monitoring King's activities.

In 1989, after two decades of effective concealment, both a book, Philip H. Melanson's *The Murkin Conspiracy*,[108] and a BBC documentary, "Who Killed Martin Luther King?"[109] began to lift the lid on the King assassination. They include evidence that the identities adopted by James Earl Ray were far more sophisticated than previously thought and, in at least one instance, must have been obtained from a top secret security file accessible only to military and intelligence agencies.[110] A convicted murderer in an Oklahoma federal prison has admitted participating in the King conspiracy and has said that it involved FBI and CIA agents, "mob" elements, and James Earl Ray.[111]

King's ever-deepening resistance to the Vietnam War and his preparations for the Poor People's Campaign were as threatening to the United States power structure as Jesus' journey to Jerusalem was to the Roman high-priestly establishment. Jesus and Martin Luther King were both executed for proclaiming to their suffering people that it was "a time to bear testimony," a time to speak and live the truth "before kings and governors" (Luke 21:12-13). By following their example and journeying also to bear testimony in Jerusalem or Washington, the disinherited would be given "a mouth and wisdom which none of your adversaries will be able to withstand or contradict" (Luke 21:15). What Jesus, and his disciple, Martin, have said to us all is that on that way to a new Jerusalem, and a new Washington, "By your endurance you [as a people] will gain your lives" (Luke 21:19).

"TILL ALL HAS TAKEN PLACE"

What meaning does the final editor of Luke see in this first, "Time of Testimony" section of the eschatological discourse (Luke 21:12-19)?

By retaining two key verses from Mark with only slight revisions, Luke has made more explicit Jesus' teaching of the cross: "You will be delivered up even by parents and brothers and kinsmen and friends, and some of you they will put to death; you will be hated by all for my name's sake" (Luke 21:16-17; from Mark 13:12-13). Those who follow Jesus' nonviolent way can expect not only imprisonment but death. They will be turned over to the authorities, even by those closest to them. As a result of their nonviolent stand, hatred will come from all sides.

On the one hand, these sayings from Mark have made the hope expressed in the Special Lucan verses (21:14-15, 18-19) more realistic, in a way that is totally consistent with Jesus' emphasis on the cross as the essence of transformation. The Special Lucan verses seem overly optimistic without these verses from Mark, and are in fact strengthened by them.

On the other hand, Mark's sayings can also be read, from Luke's post-70 point of view, in such a way as to account more readily for the destruction of Jerusalem. The Marcan sayings can be interpreted so as to suggest that Jesus' large following from Galilee to Jerusalem, as still seen in Luke's Palestinian sources, would necessarily become, as seen in Luke's Gentile context with the addition of Mark's perspective, a small, besieged community of his disciples, now opposed by the masses who instead side with the authorities: "You will be hated by all for my name's sake." This second interpretation, which Luke probably added to the first, is more consistent with Mark's eleventh-hour perspective from Galilee than it is with Jesus' original hopes for Jerusalem, as retained by the Palestinian church of the 50s while still struggling to realize those hopes and avoid a disaster.

In the second section of the eschatological discourse, which I have titled from its contents, "The Desolation of Jerusalem" (Luke 21:20-24), the alternative of destruction is set forth in explicit terms. This contingent prophecy serves as a climactic warning from Jesus to the people of Jerusalem to turn their nation in a nonviolent direction. Otherwise, as the final verse states, this people "will fall by the edge of the sword, and be led captive among all nations; and Jerusalem will be trodden down by the Gentiles, until the times of the Gentiles are fulfilled" (Luke 21:24).

That Jerusalem "will be trodden down by the Gentiles" because of the people's disobedience to Yahweh, and that it will in turn eventually be freed from the oppressive yoke of hostile nations, when "the times of the

Gentiles are fulfilled," are traditional themes of the prophets commenting on the rise and fall of occupation forces.[112] Even if the nation does not turn and the worst comes to pass with destruction, oppression, and exile, all this will last only "until the times of the Gentiles are fulfilled." "As in the prophets, the Gentiles are God's organ of punishment" for the people, "but they become guilty of arrogance (Isa. 10:5-19 etc.) and are finally in their turn judged."[113]

In section three of Luke's discourse (21:25-28), we come to cosmic symbols of the earthly fall of the Gentile nations: "signs in sun and moon and stars, and upon the earth distress of nations in perplexity at the roaring of the sea and the waves" (Luke 21:25). Gaston points out that imagery of the sea and the waves had

> long been used in Israel to mean the Gentile world. Thus it is found in parallelism with the nations in Is 17:12, "Ah, the thunder of many peoples, they thunder like the thundering of the sea! Ah, the roar of nations, they roar like the roaring of mighty waters!" or in Ps 144:7, "rescue me and deliver me from the many waters, from the hand of aliens" (cf. Ps 98:7f; 144:1-3; Ezek 26:19; Rev 17:15).[114]

Caird notes a similar symbolism in the shaking of the powers of heaven in the verse that Luke has added from Mark's gospel (Luke 21:26b):

> The powers of heaven are the heavenly bodies, identified with the gods of oriental and Greco-Roman religion, and regarded by the Jews as angelic beings created by God and allowed by him to preside over the destinies of pagan nations (Deut. 32:8, Isa. 24:21, 34:1-4). Thus the shaking of the powers of heaven denotes not so much the ruin of the physical universe as the overthrow of pagan imperial supremacy.[115]

Even if Jerusalem falls to Rome, there is nothing permanent in Gentile domination. That, too, will fall, and Jerusalem will be liberated: "Now when these things begin to take place, look up and raise your heads, because your redemption is drawing near" (Luke 21:28). "Redemption" in the *Revised Standard Version* is rendered as "liberation" in the *Jerusalem Bible* and the *New English Bible*. What is signified by both terms is the gaining of freedom from oppression.

It is in this context of Jerusalem's liberation from Gentile oppression that Luke has introduced a verse from Mark on the coming of *Bar Enasha* (Luke 21:27), immediately after the successive symbols of a judgment on Gentile power: roaring of the sea and waves, shaking of the powers of heaven. We need to pay close attention to what Luke has thereby revealed about his understanding of the coming of *Bar Enasha*. For Luke, *Bar Enasha* comes *twice* in historical judgments.

As we saw, Luke already used the symbol of *Bar Enasha* in his first eschatological discourse, in chapter 17, in relation to Rome's destruction of Jerusalem. Whereas Jesus had warned of a day of judgment on Jerusalem, when its most privileged citizens would be as oblivious as were those in the days of Lot and Noah, Luke linked the judgment on Jerusalem specifically with *Bar Enasha*:

> "But on the day when Lot went out from Sodom fire and brimstone rained from heaven and destroyed them all. – So will it be on the day when *Bar Enasha* is revealed" (Luke 17:29-30).

In the next verses, the people are urged to flee without looking back, "on that day" (17:31) when *Bar Enasha* is revealed. If they hesitate, they will become victims of the swift-marching Roman legions—carrion for the eagle-vultures. "Where the body is, there the eagles will be gathered together" (Luke 17:37).

Thus Luke has identified *Bar Enasha* with successive judgments in history: 1) the fall of Jerusalem to Rome in 70 C.E.; 2) a future liberation from Gentile oppression. This double reference to *Bar Enasha*'s judgments in history was already indicated by Luke 17:22: "The days are coming when you will desire to see one of the days of *Bar Enasha* [the day of Israel's liberation from Rome], and you will not see it." What the disciples were told they would see instead, if they followed the prophets of violence, would be that other day of *Bar Enasha*—a day of lightning judgment on their nation via the Roman legions: "For as lightning flashes and lights up the sky from one side to the other, so will *Bar Enasha* be in his day" (Luke 17:24). Yet in the second eschatological discourse, Jesus' ultimate vision in Luke includes the day of liberation from the Roman legions and all Gentile power, when "the times of the Gentiles are fulfilled," when "your redemption is drawing near." The Lucan editor of this Palestinian Christian text, by in turn introducing verse 21:27 from Mark into its midst, identifies this day of liberation from the Gentiles with the coming of *Bar Enasha*.

Recognizing Luke's double identification of *Bar Enasha* with historical judgments that correspond to Jesus' prophecies concerning Jerusalem gives valuable insight into the synoptic gospels' eschatology. The "coming of *Bar Enasha*," the Human Being, or "the day of *Bar Enasha*'s revelation," are gospel variations for describing great judgments in history, which their writers saw as carried out by the Human Being, Jesus, who is now at God's right hand. In Luke's gospel there are two such judgments by *Bar Enasha*: 1) at the fall of Jerusalem; and 2) when the Gentile nations are in turn judged and overcome, to bring about a transformed history.

Thus the coming of *Bar Enasha* in Luke does not mean a historical judgment resulting in the end of only one nation, Israel. It also means a judgment that is the end of all nations. The reason Luke has *Bar Enasha* come twice in judgment is that he is applying Jesus' prophetic, nonviolent teaching first to Israel (retrospectively), and second to the Gentile nations (prophetically). *All* unrepentant nations are judged in history from the standpoint of a new, nonviolent humanity. Unless they turn and are transformed, the nations will destroy themselves by their own violence.

A truth begins to dawn concerning the very nature of Jesus' "good news," of turning from violence toward an upside-down kingdom in which the poor and suffering are given first place and in which we love our enemies. Such transforming news is proclaimed to the poor. But to whom else is this good news of the kingdom of God proclaimed?

The conclusion of Luke's gospel is explicit on this point: "Thus it is written, that the Christ should suffer and on the third day rise from the dead, and that *repentance* and *forgiveness of sins* should be preached in his name *to all nations, beginning from Jerusalem*" (Luke 24:46-47).

The final commandment of the resurrected Jesus to the disciples is that they make disciples of all nations—that they transform the nations of the world by teaching them to turn from the logic of violence to the logic of love and forgiveness. That is the nature of the new age begun by Jesus' resurrection, a resurrection of all peoples and nations in a forgiving, nonviolent humanity. The first fruit of this age of nonviolence was to be the salvation of Jerusalem from destruction. Thus the text emphasizes "repentance and forgiveness of sins . . . to all nations, beginning from Jerusalem." To save the people of Jerusalem from destruction, God's power would come to the disciples in Jerusalem: "Stay in the city, until you are clothed with power from on high" (Luke 24:49).

The paradox with which Christian eschatology is afflicted is that it failed in its most fundamental purpose (as seen by its source, Jesus) before the gospels were ever written: the saving of Jerusalem from destruction. By justifying this destruction, rather than acknowledging it as the church's failure to realize Jesus' most immediate goal of nonviolent transformation, the final Gentile editors of the gospels in turn compromised the gospels' teaching of the resurrected Jesus: to teach all nations to turn from violence to nonviolence, embracing forgiveness rather than retaliation.

The gospel of Luke and its Special Source in Palestine both envision a time, however, when their communities will live in a transformed world, when "the times of the Gentiles are fulfilled"—when the power of domination has ended. The word translated in this verse as "Gentiles" also means "nations." Gaston's translation of Luke 21:24 reads: "And Jerusalem will be trampled by the nations until the times of the nations are fulfilled."[116] When "the times of the nations are fulfilled," that is to say finished, is the vision we have just seen at the gospel's conclusion, in the words of the resurrected Jesus. It is a vision of the passing of nations, as we know them, and their replacement by the kingdom of God on earth. It is a vision that God, working especially through each gospel's community—both Israel and the church (a part of Israel at the time) in the Palestinian context of Special Luke, the church alone in Luke—will transform this world beyond the violent power of nations. Luke can adapt Special Luke's vision of nonviolent liberation from the Gentile nations to his own Gentile Christian community, because both Palestinian and Gentile churches believe in the nations-transforming kingdom of God as a present possibility.

The "how" of that transformation we have already seen in the "time of testimony" proclaimed by Jesus at the end of his journey to Jerusalem in Luke — and in our own time, in the ever-widening Poor People's Campaign envisioned by Martin Luther King. If the people lived out their time of testimony, there would indeed be "signs in sun and moon and stars." Jesus' eight prophetic warnings would be given a positive fulfillment: Both the people and Yahweh would turn. If the people endured in their time of testimony, they would gain their lives in the life of Jerusalem and Israel. They would see their redemption drawing near. They would see the powers of the heavens shaken. They would see the coming of a New Humanity, *Bar Enasha*. They would see the signs of the kingdom of God. The kingdom of God was within their power, is within our power, but it cannot be achieved by seeking power.

That was and is the "how" of a transformed world. The "how" is a transformed people, discovering the nonviolent kingdom of God in themselves, in their midst, within their power.

The "when" of transformation is also given in the eschatological discourse. Luke and Special Luke agree on the "when." It is indicated in the final verse of the Lucan discourse, derived from Special Luke: "Now when these things begin to take place, look up and raise your heads, because your redemption is drawing near" (Luke 21:28).

In the following verses on the parable of the fig tree, added by Luke from Mark, the "when" of this approaching transformation is made explicit:

And he told them a parable: "Look at the fig tree, and all the trees; as soon as they come out in leaf, you see for yourselves and know that the summer is already near. So also, when you see these things taking place, you know that the kingdom of God is near. *Truly, I say to you, this generation will not pass away till all has taken place.* Heaven and earth will pass away, but my words will not pass away" (Luke 21:29-33; from Mark 13:28-31).

"Truly, I say to you, this generation will not pass away till all has taken place." For centuries interpreters have been confounded by this saying of Jesus, which stands out like a beacon in all three synoptic discourses, because they have tried to understand it as a prediction of something that did not happen. But prophets do not predict. They demand. They do so for the sake of God in their people. And they hope and pray that their demands will be met. Jesus is demanding a divine revolution of his people. The alternative is destruction. One or the other must come within a generation. A prophet sees that inflexible set of alternatives. We do not. What

Jesus' statement means is that either transformation or annihilation will be the choice of his generation—and ours.

When will the kingdom of God come for us in the nuclear age? It must come now. Our choice is between nonviolence and nonexistence. Our generation will necessarily choose either the nonviolent kingdom within our power or its equally inconceivable alternative.

"Truly, I say to you, this generation will not pass away till all has taken place."

EPILOGUE

The historical consequences of the early church's obscuring of Jesus' prophecy of nonviolent transformation have been momentous. Pacifist theologians identify that contradiction, from the fourth century on, as the "Constantinian heresy." However, the church's simultaneous victory over and cooptation by a previously persecuting empire had its first-century seeds. The Emperor Constantine's decision to embrace the church, symbolized by the battle of the Milvian Bridge in 313, was a late development made possible by the gospels' inner ambivalence. The most critical shift can be seen in the layers of tradition in the synoptic gospels themselves, from Jesus' own eschatology of nonviolence to Mark's, Luke's, and Matthew's mixed messages.

Jesus' prophetic symbolism of "the end" encompassed both transformation and destruction as concrete alternatives for human freedom: *either* the nonviolent coming of *Bar Enasha*, the New Humanity, toppling the dominant powers on earth (as in Mark 13:24-26, Luke 21:25-27) *or* a day similar to "the day when Lot went out from Sodom" and "fire and brimstone rained from heaven and destroyed them all" (as in Jesus' Trident prophecy, Luke 17:29). What intervened between the contingent prophecy of Jesus' symbolism and the theologies of his synoptic redactors were the critical events of the year 70, impending (for Mark) or accomplished (for Luke and Matthew), which then had to be interpreted by that same symbolism.

Mark, in the late 60s, knew that Jesus' hope of nonviolent transformation could no longer include Jerusalem, which had already doomed itself by taking up arms against Rome. Jerusalem had to be left behind. Mark hoped for a new world's coming instead through his own remnant community in Galilee. Luke and Matthew, in their final redactions a decade or two after 70, set Jesus' proclamation of the nonviolent coming of God within their broader, individual interpretations of Jerusalem's destruction as a Second Coming of Jesus, a divinely willed coming in judgment upon the Jewish nation for its not having accepted Jesus (in the church's proclamation but symbolized in Jesus' death). Mark also, in a post-70 context and in light of Luke and Matthew, would be read and interpreted increasingly on the side of judgment. In their varying efforts to explain theologically the destruction of Jerusalem, through Jesus' crucifixion, the synoptic gospels obscured, and in their increasing anti-Judaism contradicted, the prophetic transformation of Israel and of all nations at the heart of Jesus' message.

181

As Jesus' vision of transformation moved outside his own Jewish nation, it was adapted into a Gentile theology explaining that other nation's destruction as a divinely willed punishment. Because of two radical shifts of perspective as the gospels were being written, from Judaism to Gentile Christianity, and from a pre- to a post-70 vantage point, Jesus' prophetic, nonviolent calls to his own people — and by extension, to every people — became instead predictive, violent judgments, from Rome and elsewhere, upon another, already defeated people. The contingent, prophetic alternatives, to Israel and every nation, of transformation or annihilation, became the realized prediction of a ruined nation, with the anticipation of a glorious kingdom to follow it — successive events in a "history of salvation."

Through these theologies of Jerusalem's fall, and especially through an uncritical reading of them, Jesus' symbolic polarity of prophetic alternatives has been lost. Every symbol of the end is now read in terms of destruction — and worse, in terms of foreordained destruction. The nonviolent kingdom of God — Jesus' vision of a New Humanity in Israel, and in all nations — has been absorbed into the larger context of a predetermined, "end-of-the-world" judgment upon Jerusalem and the Jewish nation — a foundation for modern, deterministic predictions that God wills the destruction of the entire world by nuclear war.

In the nineteen centuries since this process began, Jews in particular have learned the horrifying power of one of their own prophetic visions, torn from their midst and made into a deterministic prediction against them by Gentile Christians. Jesus' nonviolent kingdom of God became a realm of the sword and the rack, which culminated in a Nazi reign of gas chambers and flaming ovens whose stench covered Europe. The terrible irony of this history is that, as it progressed, Christians have burned into the flesh and consciousness of Jews the iron law of violence, as climaxed by the lessons of the Christian country of Nazi Germany, whereas Jews have lived out, as an example to Christians, the redemptive, suffering servanthood of the prophet Isaiah and their other brother, Jesus. Both rulers and ruled, Christians and Jews, have learned something over these centuries from the practice of the other.

"WHERE JUSTICE ROLLS DOWN LIKE WATERS"

As the Nazi logic of extermination reached its conclusion in Auschwitz and Treblinka, the hope for a new Jewish nation was being realized in Palestine by the worldwide Zionist movement. The age-old roots of Zionism were described by Martin Buber in 1946, two years before the founding of the state of Israel, in the following way:

Modern political Zionism, in the form it has taken during my nearly fifty years of membership in this movement, was only developed and intensified but not caused by modern anti-Semitism. Indeed, Zionism is a late form assumed by a primal fact in the history of [humankind], a fact of reasonable interest at least for Christian civilization. This fact is the unique connection of a people and a country. This people, the people Israel, was once created by the power of a tradition that was common to some semi-nomadic tribes. Together these tribes migrated, under very difficult conditions, from Egypt to Canaan because they felt united by the promise to them of Canaan as their "heritage" since the days of the "Fathers." This tradition was spectacular and decisive for the history of [humankind] in that it confronted the new people with a task they could carry out only as a people, namely, to establish in Canaan a model and "just" community. Later on, the "prophets"—a calling without any historical precedent—interpreted this task as obliging the community to send streams of social and political justice throughout the world. Thereby the most productive and most paradoxical of all human ideas, Messianism, was offered to humanity. It placed the people of Israel in the center of an activity leading towards the advent of the Kingdom of God on earth, an activity in which all the peoples were to cooperate.[1]

The way to begin realizing the kingdom of God in Palestine, Buber believed, was through the creation of a bi-national state in which Jews and Arabs would have equal rights and representation. Buber joined Judah Magnes and other pacifist Zionists in Palestine in forming the Ihud (Union) Association, "united in the firm conviction that there is but one way of meeting the Palestine problem—that of Jewish-Arab cooperation."[2] In 1946, the Ihud Association concluded its proposal for a bi-national Palestine by expressing the hope that Jews and Arabs would strive together

> to make their Holy Land into a thriving, peaceful Switzerland situated at the heart of this ancient highway between East and West. A "Palestine Solution" is required for the Palestine problem. This would have an incalculable political and spiritual influence in all the Middle East and far beyond. A bi-national Palestine could become a beacon of peace in the world.[3]

Martin Buber envisioned a nonviolent coming of God in Palestine. Cooperation between Jews and Arabs was both possible and necessary "for the lasting success of the great work, of the redemption of this land."[4] For Buber, a Jewish-ruled state that would exclude or oppress Arabs was a contradiction of the Zionist vision. The prophets had long ago laid down the indispensable condition for the promise and continuation of Zion, *justice*. As the prophet Amos had put it,

> Take away from me the noise of your songs;
>   to the melody of your harps I will not listen.

But let justice roll down like waters,
and righteousness like an ever-flowing stream (Amos 5:23-24).

As I read today Amos's and Buber's prescriptions for the messianic
kingdom on earth, I am reminded again of Jesus' vision of the same kingdom nineteen centuries ago. The kingdom of God was at hand. The New
Humanity was being born. The things that make for peace were on Israel's
horizon. A divinely human world was on the edge of creation. An inconceivable power of justice and love was radiating inwardly and outwardly
from Galilee. The things that make for peace found in the Sermon on the
Mount are Jesus' attempt to describe a new reality. Personal, social, Jewish,
and universal are all dimensions of it. The God whom Jesus experienced
as a loving parent, *Abba-Ima*, is every dimension of it. The things that make
for justice and peace are a transformed and transforming reality, present
and future, within and without, personal and social, active and contempla-
tive—no farther away than one's own hand, heart, and people.

In relation to Amos's vision, I feel this reality of Jesus as if it were two
rivers flowing together, one the river of God, the other the river of human
history. The converging waters of God and humanity form one immense
river, "where justice rolls down like waters, and righteousness like an ever-
flowing stream." That was the mind of Jesus, where the kingdom of God
and the New Humanity of Israel were one in a transforming act of faith.
For us to understand Jesus' faith would be to dive into his river of God
become history, the same as his river of history become God. For to break
into Jesus' reality is to be swept into the depths of God and history integrated so totally in one transforming power of justice, love, and peace that
we know the kingdom of God is within our power—we know that a New
Humanity is coming—we know that the nonviolent coming of God is rising
within us all. Jesus understood the history and consciousness of his people
through the transforming river of God flowing in and through them; God
he saw in turn in the turbulence of the people, as their river in God's river
wound through divine providence, hope, and judgment. God and the people
of God were—in Jesus' vision of the kingdom, of the New Humanity—
joined in a single overwhelming reality, the one reality, divine and human,
the power of God pouring through the new humanity of poor Palestinian
Jews. The kingdom of God was at hand, in these people, in the transforming
power rising from beneath their poverty, their suffering, their death—justice rolling down like waters, righteousness like a mighty stream, into an
ocean of love.

THE CYCLE OF SEPPHORIS

In December 1989 I went on a transforming pilgrimage to Israel-Palestine, the birthplace of transformation. Nazareth and Sepphoris, the West
Bank and Gaza, Jerusalem and its prophets, *gospel* and *intifada* drew me

into the depths of a question that has been present since I awakened to nonviolence thirty years ago:

Can humanity be transformed through nonviolence in the nuclear age, through the discovery of a power beyond power, before humanity destroys itself?

The December journey took me to four places in particular that emphasized the question of our nonviolent transformation: Sepphoris, the remains of an ancient city beside Nazareth whose destruction may have inspired Jesus' prophetic vision of choosing either the kingdom of God or the destruction of Jerusalem; Beit Sahour, a Palestinian Christian town in the West Bank that is now the setting for a tax revolt; Beach Camp, Gaza, a refugee camp where a deep Muslim spirituality sustains daily life-and-death confrontations; and Jerusalem itself, where prophets once again confront the threatened end of their city and the world.

Although Sepphoris was near the end of my pilgrimage, that dead city is the beginning and symbol of our predicament. So I will begin this reflection with my visit there.

On the eve of my visit to Sepphoris, I stayed overnight at the Galilean home of David and Hava Hammou in Kiryat Tiv'on, ten miles from Nazareth. David Hammou is an Oriental Jew and the editor of *Iton Aher* ("Another Magazine"), a quarterly publication put out in Israel by the Yated Association, which is comprised mainly of Oriental Jewish activists. He is in constant demand as a speaker and writer on questions affecting Oriental Jews. Hava Hammou is a German Jew and a physiotherapist at a children's clinic. Her mother and father came from Germany to Palestine in the late '30s, narrowly escaping the Holocaust.

While Hava and I were visiting, David returned to the room from a telephone interview with a reporter from one of Israel's largest papers. David had been sharing his hope and belief that there will be a revolution of Oriental Jews in Israel. Sixty percent of the country's Jews are Orientals (*Sephardi*), who have emigrated from the Middle East, Asia, and Africa. Together with Palestinians, they make up the bottom of Israel's labor force. The average income of Oriental Jews is four times less than that of the *Ashkenazi*, European Jews who control Israel's politics and culture. Oriental Jews live mainly in slums. Only ten percent of them receive a university education, in contrast to seventy percent of Ashkenazi youth. Orientals' dismal prospects mirror the bleak future of Palestinians. David believes the Oriental majority in Israel will begin to identify their struggle for social and economic changes with the struggle for a Palestinian state. This Oriental-Palestinian alliance will revolutionize Israeli politics.[5]

Five years from now, David says, all of Israel's present political leaders will be forgotten. They do not understand the forces moving within their country. The problem is not only Israelis and Palestinians. The problem is also Ashkenazi and Orientals. The same problem holds true inside and outside Israel.

Just as Sadat was in one moment transformed from an enemy into a brother, so too David believes, will a PLO leader some day be transformed. Then Israel will not only recognize a Palestinian state, but in the sea-changes that occur within its own society, Israel will rediscover the Arabic part of its heritage.

The alternative to such a revolution of values is destruction. In one of his articles, David has written:

> There is no doubt that Ashkenazi Zionism is leading Israel to a dead end — internally and externally. There will be a division of Israel, both ethnically and socially. Israel will reach a dead end in terms of security. Leading Israel further and further away from the possibility of becoming an integrated state in the Middle East, one entertaining cultural and economic relations with its neighbors, will bring about a complete loss of Jewish independence and Jewish sovereignty.[6]

As David presented the alternatives of nonviolent revolution or Israel's end, Hava gestured at the television screen, with its sound turned off, on which a drama was being silently played out. Another story of the Holocaust, she said. Every week there were programs on it, dramatizations and reflections. The leaders of her society, she remarked, had become mentally ill as a result of the Holocaust. It was the source of their inability to accept the Palestinians.

The following day, as I became a pilgrim to the ruins of ancient Sepphoris, I carried within me the Hammous' softly spoken insights and prophecies of the alternatives now facing Israel.

As an experiment in the truth of Jesus' history, I walked to Sepphoris from its neighboring village, Nazareth. The winding, five-mile route through the Galilean countryside took a little less than two hours. Jesus probably walked it frequently.

As we saw in Chapter 3, Jesus grew up in the shadow of a destroyed Sepphoris, the culmination and symbol of a failed revolution. As a client-king of Rome, Herod the Great used Sepphoris as his Galilean headquarters. His royal palace and garrison there were a focus for the resentment of exploited Galilean peasants. When Herod died in 4 B.C.E. (around the time of Jesus' birth), violent uprisings occurred throughout Judea — peasants hoping to thwart the continuation of oppressive rule under Herod's sons. The attack on Sepphoris was led by the messianic Galilean revolutionary, Judas, son of Hezekiah.

Judas raised his people's army from villages "around Sepphoris" (in the historian Josephus' phrase),[7] probably including residents of Nazareth. His forces succeeded in overcoming the Herodian garrison at Sepphoris, but theirs was a short-lived victory. Its outcome provides a striking parallel to Rome's future destruction of Jerusalem in retaliation for the Jewish revolution of 66-70 C.E. Roman legions swept down on Sepphoris from Syria, re-took the city from the revolutionaries, and then, as an imperial lesson, burned Sepphoris down and made slaves of its people—just as they would do in Jerusalem in 70.

I walked to Sepphoris as a pilgrimage into Jesus' consciousness of that nearby destruction, with its prefiguration of the fate of Jerusalem which, as the gospels tell us, he then prophesied. In the ruins of Sepphoris, a city destroyed by both revolutionary and imperial violence (and rebuilt by Herod Antipas when Jesus was a young man), Jesus would have foreseen the fate of Jerusalem. Hoping to save his people in a specific, historical sense, Jesus set out to realize an alternative, transforming vision, "the kingdom of God."

I visited the site of ancient Sepphoris in the hope of finding further connections between its history and the gospels. What I discovered instead was the perennial significance of Jesus' prophetic alternatives, nonviolent transformation or destruction.

As I climbed the rocky dirt road leading up the hill of Sepphoris' archaeological diggings, I saw beside the road, under newly planted trees, a few scattered remnants of destroyed Arab houses. These modern ruins are among the scant visible remains of the four thousand or so people who lived in Sepphoris' successor community, the Arab village of Saffuriya, which dates back to the twelfth century. Just as Rome razed Sepphoris in 4 B.C.E., Israel razed Saffuriya in 1948.

On the night of July 15, 1948, during Israel's War of Independence, three Israeli planes bombed Saffuriya. As Israeli shelling and artillery bombardment continued sporadically through the night, about six thousand people (including two thousand refugees already fleeing the Israeli advance) evacuated Saffuriya to take refuge in the orchards two kilometers northeast.

The next day, 150 remaining Palestinian men fought the Israel Defense Forces (IDF) house-to-house, inflicting twenty percent casualties. After Saffuriya was taken by the IDF, the new state of Israel, in a pattern repeated at over three hundred Arab villages, destroyed the village and barred the Palestinians from returning. Trees were planted to hide the remains of the old village.[8]

The Jewish settlement of Zippori took over the land of Sepphoris and Saffuriya. In recent years American archaeological expeditions to Israel's Zippori have dug up more evidence of the ancient city of Sepphoris than remains of the twentieth-century people of Saffuriya.

The recycling of violence represented by Sepphoris-Saffuriya-Zippori has, in the nuclear age, reached an end of the line. In Jesus' contingent prophecy of the destruction of Jerusalem, Jerusalem has become the world. The ruthless, yet hopeful realism of Jesus leaves us no other alternative: transformation or annihilation. The kingdom of God is at hand. So, too, is total destruction.

A NONVIOLENT ALTERNATIVE AT BEIT SAHOUR

My first encounter with Beit Sahour (pronounced Bate Sah-hour) occurred earlier, on November 1, 1989, when a headline in that morning's *Birmingham Post-Herald* caught my eye: "State of Siege Ends in West Bank: Property Confiscated in Face of Tax Revolt." The article told the inspiring story of Beit Sahour, a Palestinian town in the Israeli-occupied West Bank, which had been under a six-week military blockade because its people refused to pay taxes to their occupying force.

"The residents of Beit Sahour were cheering last night," I read, "proclaiming victory as Israeli soldiers cleared roadblocks and ended a six-week state of siege."

The article went on to describe Israeli tax collectors' house-to-house seizure of 1.5 million dollars worth of cars, refrigerators, clothing, and other belongings from the town's residents. Forty debtors were arrested. Some were given stiff fines, others sent directly to jail. Confiscation of property continued. Still no one paid. Finally the army reopened the town.

Beside the article was a photograph of the women of Beit Sahour celebrating in their village streets. With family members in prison and their homes and shops emptied of possessions, the radiant, marching women, their hands held toward the sky in the peace sign, looked as if nothing on earth could stop their nonviolent revolution.

One month later, thanks to an invitation from Scott Kennedy of the Resource Center for Nonviolence in Santa Cruz, California, I walked with the first Mid East Witness delegation into an again-barricaded Beit Sahour. On December 8, 1989, the second anniversary of the Palestinian uprising or *intifada*, the Israeli government closed Beit Sahour to all visitors to discourage any outside support for demonstrations. The five of us managed to enter the hillside town on a side street, however, above the soldiers guarding the main access where we had already been turned back a few minutes earlier. We walked single file, ten meters between us, so as to be less conspicuous to the army's rooftop sentries posted across Beit Sahour.

Suddenly our guide motioned us to take cover. Up ahead soldiers were firing tear gas cannisters into a women's demonstration. If the soldiers saw us, they would eject us from the town as unwanted observers. We ducked into the nearest home and were welcomed warmly by its surprised family. We were in Beit Sahour.

We were thus in the heart of the *intifada* — and of the *gospel* as well.

In the month since my introduction to Beit Sahour, I had learned that this *intifada* birthplace of nonviolence was near neighbor to the birthplace of nonviolence in the gospels of Luke and Matthew. Beit Sahour is next to Bethlehem (whose filthy jail is well-known to Sahouri tax resisters). And Beit Sahour itself is the traditional site of the field where an angel of the Lord appeared to the shepherds, bringing them the transforming "good news of a great joy which will come to all the people," the birth of a messiah, or revolutionary king, whose future meaning is spelled out further in the angels' song as "peace on earth among people with whom God is pleased" (Luke 2:8-14).

According to Luke, the historical reason for Jesus' birth having occurred in Bethlehem was in itself not good, joyful, or peaceful news for his people. Likewise in Matthew, Jesus' birth, although ten years earlier under Herod, comes at a time of extreme repression. In Luke, it was the Roman Empire's forcible enrollment of a colonized people in a repressive tax census in 6 C.E. ("when Quirinius was governor of Syria," Luke 2:2) that made it necessary for Joseph and Mary to travel almost a hundred miles from Nazareth to Bethlehem. Because Joseph's family of David was from Bethlehem, not Nazareth, he and Mary, like thousands of other displaced Jewish peasants, were forced by Roman decree to leave their current home and undertake a difficult journey to an ancestral district in order to be properly enrolled. This census enrollment, whose purpose was to lay the groundwork for Rome's exploitative taxation of the colonized Jewish nation, was the cause of a tax revolution in 6 C.E. led by Judas the Galilean.

The Lucan context for the "good news" first given to all the people at the shepherds' field (now Beit Sahour) is, therefore, a setting of imperial government repression. The Greek word *euangelion* ("glad tidings"), later translated as *godspel* ("good tale" and "good news"), had become a propaganda term for Roman military victories. The imperial meaning of "glad tidings" or "good news," celebrating a military triumph, was played upon by Mark, Luke, and Matthew, who turned the word around to announce their genuinely "good news" of a nonviolent victory. In Luke's case, the envisioned good news of peace on earth proclaimed in the infancy narrative comes within, but counter to, the intense repression of a taxation system laid upon a subject people.[9]

To the modern, predominantly Christian residents of Beit Sahour, the shepherds' field had become once again a place of conflict between "good news to all the people" — today the good news of the *intifada* as heard and carried out in Beit Sahour — and the repressive, propagandistic news of a military power occupying their land, taxing their possessions, and killing their children.

The Arabic word *intifada* literally means "shaking off" — shaking off the occupation. In the Sayings Gospel Q, Jesus tells the disciples to "shake off" the dust from their feet if a village does not listen to their message of peace (Matt. 10:14; Luke 9:5). In Q, this shaking off of dust means that the rejected advocates of peace "clear themselves of all further responsibility for the doomed city. . . . It was an act towards a whole city, not towards individuals."[10]

The *intifada* provides a comparable case of "shaking off." The message of peace has been rejected by those who militarily occupy the land of 1.5 million Palestinians in the West Bank and Gaza. This occupation is then "shaken off" by Palestinians who, in the words of Elias Chacour, are saying to Israel, "Enough! We do not agree to be occupied anymore. We have lost not only our land, homes, work, and families, but also our dignity and our future. We are going to 'shake off' this occupation, letting you and the whole world know that we want our freedom."[11]

Thus the shaking off of oppression is literally "good news" to the oppressed. But those who reject its message may experience judgment. The Beit Sahour story, mirroring and updating its own shepherds' field story from the gospels, had in turn become good news to "all the world" — or at least enough of the world to have caused the occupying government to cordon off the town from outside observers.

But now we were in Beit Sahour, in the home of a warmly welcoming Palestinian family — and soon in several such homes, as the town's communications and logistics network moved the five of us swiftly along to different households, so that during our two days there we might have the widest possible sharing with the people.

We learned quickly the basis for the nonviolent power of Beit Sahour. The town is an extended family. The people of Beit Sahour are one.

Beit Sahour, in fact, is composed mainly of five huge Palestinian families, which have lived and inter-married there for centuries. The town is an effective reminder of the basic truth of our global home — one family, one world, one life — the profoundly simple and transforming truth which nonviolence calls upon in each of its actions. Beit Sahour is that basic truth of oneness in continuous nonviolent action, the active expression of one living family. To be in Beit Sahour for even a few hours is to experience what is possible and necessary for us all.

On my first night in Beit Sahour I was taken door to door to meet as many members as possible of the Rishmawi clan, that larger Beit Sahour family in one of whose homes I was being given hospitality. I was soon immersed in a transforming vision made up of Rishmawis, Jesus, and Gandhi.

Although I met many Rishmawis that night, including the leaders cited in the Birmingham newspaper article that had introduced me to Beit Sahour, it seemed as if I was meeting just as many other Rishmawis by their absence. Every home I visited had immediate family members in prison. I was told their stories — by their fathers, their wives, their children. Beit Sahour's *intifada* had its costs. One of these was prison. It was a cost readily accepted by the people of Beit Sahour as the price for their whole people's freedom.

Throughout this house-to-house lesson on the "cost of discipleship," I not only felt the spirit of Jesus and Gandhi, I saw Jesus and Gandhi.

Because Beit Sahour is the shepherds' field of Luke's gospel, and because a number of its citizens have become master carvers (whose work is sold especially to Christian pilgrims in Bethlehem), the town is full of olive wood figures of Jesus, Mary, and Joseph. The Israeli government, by its tough confiscation tactics, must have acquired a multitude of holy families, to be placed in storage.

I was given one carving by a Beit Sahour artist after I had watched him in his basement workshop, in an incredibly short time, "release" the figure he had in his mind from a block of wood. As he completed the carving, a process in which I had become absorbed, I was startled by the baaaing of sheep—the carver's sheep, kept in a basement stall immediately behind me. The artist-shepherd's sheep were keeping watch over the scene.

Gandhi also was visibly present in each home I entered. As I heard story after story of nonviolent resistance to the occupation, I saw simultaneously in the background images of Gandhi: Gandhi burning government-imposed ID cards in South Africa, Gandhi striding toward the sea in the Salt March, Gandhi fasting for Hindu-Muslim unity . . . Every family in Beit Sahour seemed to be watching the film "Gandhi," being shown that night with Arabic subtitles on Jordanian television.

The juxtaposition of the Rishmawis' nonviolent testimony, of lives both present and absent, of *gospel* and *satyagraha* images, was overwhelming— and as I recall it now, remains overwhelming. The world of nonviolence— spanning prison walls, borders, cultures, and religions—seemed present in each Beit Sahour home. I take it now, as then, not as illusion but as a revelation of what we are all called to be as a people, in a oneness of nonviolence.

On our second day in Beit Sahour, our Mid East Witness group was cut from five persons to three as Israeli soldiers succeeded in apprehending Scott Kennedy and Deena Hurwitz and ejecting them from town.

The way in which this event ended was a parable of nonviolence.

The soldiers had again been breaking up a women's demonstration when they spotted the two illicit American witnesses on the street, first Scott, then a little while later, Deena. As the soldiers first drove Scott out of town in their jeep, one of them recalled angrily having refused him entry to Beit Sahour at the military checkpoint the day before. What especially concerned the soldier, however, was another, still obviously missing member of our group.

"Where's the rabbi?" he demanded.

He meant Rabbi Michael Robinson of Sebastopol, California, who had engaged him in a friendly conversation even as he was being barred from the town. Mike felt deeply the confusion and suffering of these young Jewish soldiers forced to carry out criminal orders. But this soldier could only see such a rabbi's presence in Beit Sahour as a distinct threat.

"Where's the rabbi?"

Scott had not seen Mike since the night before. But as the security jeep drove out Beit Sahour's main street, Scott saw a familiar figure standing in front of the Greek Orthodox Church—smiling and waving at him, but unnoticed by the soldiers.

It was "the rabbi" — now wearing a red checkered *kuffiyeh* or headscarf, transformed for the present into a Palestinian.

Yet that was also the rabbi's nonviolent threat to the soldier who failed to recognize him, his willingness to stand in the place of the other.

Where's the rabbi?

Where the soldier for his transformation also needed to be, in the *kuffiyeh* of Beit Sahour.

On a later visit to Beit Sahour Deena Hurwitz would engage one of the young soldiers there in a sensitive dialogue that would continue for weeks in other settings. The soldier estimated that less than half of the Israeli army agreed with the repression of Palestinians they were ordered to carry out. A courageous group of Israeli soldiers, *Yesh Gvul* ("There Is a Limit"), has refused to serve in the Occupied Territories, and, as a result, they have gone to jail instead.

On Sunday, December 10, Ann Hafften, Mike Robinson, and I said farewell to our friends in Beit Sahour and rejoined Scott and Deena in Jerusalem, where they had gone after the soldiers had released them in Bethlehem. Our Mid East Witness delegation then proceeded together to our second destination, Gaza. There Palestinian friends smuggled the five of us into different refugee camps.

TRANSFORMING SIGNS IN GAZA

Gaza. I say the name and its reality returns. The Gaza Strip: just that, a strip of land on the Mediterranean coast twenty-eight miles long and five miles wide, inhabited by 650,000 Palestinians, occupied by the Israel Defense Forces since the IDF's victory in the Six-Day War in 1967. Most of the Palestinians are refugees, having already fled or been expelled from their original homes in Israel. They are now squeezed into eight United Nations refugee camps, which are patrolled by IDF soldiers. Gaza's Palestinians are a stateless people, without passports from their Israeli occupiers, just as they had none earlier from Egypt.

The question of transformation took on awesome proportions in Gaza. Yet at those very moments when Gaza's violence seemed to freeze the heart, a nonviolent alternative was already present and emerging. The transformation of Gaza may transform the world.

For two days and nights I was hidden by a Palestinian Muslim family in their home at the center of Beach Camp, one of the Gaza Strip's three largest refugee camps. Roughly fifty thousand Palestinian refugees are wedged into Beach Camp's one-kilometer-long strip beside the Mediterranean.

Beach Camp had been closed to the outside world by the Israel Defense Forces for 318 days in the two years of the *intifada*. Like the rest of Gaza, it had been under curfew from 8:00 P.M. to 4:00 A.M. every night since the *intifada* began. People on the street in those hours were liable to be shot.

But many had also been shot in Beach Camp during non-curfew hours, as Israeli patrols swept through several times a day. Beach Camp was under a constant state of siege.

I saw the reality of Beach Camp through the cracks of shutters. On my first afternoon in the camp, as my host family was serving tea, the eldest son, Mohammed, seemed to be listening intently. He put his fingers to his lips and motioned to me to follow him into the next room. There slowly, cautiously, he opened the shutters a fraction of an inch. Then he stood aside. I looked out. The dusty road, which had been teeming with people when Mohammed brought me in by car an hour earlier, was now deserted and silent. Then I saw the soldiers appear in the crack.

The soldiers came in two jeeps. They wore camouflage uniforms and flak jackets. All of them carried rifles at the ready. They fanned out from the jeeps, stopping periodically with their rifles trained on the silent houses. Two older women walked carefully at a distance, not looking at the soldiers.

Sometimes the soldiers would run to a corner. The jeep would follow. After sweeping through the empty area and firing a random shot or two, the soldiers would mount the jeep to move to another area.

No one challenged the soldiers. The scene was like a village in Vietnam, with U.S. troops on a search-and-destroy mission. Now, as then, occupying troops and weapons are financed by United States dollars. Without billions of United States military aid, Israel's occupation of the West Bank and Gaza could not be sustained.

Night fell.

While soldiers outside the courtyard walls continue to fire their rifles and sweep through the dark roads, Mohammed's family and friends sit around the room sharing quiet, halting conversation with me. A Beach Camp teacher translates their Arabic and my English.

At one point we hear two shots fired just outside. We fall silent.

We know the soldiers could burst in at any moment. They have done so before, to humiliate the elders by forcing them to wash away slogans written on the walls outside by the shebab *(the Palestinian youth). If the soldiers enter, they will find me. That would mean serious repercussions for the family.*

After five minutes of silence, Mohammed says something softly and everyone laughs.

The interpreter leans over, smiles, and whispers to me, "We are afraid."

The conversation resumes. I ask Mohammed about differences between Beach Camp and other places of the intifada.

Why did I see no burning tires, no rock barricades set up by the shebab?

Mohammed explains: When tires are burned in Beach Camp, the soldiers take them and throw them over the walls into the people's homes. The burning tires are very bad for the respiration of older people. They are bad for everyone's health.

So the camp leadership and the people have agreed that tires should not be burned except after someone has been killed by the soldiers. Then they will be burned to express the people's anger. But normally there is no burning of tires in Beach Camp.

I saw no rock barricades because during the last extended curfew the soldiers came with trucks and machines that stripped the roads of stones and scrap objects that could be used to blockade their patrols.

The 3-year-old son of a friend of Mohammed comes in and snuggles between his father's knees. He watches me in fear, wondering if I am like the soldiers outside.

Mohammed tells me the story of a confrontation between the Beach Camp shebab *and the soldiers. One day the* shebab *had run forward, throwing stones at a heavily fortified local building occupied as a command post by the soldiers. The Israeli forces fired back with their rifles, picking off the* shebab *one by one until there were fifty wounded and one young girl dead.*

Mohammed says every family in the camp has had at least one shebab *shot or beaten by the soldiers.*

While his 13-year-old brother is serving us a delicious dinner, Mohammed asks if he will please show me the bullet scar on his cheek where he has been shot by the soldiers. The boy bends over, pointing to the scar. Then he opens his mouth. I can see the hole left from a bullet-shattered tooth.

Because the intifada *has renounced any use of guns against the occupiers, it has neutralized Israel's far superior firepower of artillery, tanks, Phantom fighter planes, nuclear warheads, and a virtually inexhaustible supply of U.S. weapons technology. By its opponent's choice of predominantly nonviolent tactics, the Israeli army has been forced to fight the* intifada *with the reduced violence of clubs, gas, and "rubber" bullets (their core is in fact metal).*

But I am shown how immense the cost in suffering from this "low-intensity conflict" has been to the shebab. *As other young men, curious to meet the visiting American, filter into the room, Mohammed points out their scars — and in some cases, shortened limbs.*

The wounds are shown in silence. This is the accepted cost of the intifada. *They all know that if they give up resisting the occupation, the cost will be far greater.*

On my second afternoon in Beach Camp, I witnessed the *shebab* in their David-versus-Goliath role. The term *children of the stones* took on flesh.

Again I was given a vantage point where, without being detected, I could witness the events going on outside. This time Mohammed invited me to climb a high ladder braced in a corner of the courtyard where wall louvers met beneath a corrugated tin roof. By standing near the top of the ladder and shifting my attention from one slightly opened louver to the other, I could see below me a dusty crossroads of the camp and any activity for several blocks in each direction.

The walls of Palestinian family homes, blemished with rubbed-out slogans, framed the encounter I saw developing at the center of Beach Camp.

In the middle of the dusty intersection are eight young men, the shebab. *In the course of the next hour, their number will grow to as many as fifteen or drop to as few as two, as the young men come and go. The* shebab *range in age from 9 or 10 years up to their early 20s.*

The sky is darkening. Rain seems about to fall but never does.

Sporadic shooting can be heard. The shooting gets louder.

A donkey is braying wildly on a side road, pulling hard on its tether.

A little boy, perhaps 2 years old, runs out from an alley into the middle of the road. He makes a quick V sign in the direction of the shooting, then scampers back into the arms of his pursuing mother.

Each of the shebab *at the crossroads has a rock or two held lightly in hand. There are no stockpiles by the side of the road. As I watch one of the* shebab, *he throws away his only rock and remains standing, waiting, at the center of the road.*

I realize that this young man is preparing to be shot.

A small plane is circling overhead. I ask Mohammed, who is in the courtyard below me, what the plane is doing. He says it is a military surveillance plane telling the soldiers where the shebab *are located.*

A United Nations ambulance passes through the crossroads. The flag on its rear fender is lit up and flying. The U.N. ambulance is followed by a Red Crescent Society ambulance.

Eventually the two ambulances return. They sit with motors running at one spoke of the intersection, a few feet from the shebab, *who pay no attention to them.*

The ambulances are waiting to take whichever of the shebab *will be shot today.*

But while the sounds of shooting continue, this afternoon the soldiers do not come to the crossroads I am watching. The toll from other sites in Beach Camp, Mohammed says later, is three shebab *shot—one of them hit in the eye and taken prisoner by the soldiers.*

This has been the 734th afternoon of the intifada *in Beach Camp.*

I have become more and more conscious, during my two days and night in Beach Camp, of the presence of the tower. The tower, or minaret, rises from a corner of the mosque across from Mohammed's home. But from the family courtyard, the tower seems to be almost directly above us. At least that is the sense of its presence. At night, as I walk across the courtyard, the tower and the moon are together in the dark sky over us.

At the top of the tower there is a crescent open to the sky, and beneath the crescent a roofed balcony. It is from the loudspeakers on this balcony that the tower calls the people of Beach Camp to prayer five times a day, in a thunderous, static-crackling voice:

"ALLAH AKBAR!"

("God is great!")

"ALLAH AKBAR!"

The day's first call to prayer is at dawn. We awaken to it each morning. I hear the sunset call to prayer, on my second day in Beach Camp, against the background noise of rifle fire.

As I watch the *shebab* standing at the crossroads waiting, with the sounds of death approaching, the tower in the darkening sky calls us all to remember:

"ALLAH AKBAR!"

I wonder how many *shebab* have been shot or beaten while listening to "ALLAH AKBAR!" from the tower, or hearing it within themselves.

The *intifada*, I learned, was capable of greater violence than the stone-throwing of the *shebab* in the face of rifle fire.

After the five members of our Mid East Witness delegation had reunited, a representative of the United Nations Relief and Works Agency (UNRWA) drove us through Gaza. We toured Raffah, an area where reportedly more than forty "collaborators" had been killed by Palestinian "strike forces."

At Raffah we entered an UNRWA clinic. Posted on an electrical pole was a leaflet that we stopped to read. It was a warning against anyone collaborating with or helping the enemy.

A moment later we saw the enforcers of this warning to collaborators, presumably also the posters of the leaflet. I cite here Scott Kennedy's graphic description:

> As we turned from reading the notice, 4-6 young people, dressed from head to toe in black, carrying axes in one hand, with chains around their necks, knives tucked into their belts, and Palestinian flags on their shoulders, strode by. Even their feet were covered with plastic bags to make it impossible to identify them. Their faces were completely covered, but for tiny slits on their eyes. As they passed by us in single file a few feet away, without slowing or turning, I could hardly believe my eyes. We were witnessing one of the masked "strike forces" about which so much is written in the Israeli and other press. Such groups are responsible for enforcing discipline in the *intifada* and dispensing "justice," including the "cleansing" of collaborators.[12]

From conversations with Palestinians, I found the "strike forces" widely accepted in the Occupied Territories as a necessary evil to deal with those who repeatedly work with Israeli authorities to imprison or kill other Palestinians.

The process was for the "strike forces" first to issue a general warning, such as the one we had read. Then three successive, individual warnings were to be given to those identified as collaborators, by people who knew them. The fifth and final step — execution.

The *intifada* did not arise from an ideological commitment to nonviolence. It arose as a people's response to decades of lethal violence, within one of the most explosive situations in the world, in Gaza and the West Bank. The specific act which gave birth to the *intifada* could just as easily have moved thousands of Palestinians to take up arms rather than to renounce guns against their occupiers for the sake instead of strikes, boycotts, tax resistance, the flying of the Palestinian flag. . . . The *intifada* came as a people's transforming, primarily nonviolent response to a desperately violent situation.

It requires a spiritual explanation.

Before I left Beach Camp, a friend of Mohammed told me the story of how the *intifada* began.[13]

On December 8, 1987, four Palestinians were killed and seven injured when an Israeli military tank transport vehicle ploughed into a line of cars at the entrance to the Gaza Strip. Palestinians believed the crash and killings were deliberate.

A funeral for the four victims was held at Gaza's Jabalia refugee camp on December 9. The thousands of Palestinians who attended the funeral united in protest to the deaths. The people burned tires as a memorial to the four victims. They flew the Palestinian flag everywhere they could, violating the Israeli law against the flag's ever being shown. Finally, they threw stones at Israeli soldiers, who fired back with their guns. A 17-year-old Palestinian boy was killed.

On December 10 the people in Beach Camp also took many tires and burned them as a funeral memorial. When the soldiers came in response, the people threw stones at them. Then thousands of Beach Camp refugees went out on their roads, carrying symbolic coffins topped with wreaths of flowers and pictures of the four December 8 victims.

The people marched down their suddenly liberated roads chanting "ALLAH AKBAR! ALLAH AKBAR! ALLAH AKBAR!"

Within hours, a spiritual tidal wave had rolled through the Gaza Strip, across to the West Bank, and eventually back over the "Green Line" (dividing Israel and the Occupied Territories) into the Arab population of Israel itself.

The prisoners were free.

The *intifada* was born.

"ALLAH AKBAR!"

Can the former prisoners continue now to shake off their occupation in such a way as to free their jailers as well? The question may seem absurd. The prisoners' natural response would be to raise an indignant counter question: What responsibility do we have for our jailers?

But if God is truly great — great enough to save humanity from its self-destruction — then the prisoners do have a responsibility toward their jailers. The human beings below the tower, all of us, need to pray and act deeply enough to draw fully on the transforming greatness of God's being. Otherwise, the fate of Sepphoris and Jerusalem in Jesus' time will become the fate of the earth today.

In the nuclear age especially, we need to be transformed by the greatness of God to love those whose injustice we shake off, so that we and they might be saved together from our mutual violence.

"And remember the favor of Allah on you when you were enemies, then Allah united your hearts so by Allah's favor you became brothers and sisters; and you were on the brink of a pit of fire, then Allah saved you from it; thus does Allah make clear to you Allah's revelations that you may follow the right way" (*The Holy Qur'an*, III.103).

"ALLAH AKBAR! God is great! We are all one!"

TURNING FROM A HERITAGE OF VIOLENCE

Every nation is paralyzed by its own violent past, until it repents. "Unless you repent, you will all likewise perish" (Luke 13:3). Through that *teshuvah*, that turn from its own violence, a nation is then freed to forgive the violence done to it by other nations and to become a power of nonviolent transformation in the world. Self-justifying mythologies from Columbus to the American frontier have covered European and white American settlers' genocide of Native Americans and the enslavement of African Americans. Thus an unrepented past paralyzes Washington from making peace through justice with its own Native American and Afro-American citizens or with third-world peoples in El Salvador, Nicaragua, and Iraq. The violence in United States cities such as East St. Louis, Illinois, and in the nations of the Third World mirror each other, both symptoms of a systematic, economic racism practiced by first-world power elites. "Ay-rabs" have now become the "niggers" of United States foreign policy: "Gonna shoot them fucking Ay-rabs til they're dead," as I have heard U.S. Marines "sound off" in unison, as they double-timed their way past our home beside the fence of the Trident submarine base at Bangor, Washington. Every nation is called to acknowledge and turn from such hate-filled violence in its own attitudes, and in that turning, to forgive the violence done to it by other nations. By covering or justifying our own violence, we make impossible the national repentance and forgiveness of others necessary for a global salvation from violence.

But if violence is a national heritage in country after country, how much genuine hope can we place in each of those nations repenting its violence and turning toward justice and peace? If violence is so deeply a part of the past of nations, how can we realistically hope for a collective *teshuvah*, a turning from global suicide to our Nonviolent God?

In a meditation on *teshuvah*, the great rabbinic teacher Adin Steinsaltz has written:

> The principle of teshuva is that the "returner," the *ba'al teshuva*, can not only "erase" things from [one's] past, but can actually change the past. When it is said that through teshuva, deliberately committed

sins are transformed into innocent errors and even into merits, this means that the present not only ignores the past but also rewrites it. And even though this transformation of the past does not alter the facts, it does change their significance and direction.

... Teshuva is perceived as primal experience, an experience that existed as a possibility even before Creation, as it says in Psalms, "Before the mountains were brought forth, before You brought Earth and the universe into being. ... You said: Return, O children of [humankind]."[14]

In other words, in the very foundation of the world and its causal system was interwoven a non-causal element, the element of teshuva.[15]

The power in the divine mystery of *teshuvah* to free one from an iron chain of events has often been celebrated in terms of personal conversion, for example, in the hymn "Amazing Grace," written by a repentant slave trader. But nations can also turn profoundly toward God, as the United States began to do in the civil rights movement. A national and international *teshuvah* from violence is, I believe, the nonviolent coming of God which we are all invited to embody at the close of this second millennium after the birth of Jesus.

I saw signs of that coming transformation of us all in Jerusalem.

THE WOMEN IN BLACK AND MOTHER INTIFADA

I wonder if the weeping "daughters of Jerusalem" to whom Jesus appealed in the first century to save Jerusalem from destruction (Luke 23:28-31) have not been reborn in the twentieth century as the "Women in Black," determined to save Jerusalem from another destruction. Dressed in black, the women stand, one hundred strong, in an hour-long silent vigil every Friday afternoon in French Square, a busy Jerusalem intersection. They hold black, cardboard hands that have white letters on them, in Hebrew and English, saying simply, "End the Occupation." The women stand in a circle on an island in the center of the square, facing outward, confronting Friday's heavy, pre-Sabbath traffic. They are young, old, middle-aged; some are pregnant, some have children in arms, others have children beside them. One handicapped woman comes every week in her wheelchair. The women began their vigil as a handful in the early days of the *intifada*. Now one hundred Women in Black come every week. Most of the Women are Jewish Israelis. Some, however, are Arab citizens of Israel. Besides the weekly vigil, the Israeli women have organized peace conferences and marches with Palestinian women. They also organize support for women political prisoners held by Israel. The French Square vigil in Jerusalem has inspired other Women in Black vigils in Haifa and Tel Aviv, still others in the United States, Canada, Europe, and Australia, for a total of thirty weekly vigils, all with the same, stark message: "End the Occupation."

At the Jerusalem vigil the red light at the intersection is a long one, so the women stand vulnerable to the reactions of drivers a few feet away, who take in the demonstration as they wait for the light to change. The drivers' verbal responses to the circle of dissenting, black-clad women is, as one Woman in Black, Gila Svirsky, puts it, "sometimes excruciating." Svirsky goes on to describe an experience that "no one who has ever gone through will easily forget":

> Take a long breath and listen to the ugly words. I repeat them not for effect, but to report the nature of the response when women as women take an unpopular political position.
>
> The words go like this: "All you girls need is a little rape to make you feel better." "Whores of the Arabs—that's what you are." "What's the matter, ladies, fucking Arafat is better?" "Shove it, babies, good and hard." And the endless staple of "Fuck you."
>
> Believe me when I say that these words are addressed to us as women. In mixed male and female demonstrations, the abuse is politically oriented, with such words as "traitors," "anti-Semitic Jews," "no memory of the Holocaust," etc. It is horrifying to us who stand there. We feel vulnerable as we have never felt before. Some people throw things—fruit, eggs, water from canteens—whatever they have handy. There are no police to guard our safety. "Exposed," "naked," "on the front line" is how I hear us describing ourselves.[16]

The power of these silent women both to elicit and endure a deep-seated violence, which their Palestinian sisters and brothers know in more lethal forms, is remarkable. What have they done to provoke such abuse? As Gila Svirsky sees it:

> We are exponents of a hateful position, publicly chastising our Government and our men who fight its battles. . . .
>
> But why do they become so aggressive? It is our power, I believe. Surely it is our strength, lined up for all to see. When I came late one day, I could see us from a distance, standing proud and strong, looking as if we had endless reserves of strength and courage.[17]

The power of the Women in Black brings to mind the power of another woman, *Mother Intifada*. Painted by the Palestinian artist Sliman Mansour, *Mother Intifada* was given to me by Mohammed, on a poster, the morning I departed from his home in Beach Camp. Now she has become the cover of this book, an image of the nonviolent coming of God. *Mother Intifada*, like the Women in Black, has the power of creation. She has that power in herself and in the people she is delivering from fear and oppression. So too are the Women in Black renewing the conscience of their people, freeing them from different fears—and in so doing, taking on themselves the violence of those fears. The Jewish Women in Black and the Palestinian *Mother Intifada* are co-creative images of our Infinitely Compassionate God and the nonviolent humanity She is bringing to life.

"AND SHALL YOU INHERIT THE LAND?"

On my final day in Jerusalem I am told by Kathy Bergen, a peacemaker skilled in Israeli-Palestinian relations, that I should meet Yeshayahu Leibowitz.

Who, I ask, is Yeshayahu Leibowitz?

Kathy says he is a strictly Orthodox, 87-year-old philosopher and biochemist at the Hebrew University. He has been the editor of the *Hebrew Encyclopedia*. The books he has written include *The Jewish People and the State of Israel* and *Belief, History, and Values*. Leibowitz is known for having said that, after the Six-Day War, Israel should have used a seventh day, *Shabbat* (the Sabbath), to withdraw from the territories it had just occupied. She adds that Yeshayahu Leibowitz is the successor to Martin Buber.

After numerous efforts I finally reach Professor Leibowitz by phone in early afternoon, with scant time remaining before my departure from Jerusalem. He kindly agrees to see me that afternoon at his home in the center of Jerusalem.

As Yeshayahu Leibowitz sits down behind his desk, I notice on it, set in a small frame, the familiar photograph of a Jewish girl with a haunting look. I nod in the direction of the picture and say, "Anne Frank."

"That," he says in return, "is a picture of my wife."

I look at the photograph more carefully, more conscious of the woman sitting quietly in the next room. In her eyes as a girl, gazing from the faded black and white photo, is what still seems to be the haunting look of Anne Frank. Is it because any Jewish girl growing up in that time would have known a reality similar to Anne Frank's? Neither of us refers again to the picture, but the girl's eyes continue to dwell on me during our conversation.

Professor Leibowitz begins to speak about his deeply divided society.

"The brutal fact is that there are two peoples, Jews and Palestinians, both feeling deeply in their hearts that this is their country. This is a terrible situation.

"There are only two solutions for this predicament. One solution, which is an inevitable corollary of our maintaining the occupation and retaining the ruler-ruled relationship, is perpetual war, *to the finish*. This won't be just a war between Israel and two or three million Palestinians but a war between Israel and the Arab world from Morocco to Kuwait, despite internal differences within the Arab world.

"The alternative to this is the division of the land between the two peoples without arguing whether this solution is 'just' or 'unjust,' 'logical' or 'illogical,' 'good' or 'bad.' It is the only alternative to war and the only means to do away with the ruler-ruled relationship between the two peoples.

"It is absolutely essential — in the interests of the Jewish people and their State — to get out of the territories inhabited by one and a half million Palestinian Arabs, even without a guarantee for an ensuing peace. It is not our business, nor our obligation, nor our right, to determine what the Palestinians should do or will do with their country after our withdrawal.

"Basing security on geography always fails. There is only one kind of security — a true peace between neighbors."

I ask Professor Leibowitz what he thinks of the *intifada*.

"The *intifada* is a war of independence by the Palestinian people. They wage this war without arms. It is an act of heroism. There have been 150 children murdered by the army of Israel."

He pauses, looking at me through his thick-lensed glasses. Then he continues speaking slowly and deliberately, watching to see if I understand each point.

"As for the 'religious' arguments for the annexation of the territories, they are nothing but sham and unconscious (or even conscious) hypocrisy, making Jewish faith a cover-up for Israeli nationalism.

"A false religiosity identifies the satisfaction of nationalistic aspirations with the service of God and makes the state — which is nothing but an instrument for satisfying human needs — a supreme religious value, a horrible devaluation of Judaism, similar to the substitution of the calf for God.

"Not every kind of return to Zion is a religious deed. There may be a return to Zion which is characterized by Jeremiah as 'you came and defiled my land and made an abomination of my property.'[18]

"Even establishing and maintaining Israeli sovereignty over the Temple Mount and the Western Wall in themselves have nothing in common with religious values: there was, and there is, a kind of Jewish possession of the Temple which is characterized by the prophet as 'defilement by villains (from your own people).'

"Jewish sovereignty over *Eretz Israel* ["Greater Israel," a term used to claim the Occupied Territories as Israel's divinely given heritage] as a fact of exercising mere political power is not at all what is meant by the 'faith of our past generations' on which lean the supporters of our 'integral Eretz Israel.' Nor does it express 'the historical linkage' between the Jewish people and the land in Jewish tradition.

"Jewish traditional thought never envisaged a renewal of Jewish sovereignty over the land without an intrinsic connection with a revival of the rule of the Torah in the Jewish community.

"Some 2,600 years ago Ezekiel foresaw the arguments of the rabbis and leaders of *Gush Emunim* [the movement to establish Jewish settlements in the Occupied Territories], and even the words and terms they use, and he reacted strongly: 'These were the words of the Lord to me: "Man, the inhabitants of these wastes on the soil of Israel say, 'Abraham was one, and he inherited the land; but we are many—*the land is given to us for an inheritance*.' Tell them therefore, that these are the words of the Lord God: "You eat with the blood, you lift your eyes to your idols, you shed blood— *and shall you inherit the land?...*" ' "

As Professor Leibowitz emphasizes Ezekiel's question from the Lord God, I think of the land stolen from Native Americans by white settlers ... of the land worked by African Americans for their slave masters ... of the land which third-world peoples till for first-world corporations, while their own children die of malnutrition and disease.

"You trust to your sword, you commit abominations, you defile one another's wives—*and shall you inherit the land?*"[19]

Again he emphasizes the question, a question which has now encompassed the earth. The land to which the Lord God is referring is not just the land of Israel-Palestine. It is the entire earth, claimed as our exclusive possession by us who trust to our swords. How can we claim to possess this land, the earth, even as we commit abominations on it and lay waste to it? *And shall you inherit the land?*

He brings us back to the Israeli-Palestinian conflict: "These words were not directed solely to the contemporaries of Ezekiel, some 100 generations ago. They are addressed to the present generation of 'the liberators of the Holy Land.' There is no greater abomination than turning a divine promise into a gratuitous gift, disregarding the conditions attached thereto.

"The idea of withdrawal from the territories sometimes raises an outcry of anguish: 'Did the best of our young men die in vain in the Six-Day War and the Yom Kippur War? Shall we desecrate the soil drenched with their blood by handing it over to the goyim?'

"To this let us answer: of the fallen in most wars in history it can be said that their death was meaningful, and nevertheless they died in vain. Their death was meaningful if they died in defense of their people and country. They died in vain because in most cases their deaths (even in a victorious war) did not decide the cause for which they fell, nor did it prevent a later war.

"Our brethren and our sons who died in our wars saved us from mortal peril at those moments, but their victories and their deaths did not eliminate, nor did they even weaken, the permanent danger to the existence of our State and its people. That will persist until a true peace is reached."

I say to Professor Leibowitz that he speaks like a prophet.

"I am not a prophet. I am speaking of politics. A prophet is religious."

I ask if a prophet may not be one who, as he does, has a deep sense of God's presence and speaks powerfully out of that experience.

He again declines: "There are too many people who think they have a sense of God and use it to justify murder."

I ask about the books he has written. He hands me a copy of his *Notes and Remarks on the Weekly Parashah*, a collection of talks on the Torah which he gave as a series on Israel Television in 1985 and 1986. I open it at random and read the following paragraph:

> I would like to remind you that a few weeks ago I had the opportunity to apply the notion of "ought" or "deserves to be" (or "should be") to another matter — prophecies about the future: "A prophet foretells but what ought to take place." The prophet presents a future which must be striven for, and which one must attempt to bring to fruition, without any guarantee that this will actually be realized. The term "deserves" (or "ought") refers to the *mitzvot*, to law and justice, and to forecasting the future. Every prophecy deserves to happen — and it depends on [humankind] whether those things which deserve to happen will or will not happen.[20]

What this "successor to Martin Buber" (a title he would also disdain) has written on prophecy seems to flow from his own prophecies on the state of Israel's "true peace" into Jesus' prophecies of the kingdom of God: A prophet foretells what ought to take place, a future which must be striven for . . . *Thy kingdom come, thy will be done* . . . One must attempt to bring it to fruition . . . *Love your enemies* . . . Without any guarantee that this will actually be realized . . . *Unless you repent, you will all likewise perish* . . . Every prophecy deserves to happen, and it depends on us humans whether those things which deserve to happen will or will not happen . . . *The kingdom of God is within your power.*

I read the original paragraph over again, this time aloud. As I finish reading, I look up from the book, into the eyes of Yeshayahu Leibowitz.

"By your own words," I say, "you are a prophet."

He is looking at me intently. We are both smiling.

NOTES

1. BEGINNING AT THE END OF THE LINE

1. The story of Franciszek Zabecki, member of Poland's underground Home Army and traffic superintendent of Treblinka railway station, is told by Gitta Sereny, *Into That Darkness* (New York: Vintage Books, 1983), pp. 148-56, 247-50.

2. Scripture scholar Lloyd Gaston has written an exhaustive, five-hundred-page analysis of Mark 13:1-2 and Jesus' other prophecies of the Jewish-Roman War, *No Stone on Another* (Leiden: E. J. Brill, 1970). His book is remarkably illuminating and little read. In Chapter 5, "Jesus, Jerusalem, and the End of the World," we will consider Jesus' prophecies in the light of Gaston's work.

3. John Pairman Brown, *The Liberated Zone* (Richmond: John Knox Press, 1969), pp. 111-12.

4. The Cooper Green Hospital's lack of resources is symptomatic of the poor medical care available nationwide to African Americans. See Associated Press, "Many Blacks Dying Due to Lack of Care," *Birmingham Post-Herald* (November 29, 1990), p. A-11.

5. Shelley Douglass, "Buried Treasure," *Ground Zero*, vol. 9, no. 2 (Fall 1990), p. 1.

6. Archbishop Raymond Hunthausen, "Our Nuclear War Preparations Are the Global Crucifixion of Jesus," *National Catholic Reporter* (February 12, 1982), p. 42.

7. Martin Hengel, *Crucifixion* (Philadelphia: Fortress Press, 1977).

8. Josephus, *The Jewish War*, trans. G. A. Williamson, revised by E. Mary Smallwood (Harmondsworth, Middlesex, England: Penguin Books, 1985), p. 326 (5.11.1; 449-50).

9. Edward N. Luttwak, *The Grand Strategy of the Roman Empire* (Baltimore: Johns Hopkins University Press, 1984), p. 3.

10. Zbigniew Brzezinski, "America's New Geostrategy," *Foreign Affairs* (Spring 1988), p. 680.

11. Ibid., p. 680.

12. Ibid., p. 683.

13. Ibid.

14. Ibid., p. 697.

15. *Discriminate Deterrence*, Report of the Commission on Integrated Long-Term Strategy, Fred C. Iklé and Albert Wohlstetter, co-chairmen (Washington: G.P.O., January 1988). The other members of the commission were Anne L. Armstrong, Zbigniew Brzezinski, William P. Clark, W. Graham Claytor, Jr., Andrew J. Goodpaster, James L. Holloway, III, Samuel P. Huntington, Henry A. Kissinger, Joshua Lederberg, Bernard A. Schriever, and John W. Vessey.

16. Ibid., p. 5.

17. Ibid., pp. 13-15.

18. Luttwak, p. xii.

19. *Discriminate Deterrence*, p. 15.

20. Ibid.

21. Luttwak, p. 24.

22. *Discriminate Deterrence*, p. 16.

23. Ibid.

24. Ibid.

25. Keenen Peck, "First Strike, You're Out: An Interview with Daniel Ellsberg," *The Progressive* (July 1985), pp. 31-32.

26. Daniel Ellsberg, Introduction to *Protest and Survive*, ed. E. P. Thompson and Dan Smith (New York: Monthly Review Press, 1981), pp. v-vi.

27. Ibid., p. x.

28. I am grateful to Marcus Borg for the formulation of this question.

29. M. K. Gandhi, *The Message of Jesus Christ* (Bombay: Bharatiya Vidya Bhavan, 1971), p. 67.

30. David J. Garrow, *Bearing the Cross: Martin Luther King, Jr., and the Southern Christian Leadership Conference* (New York: William Morrow, 1986).

31. "The Power Within: An Interview with Brian Willson," *Sojourners* (April 1988), p. 27.

32. Michael Kroll, "The Odyssey of Brian Willson," *San Francisco Examiner Image* (October 18, 1987), p. 23.

33. Ibid.

34. Ibid., p. 37.

35. Through a Freedom of Information Act request made in 1986 the San Francisco Pledge of Resistance confirmed that the government of El Salvador had a contract to receive munitions through the Concord Naval Weapons Station, including white phosphorus bombs and ammunition for a General Electric machine gun mounted on helicopter gunships. Brian Willson met with captured U.S. mercenary Eugene Hasenfus while he was in jail in Nicaragua and learned also of the air drop routes of U.S. military supplies from bases in El Salvador to their ultimate destination, contras in Nicaragua. Concord trains carried the weapons used for killing in both El Salvador and Nicaragua in violation of the Nuremberg Principles and treaty obligations embodied in the United States Constitution, Article 6, Section 2. This information is from Brian Willson's written presentation to the November 18, 1987, hearing conducted by the House Armed Services Subcommittee on Investigations. Of his forty-eight pages of prepared testimony, forty-four were censored from the Subcommittee's record.

36. Angus MacKenzie, "Weapons Train That Maimed Pacifist Was under Navy Orders Not to Stop," *National Catholic Reporter* (January 28, 1988), p. 15. The details in the four following paragraphs are drawn from investigative reports done by the Navy, the Department of Transportation, the Federal Railroad Administration, and the Contra Costa county sheriff's office, all cited in the *NCR* article.

37. Cited by Brian Willson, "The Power Within," p. 28.

38. Angus MacKenzie, "Conversion: The Cost of a Fired FBI Agent's Journey to Catholic Nonviolence," *National Catholic Reporter* (November 27, 1987), p. 1.

39. Associated Press, " 'No ill will,' Says Protestor Who Lost His Legs to a Train," *Bremerton Sun* (September 12, 1987).

40. "The Power Within," p. 27. The logic of violence has continued to be frus-

trated by a nonviolent presence at Concord. In the years since the train ran over Brian Willson, the sustained vigil of Nuremberg Actions-Concord has brought thousands of people to the base: vigiling, praying, fasting, leafletting the workers,. and nonviolently blocking the munitions trains and trucks twenty-four hours a day. As of October 1990, nearly fifteen hundred people had been arrested for taking part in the train blockades.

In mid-August 1990 Brian Willson and four other plaintiffs (Duncan Murphy, David Duncombe, the third veteran blocking the September 1, 1987 train, banner-holder Michael Kroll, and Holley Rauen, accepted a settlement of $920,000 in damages in their lawsuit against the United States government for its culpability in the use of lethal force.

41. The government's total estimated life-cycle costs for Trident-2 missile capability through the year 2032 are $154.6 billion. *Navy Strategic Forces: Trident II Proceeding Toward Deployment; Report to the Chairman, Committee on Armed Services, House of Representatives* (Washington: United States General Accounting Office, 1988), p. 31.

42. "If you know or suspect that heavily-encased Class A explosives, such as bombs or artillery projectiles, are being exposed to heat or flames, expand the isolation area in all directions to: 4000 feet (3/4 mile) for a Tractor/Trailer load; 5000 feet (1 mile) for a Railcar load." *Emergency Response Guidebook for Initial Response to Hazardous Materials Incidents* (Washington: Office of Hazardous Materials Transportation, Research and Special Programs Administration, U.S. Department of Transportation, 1987), Guide 46.

43. "WASHINGTON—Alabamians will do a disproportionate amount of the fighting and dying if war breaks out in the Persian Gulf.

"Population figures released by the U.S. Census Bureau [the week of January 6, 1991] confirmed that residents of Alabama are much more likely than the national average to go into full-time military careers and to be assigned to overseas duty. . . .

"When put on a per capita basis, Alabama has the fifth-highest level of citizens in overseas military service of any state in the nation."

Capt. Johnny B. McDonald, director of the U.S. Army's recruitment program in the Birmingham area, acknowledged in this article that unemployment was a big factor in Alabama's high enlistment rate.

Thomas Hargrove, "Numbers Prove Alabama's Stake in Mideast," *Birmingham Post-Herald* (January 10, 1991), p. A9.

In the fall of 1990, after the census enumeration had been made, Alabama ranked third in Persian Gulf call-ups among states in the Southeast, the region which was hardest hit by the reserve and National Guard mobilizations for Operation Desert Shield.

Associated Press, "South Hardest Hit by Call-Ups, Study Says," *Birmingham Post-Herald* (January 7, 1991), p. A3.

44. "The Other Side of the Trident Tracks: A Dialogue with Buck Jones and Jim Douglass," *CALC Report* (December 1988), p. 8.

45. Ibid.

2. THE NEW HUMANITY

1. Pyarelal, *Mahatma Gandhi: The Last Phase* (Ahmedabad: Navajivan Publishing House, 1958), pp. 809-10.

2. Timothy Garton Ash, *We the People: The Revolution of 89* (Cambridge: Granta Books, 1990), p. 20.

3. Ibid., pp. 68-69.

4. George Lakey, "Guerrilla Training, Nonviolent Style," *The Nonviolent Activist* (December 1990), p. 9.

5. Ralph David Abernathy, *And the Walls Came Tumbling Down* (New York: Harper & Row, 1989).

6. David J. Garrow, *Bearing the Cross: Martin Luther King, Jr., and the Southern Christian Leadership Conference* (New York: William Morrow, 1986). Taylor Branch, *Parting the Waters: America in the King Years 1954-63* (New York: Simon and Schuster, 1988).

7. "I See the Promised Land," in *A Testament of Hope: The Essential Writings of Martin Luther King, Jr.*, ed. James M. Washington (San Francisco: Harper & Row, 1986), pp. 280, 286.

8. J. H. Charlesworth, "Jesus and Jehohanan: An Archaeological Note on Crucifixion," *The Expository Times* 84 (1973), pp. 147-50. Charlesworth counts thirty-five individual deaths and nine violent deaths, and I count thirty-six and ten, the difference being his exclusion and my inclusion in both categories of the child who died with its mother in a neglected childbirth.

9. John L. McKenzie, *The New Testament Without Illusion* (Chicago: Thomas More Press, 1980), p. 116.

10. Maurice Casey, *Son of Man* (London: SPCK, 1979). Barnabas Lindars, SSF, *Jesus Son of Man* (London: SPCK, 1983). Geza Vermes laid the foundation for Casey's and Lindars's work by initiating a discussion of *bar enasha* as an idiomatic Aramaic speech pattern in his "The Use of Bar Nash/Bar Nasha in Jewish Aramaic," *Post-Biblical Jewish Studies* (Leiden: E.J. Brill, 1975), pp. 147-65. Vermes's thesis that *bar enasha* is exclusively a self-reference was modified by Casey's emphasis on the undisputed generic meaning of the expression, "human being," but with the nuance of "anyone, including myself." Lindars has sought a meaning between an exclusive self-reference and universal generic usage. See also the incisive summary of their debate by Donald J. Goergen, *The Mission and Ministry of Jesus* (Wilmington: Michael Glazier, 1986), pp. 189-92.

11. McKenzie, *New Testament Without Illusion*, p. 116.

12. John L. McKenzie, *Dictionary of the Bible* (Milwaukee: Bruce Publishing Company, 1965), p. 831.

13. Letter from Walter Wink to Jim Douglass, May 5, 1988.

14. "I See the Promised Land," p. 280.

15. The Stringfellow anecdote comes from Scott Kennedy, who was the source of the question.

16. William Stringfellow, *An Ethic for Christians and Other Aliens in a Strange Land* (Waco: Word Books, 1973), p. 153.

17. Hal Lindsey, *The 1980's: Countdown to Armageddon* (New York: Bantam Books, 1982), pp. 5-6.

18. A. G. Mojtabai, *Blessèd Assurance: At Home with the Bomb in Amarillo, Texas* (Boston: Houghton Mifflin Company, 1986), p. 154.

19. Quoted in Mojtabai, p. 55.

20. Letter from Walter Wink to Jim Douglass, March 17, 1989 (emphasis in original).

21. David J. Garrow, Foreword to *The Montgomery Bus Boycott and the Women*

Who Started It: The Memoir of Jo Ann Gibson Robinson, ed. David J. Garrow (Knoxville: University of Tennessee Press, 1987), p. x. Garrow calls the Robinson letter to Mayor Gayle "the most remarkable sheet of paper I had ever seen in some eight years of research on the civil rights movement." The letter is reproduced as the frontispiece to his Foreword to the Robinson memoir.

22. Ibid., p. 39.

23. Ibid., p. 47.

24. Branch, *Parting the Waters*, pp. 139-40.

25. Ibid., pp. 140-41.

26. Martin Buber, *Two Types of Faith* (New York: Macmillan, 1951), p. 100.

27. T. W. Manson, "Realized Eschatology and the Messianic Secret," in *Studies in the Gospels*, ed. D. E. Nineham (Oxford: Basis Blackwell, 1957), p. 218.

28. "The Son of man is delivered up (Mk. 9:31) so are the disciples (13:9, 11). He is brought before the authorities (8:31, 10:33); so are they (Mk. 13:9, cf. Lk. 12:11). He is treated with hatred and contempt (8:31, 9:12): the disciples may expect the same treatment (Mk. 13:13, Lk. 10:16, cf. Matt 5:11, Lk. 6:22). He is scourged (Mk. 10:34): so are the disciples (13:9, cf. Matt. 10:17). He is put to death (8:31, 9:31, 10:34): the disciples are repeatedly warned that they must be prepared for the same fate (8:34 f., cf. Matt. 10:38f., Lk. 14:27, 17:33), though not all of them may be called upon to suffer it (Mk. 9:1). We may also compare the saying about the Son of man in Mk. 10:45 with that to the disciples in Mk. 8:35." Ibid., pp. 218-19.

29. James R. Brockman, *The Word Remains: A Life of Oscar Romero* (Maryknoll, New York: Orbis Books, 1982), p. 208.

30. Ibid., p. 205.

31. Ibid., p. 210.

32. Ibid., p. 217.

33. Ibid., p. 223.

34. Letter from Walter Wink to Jim Douglass, March 17, 1989.

35. "It appears that the ancient Israelite tradition of popular anointed kingship, though dormant during the Persian and Hellenistic periods, remained alive. It certainly reemerged in vigorous form just before and after the life of Jesus of Nazareth. In response to foreign domination, severe repression, and illegitimate Herodian kingship, peasant attempts to set things right took the form of messianic movements." Richard A. Horsley and John S. Hanson, *Bandits, Prophets, and Messiahs: Popular Movements at the Time of Jesus* (Minneapolis: Winston Press, 1985), p. 131. Among the diverse movements and Judaisms at the time of Jesus, there was no single definitive Jewish messianic expectation. See also *Judaisms and Their Messiahs at the Turn of the Christian Era*, ed. Jacob Neusner, William S. Green, and Ernest Frerichs (Cambridge: Cambridge University Press, 1987).

36. Letter from Wink to Douglass, March 17, 1989 (emphasis in original).

37. Ibid.

38. "Luke 22:69, Luke's special source again, has a different image than Mt/Mk—much closer to Dan. 7—the movement seems to be one of *ascension* to God's throne, whereas Mt/Mk have the ascended one *returning* to *earth* from heaven. This is the source of the 2nd coming idea in its literal form. Luke's picture is much different: the human being is exalted to heaven. Perhaps the difference seems small; I tend to make a lot of it later on in my own work." Ibid. (emphasis in original). I look forward eagerly to reading Walter Wink's development of these insights on

Jesus' *Bar Enasha*, which he has so generously shared with me by correspondence, when he completes a major work on this subject.

39. T. F. Glasson, "The Reply to Caiaphas (Mark XIV.62)," *New Testament Studies* 7 (1960-61), p. 89.

40. T. F. Glasson lists ten well-known exegetes who agree on this point in his " 'The Second Advent' — 25 Years Later," *Expository Times* 82 (July 1971), p. 309.

41. C. H. Dodd, *The Parables of the Kingdom* (Welwyn: James Nisbet, 1958), p. 96.

42. John A. T. Robinson has pointed out that the only instance in the gospels in which Jesus is expected to come as Lord rather than as the Human Being is, "Watch therefore, for you do not know on what day your Lord is coming" (Matt. 24:42), where the vocabulary is taken from the parable behind it (Mark 13:35). *Jesus and His Coming* (London: SCM Press, 1957), p. 141. The coming Human Being statements are listed by T. W. Manson, *The Sayings of Jesus* (London: SCM Press, 1949), p. 250, footnote 31.

43. In his analysis of the Aramaic roots of "son of man" in the synoptic gospels, Geza Vermes identifies all of the *coming* "son of man" statements as either citing Daniel 7:13 explicitly or alluding to it indirectly. Geza Vermes, *Jesus the Jew* (New York: Macmillan, 1972), pp. 178-79.

44. T. W. Manson, "The Son of Man in Daniel, Enoch and the Gospels," *Bulletin of the John Rylands Library* 32 (2) (March 1950), pp. 174-75. It is Manson who has argued most extensively for the collective interpretation of the Human Being in a series of works. See also footnotes 27 and 28, and T. W. Manson, *The Teaching of Jesus* (Cambridge: Cambridge University Press, 1959).

45. G. B. Caird, *Jesus and the Jewish Nation* (London: University of London, 1965), p. 20.

46. Lloyd Gaston, *No Stone on Another* (Leiden: E. J. Brill, 1970), pp. 394-95.

47. Branch, p. 215.

48. Ibid., pp. 215-16.

49. Caird, p. 8

50. T. F. Glasson and John A. T. Robinson make a strong case that the phrase "from now on" stood originally in Mark's text as well. T. Francis Glasson, *The Second Advent* (London: Epworth Press, 1963), pp. 56-59. John A. T. Robinson, *Jesus and His Coming* (London: SCM Press, 1957), pp. 49-50.

51. Rudolf Bultmann, *Theology of the New Testament* (New York: Charles Scribner's Sons, 1955), p. 30.

52. Philosopher-theologian Howard Thurman drew on his own experience as an African American to illustrate this point in his beautiful book, *Jesus and the Disinherited* (Richmond: Friends United Press, 1981).

53. Robinson, p. 20.

54. Ibid., pp. 75-76.

55. Elizabeth Schüssler Fiorenza, *In Memory of Her* (New York: Crossroad, 1985), pp. 138-39.

3. TRANSFORMATION OR ANNIHILATION

1. This is the title of Gordon Zahn's biography of Jagerstatter: Gordon Zahn, *In Solitary Witness: The Life and Death of Franz Jagerstatter* (New York: Holt, Rinehart and Winston, 1964).

2. Ibid., pp. 111-12.

3. The February 1984 White Train to Bangor consisted of three security cars, four buffer cars, and ten cars designed to carry nuclear weapons. Each of the train's weapons cars is divided into three sections. A former nuclear weapons worker has estimated that each of these sections holds four warheads—thus twelve per car, and 120 warheads in this ten-car train. The Trident-1 nuclear warhead then being delivered to Bangor has an explosive equivalent of one hundred kilotons of TNT, or roughly eight times the power of the Hiroshima bomb, which was about 12.5 kilotons. A White Train carrying 120 Trident-1 warheads would therefore have the explosive equivalent of 960 Hiroshimas.

4. Karol Schulkin, "The Arms Race Has Come Home," *Ground Zero*, vol. 3, no. 2 (May/June 1984), pp. 5-7. For a subscription to the Ground Zero newspaper (four issues per year), write to Ground Zero Center for Nonviolent Action, 16159 Clear Creek Road, N.W., Poulsbo, WA 98370. A beautiful videotape, "The Arms Race Within," has been made of the February 1985 White Train arrival at Bangor. It is available from Idanha Films, PO Box 17911, Boulder, CO 80308.

5. Memorandum by R. G. Romatowski, Manager, Transportation Safeguards Division, Albuquerque Operations Office, Department of Energy, to Major General William W. Hoover, USAF, July 30, 1984. Obtained through the Freedom of Information Act by Glen Milner. The significance of the memorandum's term "special trains" is recognized in the introduction to Chapter 5, "Jesus, Jerusalem, and the End of the World."

6. An illustration of the effectiveness of Nukewatch's trucks campaign is the story of Nancy Copeland-Cannata, who on October 11, 1990, went outside to water the plants on her front porch in Greensburg, Kansas, and discovered a DOE H-bomb convoy parked on her street. Because she was thoroughly familiar with Nuke-watch materials, Copeland-Cannata had no difficulty in recognizing the H-bomb delivery trucks, which had inexplicably stopped beside her house. She immediately phoned the editor of her local paper and peace activists elsewhere. Then she took pictures of the trucks and their escort vehicles, engaging one of the drivers in a reluctant conversation while he refueled at a food mart. With her 16-year-old son, Cody, she circled the trucks, inspecting their special roof antennas, armor-plated cab walls, and bullet-proof windows. The next morning Cody reported the event in detail at his current-events class. Nancy Copeland-Cannata, "New H-Bomb Trucks' Cover 'Blown' in Kansas Neighborhood," *Oklahoma Peace Strategy* (November 1990), pp. 5-8. Nancy and Cody Copeland-Cannata's street was not a likely place for the DOE truck convoy to remain unidentified. Nancy and her children had already been a contributing factor to the Department of Energy's decision to stop sending the White Train. In the mid 1980s, they had driven repeatedly two and a half hours in the middle of the night to Harper, Kansas, to watch for the White Train at a key junction and alert others. By serving as an early warning for hundreds of White Train vigilers up the tracks, they were instrumental in stopping the train.

7. Josephus, who is known for exaggerating figures, states that the Roman siege of Jerusalem in 70 c.e. resulted in 1,100,000 Jewish dead and 97,000 prisoners. Josephus, *The Jewish War* 6.9.3 (420).

8. Emil Schürer, *The History of the Jewish People in the Age of Jesus Christ*, rev. ed. Geza Vermes and Fergus Millar (Edinburgh: T. & T. Clark, 1973), vol. 1, pp. 553, 556.

9. A straight line drawn from modern Nazareth to the ruins of Sepphoris would

extend a little less than four miles. In December 1989, as narrated in the Epilogue, I made a pilgrimage from Nazareth to the archaeological diggings of Sepphoris. Following modern roads, I walked a distance of five miles.

10. Except for a confused reading in the Cambridge Manuscript of John 11:54, noted by John Pairman Brown, "Techniques of Imperial Control," *The Bible and Liberation*, ed. Norman K. Gottwald (Maryknoll, New York: Orbis Books, 1983), p. 362. The generally accepted text has Jesus and his disciples visiting not Sepphoris but Ephraim.

11. Aharon A. Kabak, *The Narrow Path*, trans. by Julian Louis Meltzer (Tel Aviv: Massada Press, 1968), p. 157.

12. Josephus, *The Antiquities of the Jews* 17.10.5 (271), trans. William Whiston, *The Works of Josephus* (Peabody, Massachusetts: Hendrickson, 1987), pp. 469-70.

13. Brown, p. 362.

14. Seán Freyne, *Galilee from Alexander the Great to Hadrian 323 B.C.E. to 135 C.E.* (Wilmington: Michael Glazier, 1980), pp. 126-28. Freyne reconstructs what he can of Sepphoris prior to 70 C.E. with rabbinic materials from the second century. These are found mainly in A. Büchler, *The Political and Social Leaders of the Jewish Community of Sepphoris in the Second and Third Centuries* (London: Jews' College Publication, 1909).

15. Freyne, p. 127.

16. Josephus, *Antiquities* 17.10.9-10 (286-98), pp. 470-71.

17. Brown, p. 366.

18. Abraham J. Heschel, *The Prophets* (New York: Jewish Publication Society of America, 1962), p. xvi.

19. Ibid., pp. 221-31.

20. Brown, p. 361.

21. Carl H. Kraeling, *John the Baptist* (New York: Charles Scribner's Sons, 1951), p. 44. Lloyd Gaston, citing H. Sahlin in Gaston's *No Stone on Another* (Leiden: E. J. Brill, 1970), p. 312, also identifies Israel as the object of John's saying but by a different logic. Gaston believes John must have spoken originally of the ax laid at the root of a single tree, Israel. This contingent prophecy in its transmission was then combined with another tree-saying applying to individuals, which stands by itself in Matthew 7:19, "any tree that does not produce good fruit is cut down and thrown on the fire," thus causing John's statement to become plural and obscuring its meaning.

22. "That MT and LK differ with regard to John's audience is of little consequence in determining who that audience was, since an examination of the speech itself shows the audience clearly enough. ... There is only one group that it fits well and that is the ruling priestly aristocracy in Jerusalem which perpetrated the most heinous social injustices." Paul Hollenbach, "Social Aspects of John the Baptizer's Preaching Mission in the Context of Palestinian Judaism," *Aufstieg und Niedergang der römischen Welt*, ed. Hildegard Temporini and Wolfgang Haase, vol. 2, 19, 1, ed. W. Haase (Berlin–New York: W. de Gruyter, 1979), pp. 860-61.

23. Letter from Walter Wink to Jim Douglass, July 4, 1988. So also Joachim Jeremias, *New Testament Theology* (New York: Charles Scribner's Sons, 1971), p. 48.

24. Hollenbach, pp. 870-73.

25. Kraeling, pp. 95-122.

26. Ibid., p. 117.

27. Millar Burrows, *The Dead Sea Scrolls* (New York: The Viking Press, 1956), pp. 328-29. On the evidence of this psalm, VI (iii.19-36), Burrows connects John's proclamation with the river of fire in a way similar to Kraeling's earlier hypothesis (done without benefit of the scrolls): "[John's] prediction that the one coming after him would execute judgment by fire is undoubtedly related in some way to the Zoroastrian idea of a final conflagration in which the mountains will melt and pour over the earth like a river; and this idea is vividly presented in one of the Thanksgiving Psalms in terms of the 'torrents of Belial' that will consume in flame even the foundations of the mountains" (pp. 328-29). Burrows includes the full text of the psalm on pages 404-5.

28. Rather than "the Universal Judge," as Ernst Käsemann believes in his *Essays on New Testament Themes* (Philadelphia: Fortress Press, 1982), p. 142. "That John expected a representative of God and not God himself is indicated by his description of the Coming One. John would scarcely have spoken of God as 'he who is mightier than I.' God is not 'the mightier One'; he is the Almighty. Likewise the Coming One will wear sandals, and John feels unworthy to unloose them." Walter Wink, *John the Baptist and the Gospel*, doctoral diss., Union Theological Seminary, 1963, p. 50. Wink's unpublished dissertation is the basis for his book *John the Baptist in the Gospel Tradition* (Cambridge: Cambridge University Press, 1968). The dissertation contains a survey of works on John not included in the book. I am grateful to Walter Wink for sharing his dissertation with me.

29. Josephus, *Antiquities* 18.5.2 (118), p. 484. Kraeling has explained the political motives behind John's arrest and execution. Herod Antipas had decided to divorce his wife, daughter of the Nabataean King Aretas IV, in order to marry Herodias, his brother's wife. John's denunciation of Herod's marriage (Mark 6:18) was politically explosive because he was preaching in Peraea, which was controlled by Herod but surrounded by Nabataean spheres of influence. John's powerful voice against Herod's rejection of the Nabataean princess "meant aligning the pious Jewish inhabitants of Peraea with those of Arabic stock against their sovereign and thus fomenting insurrection" (Kraeling, p. 91).

30. Lloyd Gaston has argued that because Luke 7:18-23 is a pronouncement story it is illegitimate to see any biographical implications in John's question (Gaston, p. 286). However, to see the question's function in a pronouncement story is not to rule out the memory of such an event as a basis for this particular use of it. Moreover, as W. G. Kümmel points out, "the Baptist appears here in no way as a witness to Christ, but as an uncertain questioner, which contradicts the tendency of the early Church to make him such a witness. ... So it is the most probable assumption that the story in its essentials represents an old reliable tradition." Thus also M. Dibelius, H. G. Marsh, W. Manson, and C. J. Cadoux in works cited by Kümmel. Werner Georg Kümmel, *Promise and Fulfilment*, trans. Dorothea M. Barton (London: SCM Press, 1957), pp. 110-11.

31. Martin Buber, *Two Types of Faith* (New York: Macmillan, 1951), p. 117.

32. Ibid., p. 122.

33. Ibid.

34. Ibid., p. 123.

35. The Greek word *pais* can mean both, as can the Hebrew *ebed*. Mark 1:11 may have translated the Isaianic servant as "son" in order to combine the text from Isaiah with Psalm 2:7, "You are my son." Oscar Cullmann, *The Christology of the*

New Testament, trans. Shirley C. Guthrie and Charles A. M. Hall (Philadelphia: Westminster Press, 1959), p. 66.

36. James W. Douglass, *The Nonviolent Cross* (New York: Macmillan, 1968), pp. 61-62.

37. Charles H. H. Scobie, *John the Baptist* (London: SCM Press, 1964), pp. 163-77.

38. Scobie, p. 164, citing W. W. Moore, "Aenon," *Hastings' Dictionary of Christ and the Gospels*, vol. 1, p. 35.

4. THE TRANSFORMATION OF POWER

1. Cited by Bill Hall, "The Third World Debt Crisis," *The Nonviolent Activist* (December 1987), p. 3.

2. Bernard Guri, coordinator of agriculture and development for the Catholic church in Ghana, once explained to an affluent Christian parish in London a connection between its wealth, third-world poverty, and the destruction of the environment:

> My village is in the north of Ghana. You had better redraw your maps because they say the land around my village is savannah. But it is desert. Every year the desert creeps forward. There are many reasons. But one important one is that my people cut down the trees. This allows the soil to erode and so the desert creeps. There are fewer trees, so they do not give off the moisture which helps precipitate rain. So the desert grows.
>
> We in the Third World are destroying our environment. We cut the wood to make fuel to cook. We cut the wood to sell to the cities to make our living. In 15 years time there will be no trees left in Ghana. It will all be a desert. All this helps towards the greenhouse effect which will melt the ice-caps and flood cities like London. We are helping to destroy the global environment.
>
> But wouldn't you cut down a tree to cook your next meal if there was no other option? . . .
>
> I tell you: there is only one way to solve the threat to the environment. Poverty must be eliminated. How? You must have less. We must have more. You must not give of your surplus. You must sacrifice to give. You must not give out of pity or guilt. You must give out of love. We need your help. But we want to be treated like fellow children of God, not animals on whom you dump food. If you listen, I will tell you how to do it (from a speech by Bernard Guri to St. Margaret's Church, Twickenham, West London, on May 10, 1989; recorded by Paul Vallely and cited in his book, *Bad Samaritans: First World Ethics and Third World Debt* [Maryknoll, New York: Orbis Books, 1990], p. 215 of manuscript, not in final text).

3. Associated Press, "Kings Bay Base Ready to Do Job," *The Atlanta Journal and Constitution* (January 21, 1990), p. C-6.

4. Joachim Jeremias, *The Parables of Jesus* (New York: Charles Scribner's Sons, 1972), p. 160.

5. Ibid., p. 51.

6. Martin Buber, *The Way of Man According to the Teaching of Hasidism* (London: Vincent Stuart, 1963) pp. 36-37.

7. In the following summary of conditions in Palestine at the time of Jesus, I have been guided especially by two sources: Richard A. Horsley, *Jesus and the Spiral of Violence* (San Francisco: Harper & Row, 1987), pp. 3-58. Douglas E. Oakman, *Jesus and the Economic Questions of His Day* (Lewiston, New York: Edwin Mellen Press, 1986), pp. 37-80.

8. Jacob Neusner, *Judaism in the Beginning of Christianity* (Philadelphia: Fortress Press, 1984), p. 32.

9. Citing Josephus, *The Jewish War* 5.9.4 (405) and 2.17.1 (405), Gerd Theissen believes tax refusal was the decisive cause of the rebellion. Gerd Theissen, *Sociology of Early Palestinian Christianity* (Philadelphia: Fortress Press, 1982), p. 43. But perhaps an even more fundamental cause was what Douglas Oakman calls "a battle for the determination of the use of the land and distribution of its products." That battle was waged among Jews as well as between the Jewish nation and the Romans. Oakman, p. 142.

10. E. Mary Smallwood, "High Priests and Politics in Roman Palestine," *The Journal of Theological Studies*, vol. 13 (1962), p. 22.

11. Harold W. Hoehner, *Herod Antipas* (Cambridge: Cambridge University Press, 1972), p. 70

12. The passage is cited in two different translations, which I have combined. Horsley, p. 47. Gaalyah Cornfeld, ed., *The Historical Jesus* (New York: Macmillan, 1982), pp. 147-48.

13. Paul Hollenbach, "Social Aspects of John the Baptizer's Preaching Mission in the Context of Palestinian Judaism," *Aufstieg und Niedergang der römischen Welt*, ed. Hildegard Temporini and Wolfgang Haase, vol. 2, 19, 1, ed. W. Haase (Berlin–New York: W. de Gruyter, 1979), p. 854, footnote 13, citing N. Avigad, "How the Wealthy Lived in Herodian Jerusalem," *BibArchRev* 2 (1976), pp. 1, 23-35. The family inscription on the stone weight is shown in an illustration in Cornfeld, p. 148. The excavated dwelling, also known as the "Burnt House" because of its having been torched by the Romans when they stormed Jerusalem in 70, can be seen in James H. Charlesworth, *Jesus Within Judaism* (New York: Doubleday, 1988), illustration 11 following page 106.

14. Marcus J. Borg, *Jesus: A New Vision* (San Francisco: Harper & Row, 1987), pp. 84-85, for the more than twenty percent Temple tithes and fifteen percent Roman taxation figures. The Roman estimate is on the minimal side. It does not include customs, tolls, and tribute. Frederick C. Grant's estimate has often been cited: "If we may hazard an approximation, where no exact figures are available, *the total taxation of the Jewish people in the time of Jesus, civil and religious combined, must have approached the intolerable proportion of between 30 and 40 percent; it may have been higher still.*" Frederick C. Grant, *The Economic Background of the Gospels* (New York: Russell & Russell, 1973), p. 105 (emphasis in original).

15. David M. Rhoads, *Israel in Revolution 6-74 C.E.* (Philadelphia: Fortress Press, 1976), pp. 177-78.

16. Ibid., p. 178.

17. Gerd Theissen portrays this movement of peasants from farm crisis to a revolutionary banditry in his "quest of the historical Jesus in narrative form," *The Shadow of the Galilean* (Philadelphia: Fortress Press, 1987), pp. 67-82.

18. Horsley, p. 47.

19. S. Safrai, "Religion in Everyday Life," *The Jewish People in the First Century*, vol. 2, ed. S. Safrai and M. Stern (Philadelphia: Fortress Press, 1976), p. 824.

20. Seán Freyne, *Galilee from Alexander the Great to Hadrian 323 B.C.E. to 135 C.E.* (Wilmington: Michael Glazier, 1980), p. 282.

21. Ibid., p. 284.

22. Borg, pp. 85-86.

23. Horsley, p. 49.

24. J. Duncan M. Derrett, *Law in the New Testament* (London: Darton, Longman & Todd, 1970), p. 28.

25. The analysis in this paragraph has been drawn from A. N. Sherwin-White, *Roman Society and Roman Law in the New Testament* (Oxford: Clarendon Press, 1963), pp. 139-41.

26. Robert W. Funk provides an insightful analysis of the Good Samaritan in *Parables and Presence* (Philadelphia: Fortress Press, 1982), pp. 29-34.

27. Josephus, *Antiquities* (18:2.2; 30).

28. J. Edward Carothers, *Living with the Parables* (New York: Friendship Press, 1984), p. 83.

29. See the January 25, 1991, Helsinki Watch report, *Pattern of Violence,* which describes the first five occasions in which Gorbachev resorted to lethal force against civilians, and Jeri Laber, "The Baltic Revolt," *The New York Review* (March 28, 1991), pp. 60-64, which describes the sixth. In the case of the Soviet army's mid-January attack in Vilnius, "there is good reason to believe that Mikhail Gorbachev chose to move against the independence movement of Lithuania at a time when most people would be distracted by events in the Middle East and when the US government, eager for Soviet support against Iraq, would mute its criticism of Soviet repression." Laber, p. 60. Thus the crumbling Soviet empire and the economically weakened United States empire have on occasion become mutually supportive partners in efforts to re-establish their domains of power.

30. *Discriminate Deterrence*, Report of the Commission on Integrated Long-Term Strategy, Fred C. Iklé and Albert Wohlstetter, co-chairmen (Washington: G.P.O., January 1988), pp. 13-15.

31. Josephus gives two conflicting accounts of this year-long struggle between Samaritans and Jews, which involved the suppression of both sides by Roman authorities. In *The Jewish War* (2.12.2; 232) the fight begins at the Samaritan village of Gema, with Samaritans killing a single Galilean in a crowd of Jewish pilgrims on their way up to Jerusalem for the feast of Passover. In *Antiquities* (20.6.1; 118) Josephus writes that "a great many" Galileans were slain by Samaritans at Gema. *The Jewish War* version stresses the disastrous possibilities of Roman intervention in this Samaritan-Jewish conflict. There, the Jewish crowds end their retaliation against Samaritans when "the Jerusalem magistrates, rushing out clad in sackcloth and with ashes poured on their heads, besought them to return and not to provoke the Romans to attack Jerusalem by reprisals on the Samaritans: they must spare their country and their Sanctuary, and their own wives and children, who were all in danger of being destroyed for the sake of avenging one Galilean" (*The Jewish War* 2.12.5; 237, trans. G. A. Williamson, rev. E. Mary Smallwood).

32. Rhoads, p. 72.

33. A. Kennedy, "Leaven," *Encyclopaedia Biblica*, 2752-54 (London: A. & C. Black, 1902). Cited by Bernard Brandon Scott, *Hear Then the Parable: A Commentary on the Parables of Jesus* (Minneapolis: Fortress Press, 1989), p. 324. I am especially grateful to Scott for his interpretation of the Parable of the Leaven, pp. 321-29.

34. Scott, p. 324.

35. Jeremias, p. 147.

36. Austin Fagothey, S. J. *Right and Reason* (St. Louis: C. V. Mosby, 1953), p. 531.

37. Like the MX, the Trident missile has pinpoint accuracy and highly explosive warheads, two of the necessary ingredients for a first-strike force. But Trident has special first-strike characteristics. Because it is underwater, far-ranging, and invulnerable to detection, Trident can sneak in to launch a massive attack of deadly accurate warheads only ten to fifteen minutes away from Soviet missile silos. The short flight time of thousands of Trident warheads homing in precisely on unlaunched Soviet or other missiles in a disarming first strike is the nightmare Trident capability the Pentagon has kept out of sight of the American public. Nuclear strategists recognize the deployment of Trident missiles as a practical argument for an enemy's either striking first itself or putting its missile force on a hair-trigger, launch-on-warning alert. For an analysis of Trident by its former missile designer who resigned his Lockheed job for reasons of conscience, see Robert C. Aldridge, "Trident: The Ultimate First Strike Weapon," *First Strike: The Pentagon's Strategy for Nuclear War* (Boston: South End Press, 1983), pp. 73-102.

38. Robert Ellsberg, ed., *By Little and By Little: The Selected Writings of Dorothy Day* (New York: Alfred A. Knopf, 1984), pp. 332-33.

39. I have described the Council's debate on war and peace in "Toward a New Perspective on War: The Vision of Vatican II," *The Nonviolent Cross* (New York: Macmillan, 1968), pp. 100-136.

40. Letter from Philip Scharper, editor, Sheed & Ward, to Rev. Austin Fagothey, S. J., September 29, 1965.

41. M. K. Gandhi, *Satyagraha* (Ahmedabad: Navajivan Press, 1951), p. 29.

42. "All who take the sword will perish by the sword" is based on an Aramaic version, or *targum*, of Isaiah 50:11. It provided Jesus with a scripturally based rejection of violence. Hans Kosmala, "Matthew XXVI:52—A Quotation from the Targum," *Novum Testamentum* 4 (1960), pp. 3-5.

43. S. Applebaum, "Economic Life in Palestine," *The Jewish People in the First Century*, vol. 2, ed. Safrai and Stern, p. 660.

44. John R. Donahue, S. J., *The Gospel in Parable* (Philadelphia: Fortress Press, 1988), p. 11.

45. John Dominic Crossan, *Raid on the Articulate* (New York: Harper & Row, 1976), p. 108.

46. Donahue, p. 183.

47. Remark by David Batker, economist and Seattle Greenpeace worker.

48. Donahue, p. 155.

49. Scott, p. 122.

50. Robert Jewett, *Jesus Against the Rapture* (Philadelphia: Westminster Press, 1979), p. 70.

51. Colin H. Roberts, "The Kingdom of Heaven (Lk. XVII.21)," *Harvard Theological Review* 41 (January 1948), pp. 7-8. Theologians have long debated whether "within" or "among" is the proper translation of the key greek word *entos*, with "among" having become the more recently dominant view. Roberts's meaning "accounts for both the opposing versions and in a sense includes them" (p. 2). Although Roberts does not go beyond the Greek text to possible Aramaic sources, G. B. Caird in his commentary on Luke suggests that *entos* "is an erratic translation

of an Aramaic preposition, which could mean 'among' or 'in the midst of.' " G. B. Caird, *The Gospel of St. Luke* (Harmondsworth, Middlesex, England: Penguin Books, 1963), p. 197. Caird paraphrases the meaning of the text similarly to Roberts's meaning: "there is no point in keeping watch for the future coming of the kingdom, since the kingdom is already present, waiting to be accepted and entered by those who have eyes to see it." Ibid.

52. In light of the Roberts and Caird interpretations, I have used the phrase "within your power" to convey the meaning of Luke's *entos humōn*, encouraged by the fact that Henry Cadbury translates comments by Tertullian and Cyril of Alexandria on Luke 17:21 in a similar vein: "[The kingdom of God] is in your hand, in your power, if you hear and do the will of God" (Tertullian, *Adv. Marcionem*, 4, 35). "Do not ask the times, but strive rather to attain the Kingdom, for it is 'within you.' That is, to take it lies among your choices and within your power" (Cyril of Alexandria, *Comment. in Luc.* No. 368, col. 841; in Migne, Patrologia Graeca, 72). Henry J. Cadbury, "The Kingdom of God and Ourselves," *The Christian Century* 67 (1950), p. 172.

53. When Brazil's president Jose Sarney made this statement in his speech to the United Nations General Assembly on September 22, 1985, "Latin Americans responded with a thundering chorus of 'Amens.' " Jaime Wright, "Against Debt and Despair," *Christianity and Crisis* (November 23, 1987), p. 413.

54. The conclusion of this up-dated Parable of the Unmerciful Servant may seem to be in contrast with that given in Matthew's text (18:23-35), and it is. Parable scholars point out that we no longer have the original text or context of any of the parables of Jesus, following their several decades of transmission through the church before the gospels were written. Matthew (in Syria in the 80s?) is not directly concerned with the earlier debt crisis of Galilean peasants, which I propose here as the most likely context for Jesus' original parable. Applying the Unmerciful Servant instead to his own divided community, Matthew has added to the parable his particular lesson of forgiveness in a conclusion which critics agree was not that of Jesus: "So also my heavenly Father will do to every one of you, if you do not forgive your brother from your heart" (Matt. 18:35). Without Matthew's tacked-on conclusion, the parable is no longer an allegory about "God the Father." The king's quick withdrawal of forgiveness in the parable is in fact a poor divine illustration of the immediately preceding response by Jesus to Peter's question on how often he should forgive his brother: "I do not say to you seven times, but seventy times seven" (Matt. 18:22). By de-allegorizing Matthew's divine king, resituating the parable in the context of Galilee's debt crisis, then transposing it to our own debt crisis, one reaches a somewhat different conclusion than Matthew did. But like his, the result is an effort to reapply in one's own time Jesus' teaching on the necessity of forgiving one's debtors.

55. Vallely, pp. 312-13 in published text.

56. The debt analysis of the next seven paragraphs has been drawn especially from conversations and correspondence with David Batker.

57. The *Revised Standard Version* gives the correct translation in a footnote.

58. Norman Perrin, *Rediscovering the Teaching of Jesus* (New York: Harper & Row, 1967), p. 151.

59. Joachim Jeremias, *The Prayers of Jesus* (London: SCM Press, 1967), p. 92. Norman Perrin, ibid. Douglas Oakman notes that in the Greek text "Luke has supplied the word 'sins' instead of 'debts.' Yet it is most interesting that Luke

continues with a material application — 'as we ourselves forgive all in debt to us' (11:4b)." Douglas Oakman, "Jesus and Agrarian Palestine: The Factor of Debt," *SBL 1985 Seminar Papers*, p. 72. Jesus' use of *hobā* would account for both Matthew's "debts" and Luke's "sins."

60. I first heard the phrase "upside-down kingdom" from former White Train watcher Hedy Sawadsky, whose life is a seeking of that kingdom.

61. George Ann Potter, *Dialogue on Debt* (Washington: Center of Concern, 1988), pp. 174-75.

5. JESUS, JERUSALEM, AND THE END OF THE WORLD

1. Raul Hilberg, "German Railroads/Jewish Souls," *Society* (November/December 1976), p. 64.

2. Note from Glen Milner to Jim Douglass, October 1988.

3. The translation used here for the final phrase of Luke 19:44 is drawn from a letter written by John Pairman Brown to Jim Douglass, July 8, 1989: "The sense [of Luke 19:44] is the Rabbinic 'repent a day before your death.'" The phrase I have used in verse 43, "will raise fortification all around you," corresponds to the *Jerusalem Bible*'s translation of this verse rather than the *Revised Standard Version*'s "will cast up a bank about you and surround you."

In regard to the origin of Luke 19:41-44, Joseph A. Fitzmyer believes that "Luke is making use of an inherited piece of tradition, which he has only slightly redacted." Joseph A. Fitzmyer, *The Gospel According to Luke X-XXIV* (New York: The Anchor Bible, Doubleday, 1983), p. 1253.

4. Norman Perrin, *The New Testament* (New York: Harcourt Brace Jovanovich, 1974), pp. 40-41, 56-57.

5. Josephus, *The Jewish War*, trans. G. A. Williamson, rev. E. Mary Smallwood (Harmondsworth, Middlesex, England: Penguin Books, 1985), pp. 358 (6.4.6; 257, 259), 360 (6.5.2; 283, 284).

6. Werner Georg Kümmel, *Introduction to the New Testament* (Nashville: Abingdon Press, 1975), p. 98.

7. Ched Myers, *Binding the Strong Man* (Maryknoll, New York: Orbis Books, 1988), p. 87.

8. Ibid., pp. 351-52.

9. Addison G. Wright, "The Widow's Mites: Praise or Lament? — A Matter of Context," *Catholic Biblical Quarterly*, vol. 44, no. 2 (April 1982), p. 261. Wright points out that Jesus' Corban statement (Mark 7:10-13), whereby human needs take precedence over religious values when they conflict, contradicts an interpretation that would have him commending the widow's action.

10. Note from Marcus Borg to Jim Douglass, August 8, 1989.

11. Myers, p. 103.

12. Amos N. Wilder, "Eschatological Imagery and Earthly Circumstance," *New Testament Studies* 5 (1958), p. 231.

13. See Walter Wink's work on the powers, *Naming the Powers* (vol. 1), *Unmasking the Powers* (vol. 2) (Philadelphia: Fortress Press, 1984, 1986), and his forthcoming *Engaging the Powers* (vol. 3).

14. Josephus, *The Jewish War*, Williamson and Smallwood, p. 359 (6.5.1; 271-76).

15. Cited by Richard L. Rubenstein and John K. Roth, *Approaches to Auschwitz:*

The Holocaust and Its Legacy (Atlanta: John Knox Press, 1987), p. 35.

16. Kümmel, pp. 119-20.

17. John L. McKenzie, Preface to Wolfgang Trilling's commentary, *The Gospel According to St. Matthew* (New York: Crossroad, 1981), p. viii. McKenzie is following K. Stendahl's characterization of Matthew.

18. W. D. Davies, *The Setting of the Sermon on the Mount* (Cambridge: Cambridge University Press, 1964), p. 315.

19. David Flusser, "Two Anti-Jewish Montages in Matthew," "Matthew's 'Versus Israel,' " in *Judaism and the Origins of Christianity* (Jerusalem: Magnes Press, 1988), pp. 552-73.

20. Ibid., p. 556. Flusser's reading of Matthew 8:10 is found in *The Jerusalem Bible* and the new *Revised Standard Version*. It is not the preferred reading in the old *RSV* or the *New English Bible*, both of which here accept different manuscripts and the Lucan parallel.

21. Ibid., p. 558.

22. I am following the interpretation of Matthew's Parable of the Marriage Feast given in *The Parables of Jesus* by Robert W. Funk, Bernard Brandon Scott, and James R. Butts (Sonoma: Polebridge Press, 1988), p. 43. In comparing Matthew with the versions of Luke and Thomas, their comment is: "The Matthean version has strayed far from the original parable. ... This allegory is alien to Jesus and looks back on the destruction of Jerusalem."

23. Joseph Fitzmyer has noted Matthew's shift in terminology from "the crowd" in the previous verse (27:24) to "all the people" as the source of the cry. "The shift seems to be deliberately intended, for the responsibility is to affect 'the children' as well." Joseph A. Fitzmyer, S. J., "Anti-Semitism and the Cry of 'All the People' (Mt. 27:25)," *Theological Studies* 26 (1965), p. 669.

24. Claude Lanzmann, *Shoah: An Oral History of the Holocaust* (New York: Pantheon Books, 1985), pp. 99-100. To clarify here the dialogue of the text, I have added speaker identifications from my memory of the film.

25. J. Lambrecht, "The Parousia Discourse: Composition and Content in Mt., XXIV-XXV," *L'Évangile selon Matthieu: Rédaction et théologie*, ed. M. Didier (Gembloux, Belgique: Éditions J. Duculot, 1972), pp. 314-18.

26. For two radically different viewpoints that coincide concerning the eagles/vultures interpretation, see: 1) Lloyd Gaston, *No Stone on Another* (Leiden: E. J. Brill, 1970), p. 353, commenting on Luke 17:37, a parallel use of the Sayings Gospel text; 2) J. Marcellus Kik, *The Eschatology of Victory* (Nutley, New Jersey: Presbyterian and Reformed Publishing Co., 1974), pp. 125-26, 102. Background on the eagle standards is provided by Carl H. Kraeling, "The Episode of the Roman Standards at Jerusalem," *Harvard Theological Review* 35 (1942), pp. 269-70, 274-78. The Jewish attitude toward Rome's eagle is illustrated by Josephus's story of the golden eagle mounted over the Temple's main gate by Herod. Two Torah scholars and their students hacked the golden idol to pieces and were in turn burned alive by Herod. Josephus, *Antiquities* (17.6.2-4; 149-67).

27. Josephus, *The Jewish War*, Williamson and Smallwood, p. 363 (6.6.1; 316).

28. The verse following that of *Bar Enasha* coming on clouds expresses Matthew's hope for the church's Gentile mission now that the age of the Temple has passed: "and he will send out his angels with a loud trumpet call, and they will gather his elect from the four winds, from one end of heaven to the other" (24:31). *Bar Enasha*'s dispatching of the angelic messengers is the heavenly counterpart to

Jesus' sending out the apostles to all nations in the final scene of the gospel (28:19). Schuyler Brown, "The Matthean Apocalypse," *Journal for the Study of the New Testament* 4 (July 1979), p. 13.

29. See Chapter 2, pp. 54-55.

30. *The Jerusalem Bible* offers this remarkable footnote comment on Matthew 16:28: "v. 28 refers to the destruction of Jerusalem which demonstrates the presence of the kingdom of Christ." Thus Matthew's worst legacy is conveyed accurately but uncritically by modern Christian scholarship.

31. For the connections between these texts, see André Feuillet, "Le sens du mot Parousie dans l'Evangile de Matthieu," *The Background of the New Testament and Its Eschatology*, eds. W. D. Davies and D. Daube (Cambridge: Cambridge University Press, 1956), p. 264. I am grateful to Philippe Batini for his translation of this important article. Feuillet's identification of the synoptic *Parousia* and the destruction of Jerusalem in various articles has served as the basis for the brilliant conclusions of two otherwise contrasting exegetical works: 1) Lloyd Gaston, *No Stone on Another*, pp. 483-87; and 2) José Miranda, *Being and the Messiah* (Maryknoll, New York: Orbis Books, 1977), pp. 203-22.

32. These judgments have clouded passages in even the Sermon on the Mount, as in the Sermon's antitheses ("You have heard that it was said . . .") where Matthew misrepresents the Torah over against Jesus. Lloyd Gaston, "The Messiah of Israel as Teacher of the Gentiles," *Interpretation*, vol. 29, no. 1 (January 1975), p. 34.

33. As Gaston has put it, "Paradoxically, the same Matthew who taught the church to hate Israel gave to the church a Jewish Jesus, encouraged in it an ethical seriousness, and helped it retain the Hebrew Bible" (Ibid., p. 40).

34. Michael G. Steinhauser, "Introduction to the Sayings Gospel Q," *Q Thomas Reader*, eds. John S. Kloppenborg, Marvin W. Meyer, Stephen J. Patterson, Michael G. Steinhauser (Sonoma: Polebridge Press, 1990), p. 5.

35. Ivan Havener, *The Sayings of Jesus* (Wilmington: Michael Glazier, 1987), pp. 43-45.

36. This paragraph's analysis is based on John S. Kloppenborg's essay, "City and Wasteland: Narrative World and the Beginning of the Sayings Gospel (Q)," which will appear in a 1991 or 1992 issue of *Semeia* entitled *How Gospels Begin*, edited by Dennis E. Smith; used with permission of the author.

37. Besides the double occurrence of the phrase at Genesis 13:10-11, Kloppenborg points to its abbreviations in the Lot narrative at Genesis 19:17, 25, 28, 29; "the phrase recurs in the retelling of the destruction of Sodom in Jubilees 16.5 and 1 Clem 11.1." Ibid., p. 10 of manuscript; used with permission.

38. John S. Kloppenborg, *The Formation of Q* (Philadelphia: Fortress Press, 1987), p. 94.

39. Richard Horsley has argued forcefully that the original sense of Matthew 19:28 and Luke 22:28-30 "would have been that the Twelve would be sitting on the thrones 'liberating/ redeeming/ establishing justice for' the twelve tribes of Israel" rather than "judging" them. Richard A. Horsley, *Jesus and the Spiral of Violence* (San Francisco: Harper & Row, 1987), p. 205. I agree that this was Jesus' understanding of the saying, but believe that it has been narrowed to the sense of judgment by the Q editor as it stands at the conclusion of that gospel.

40. John S. Kloppenborg, "The Formation of Q Revisited: A Response to

Richard Horsley," *Society of Biblical Literature 1989 Seminar Papers*, ed. D. Lull (Atlanta: Scholars Press, 1989), p. 214.

41. John S. Kloppenborg, "Literary Convention, Self-Evidence, and the Social History of the Q People" (to appear in a 1991 or 1992 *Semeia* volume edited by Kloppenborg entitled *Early Christianity, Q and Jesus*), p. 37 of manuscript; used with permission of the author.

42. "Formally and materially the most intrusive passage [of the mission charge] is 10:13-15, which is directed not at the community but at its opponents and which reflects the experience of the rejection of the Q preachers." Kloppenborg, *Formation of Q*, p. 195, citing Schulz and Laufen in support.

43. Eric M. Meyers and James F. Strange, *Archaeology, the Rabbis and Early Christianity* (Nashville: Abingdon Press, 1981), p. 56.

44. Josephus, *The Jewish War*, Williamson and Smallwood, p. 213 (3.7.31; 301-5). Even if Josephus exaggerates the total casualties and slaves, the figures would probably have been in the thousands for Japha, which he identifies elsewhere as "the largest village in Galilee" with "a great number of inhabitants in it" (*Vita* 230).

45. Robert Henry Lightfoot, *Locality and Doctrine in the Gospels* (London: Hodder and Stoughton, 1938), p. 63. In this same work (pp. 1-48), Lightfoot makes a strong case that Mark's gospel ends at verse 16:8 with respect to both form and content. This seems to have become a critical consensus, and it is supported by the manuscript evidence. It is the one I assume here. Lightfoot's difficulty with the logic of his own argument, whether Mark writing in Rome would still expect the gospel's consummation to take place in Galilee (ibid., p. 44, footnote 2), is resolved by identifying Mark's place of composition as Galilee, not Rome.

46. Kümmel, pp. 151, 186.

47. Ibid., p. 151.

48. In Luke 19:39-44; 21:20-24; 23:28-31, and 13:34-35, the latter passage also in Q, Matthew 23:37-39. Gaston, *No Stone on Another*, p. 244.

49. Gaston, *No Stone on Another*, p. 244.

50. Eusebius reports that Christians migrated from Jerusalem to Pella in Peraea before the war with Rome (*Ecclesiastical History* 3.5.2-3).

51. Lloyd Gaston, "Anti-Judaism and the Passion Narrative in Luke and Acts," in *Anti-Judaism in Early Christianity: Vol. 1, Paul and the Gospel*, ed. Peter Richardson (Waterloo, Ontario: Wilfrid Laurier University Press, 1986), p. 153.

52. Ibid., pp. 139-40. Gaston is drawing on Jacob Jervell's *Luke and the People of God* (Minneapolis: Augsburg Publishing House, 1972) for the first part of this complex Lucan thesis, the church's continuity with Judaism.

53. Two famous studies of the historical Jesus, Martin Dibelius's *Jesus* and Günther Bornkamm's *Jesus of Nazareth*, recognized the importance of the Jerusalem journey for an understanding of Jesus' life but then failed to identify its specific historical purpose. Martin Dibelius, *Jesus* (Philadelphia: Westminster Press, 1949), pp. 62-63. Günther Bornkamm, *Jesus of Nazareth* (London: Hodder and Stoughton, 1960), pp. 154-55.

54. "Jesus' saying was similar to the prophetic visions of Amos, Jeremiah, Isaiah, and Ezekiel. Apparently an actual vision occurred early in his ministry in which Satan was seen to be cast down from heaven without any human assistance." Robert Jewett, commenting on Ulrich B. Müller, "Vision und Botschaft: Erwägungen zur prophetischen Struktur der Verkündigung Jesu," *Zeitschrift für Theologie und Kirche*,

vol. 74 (1974), pp. 416-48. Robert Jewett, *Jesus Against the Rapture* (Philadelphia: Westminster Press, 1979), p. 35.

55. G. B. Caird, *The Gospel of St. Luke* (Harmondsworth, Middlesex: Penguin Books, 1983), p. 143.

56. Gaston, *No Stone on Another*, p. 322.

57. Josephus, *The Jewish War*, Williamson and Smallwood, pp. 361-62 (6.5.3: 300-309).

58. Joseph Fitzmyer points out that only six Greek words out of 47/48 in Luke 12:54-56 agree with its remote parallel in Matthew 16:2-3, which also may not have been in the original text of Matthew. He concludes that Luke 12:54-56 "is scarcely derived from 'Q' . . . and should be regarded as 'L.' " Joseph A. Fitzmyer, *The Gospel According to Luke X-XXIV* (New York: The Anchor Bible, Doubleday, 1983), p. 999.

59. Caird, *Saint Luke*, p. 169.

60. A. T. Olmstead, *Jesus in the Light of History* (New York: Charles Scribner's Sons, 1942), pp. 147-49. Also E. Mary Smallwood in her notes to Josephus, *The Jewish War*, p. 428, footnote 25.

61. Josephus, *The Jewish War*, p. 139 (2.9.4; 175-77).

62. Gaston, *No Stone on Another*, p. 342. Without such an understanding of the text's prophetic, collective warning to the nation, it becomes Jesus' incomprehensible comment on individual sin and suffering. See William H. Willimon's thoughtful struggle with this problem in his Lenten meditation, "When Bad Things Happen," *The Christian Century* (February 22, 1989), pp. 198-99.

63. Louis Jacobs, *A Jewish Theology* (Behrman House: 1973), p. 243.

64. "Repentance," *Encyclopedia Judaica*, vol. 14, edited by Cecil Roth (Jerusalem: Keter Publishing House Jerusalem Ltd., 1972), col. 73.

65. Letter and manuscript comment from Marcus Borg to Jim Douglass, August 8, 1989 (emphasis in original).

66. Ibid.

67. Samuel Pisar, "A Warning," *Preventing the Nuclear Holocaust: A Jewish Response*, ed. Rabbi David Saperstein (New York: Commission on Social Action of Reform Judaism, 1983), p. 32.

68. Martin Buber, *For the Sake of Heaven* (New York: Harper Torchbooks, 1966; originally in Hebrew as *Gog u-Magog*, Jerusalem, 1943), p. 246.

69. J. Stuart Russell, *The Parousia* (Grand Rapids: Baker Book House, 1985; reprinted from the 1887 edition issued by T. Fisher Unwin), p. 52.

70. Raul Hilberg shows how twenty canon laws, passed by the Catholic church from the fourth to the fifteenth centuries, served as precedents for Hitler's anti-Jewish measures. *Destruction of the European Jews: Student Edition* (New York: Holmes & Meier, 1985), pp. 10-11.

71. Gaston, *No Stone on Another*, p. 359. Gaston illustrates this point by citing a chain of Jeremiah passages that parallel Jesus' prophetic lament.

72. Earlier in the gospel Luke has also inserted a series of eschatological parables: 12:35-48. In chapter 21 the eschatological discourse continues through verse 36.

73. Josephus, *The Jewish War*, p. 147 (2.13.4; 259-60).

74. Ibid., (2.13.5; 261-62).

75. Josephus, *Antiquities* (20.8.6; 170-72).

76. Richard A. Horsley and John S. Hanson, *Bandits, Prophets, and Messiahs:*

Popular Movements at the Time of Jesus (Minneapolis: Winston Press, 1985), p. 161. In addition to "action prophets" such as the Egyptian, Horsley and Hanson identify a second type of prophet among the peasantry in the first century C.E.: "oracular prophets," who in the tradition of the great biblical prophets delivered messages, either of judgment or deliverance, from God to the people, especially during times of crisis. Oracular prophets included John the Baptist, Jesus, and Jeshua son of Ananias, whom we have already seen in Josephus's description of his lonely career ended by his death in the Jewish-Roman War.

77. Josephus, *The Jewish War*, p. 360. (6.5.2; 283-86). Under their twofold categorization Horsley and Hanson identify this prophet of a Temple deliverance as an "oracular prophet," whereas I am more concerned in the immediate context with Jesus' response to "sign prophets," who cut across both categories.

78. Josephus, *Antiquities* (18.4.1; 85-87).

79. Jacques Maritain, *L'Homme et l'Etat*, p. 49. Cited by P. Régamey, *Non-Violence and the Christian Conscience* (New York: Herder and Herder, 1966), p. 200.

80. Memorandum by James E. Bickel, Director, Transportation Safeguards Division, Albuquerque Operations Office, Department of Energy, August 6, 1985. Obtained by appeal under the Freedom of Information Act by Glen Milner. The purpose of the Bickel Memorandum was to announce a meeting at Kirtland Air Force Base on August 13-14, 1985, "to assure proper coordination" of the "alternate methods of delivery of warheads." Those invited to the meeting included the Commanding Officer of the Strategic Weapons Facility Pacific (SWFPAC) at the Bangor Trident base.

81. Richard Horsley, "Bandits, Messiahs, and Longshoremen: Popular Unrest in Galilee Around the Time of Jesus," *Society of Biblical Literature 1988 Seminar Papers,* ed. D. Lull (Atlanta: Scholars Press, 1988), p. 194.

82. John S. Kloppenborg, in his synopsis of Q, notes that most scholars identify Luke 17:25 as a Lucan introduction into the original Q passage. John S. Kloppenborg, *Q Parallels* (Sonoma: Polebridge Press, 1988), p. 192.

83. Robert C. Tannehill, *The Sword of His Mouth* (Philadelphia: Fortress Press, 1975), p. 118. In verses 17:26 and 17:30 of Tannehill's translation I have replaced "the Son of Man" by *Bar Enasha.*

84. Ibid., p. 121.

85. Letter from John Pairman Brown to Jim Douglass, April 28, 1988.

86. J. V. Luce, *The End of Atlantis: New Light on an Old Legend* (Norwich: Thames and Hudson, 1969), p. 47.

87. Excavations on Crete began in 1900 at the great Minoan palace at Knossos, under the direction of Sir Arthur Evans. In 1939, after the restoration of other Minoan sites, Professor Spyridon Marinatos, Director of the Greek Archaeological Service, offered the hypothesis that the end of Minoan Crete civilization soon after 1500 B.C.E. was a result of Thera's eruptions. S. Marinatos, "The Volcanic Destruction of Minoan Crete," *Antiquity* 13 (1939), pp. 425-39. The Marinatos hypothesis has been strengthened by his own more recent excavations on Thera and by the recovery and analysis of Thera's volcanic ash from the floor of the Eastern Mediterranean by two American geologists, D. Ninkovich and B. C. Heezen. All of this is described, and related to the further hypothesis that the legend of Atlantis is based on Minoan Crete, by J. V. Luce in *The End of Atlantis* (with extensive maps, charts, and illustrations).

88. John Pairman Brown, "The Sacrificial Cult and Its Critique in Greek and Hebrew (I)," *Journal of Semitic Studies* 24 (1979), p. 168.

89. John Pairman Brown, *The Liberated Zone* (Richmond: John Knox Press, 1969), p. 110.

90. Luce, *The End of Atlantis*, p. 173. Luce was led to the references and significance of Caphtor in the Hebrew Scriptures by Professor J. Weingreen. Ibid., p. 11.

91. "The story [of Sodom and Gomorrah] is filled with obvious folklore traits which indicate that it is constructed from fragmentary memories. It is now a theological narrative; the disaster is explained as a judgment of God on the sins of the cities." John L. McKenzie, *Dictionary of the Bible* (Milwaukee: Bruce Publishing Company, 1965), p. 827.

92. "Orpheus," *Argonautica* 1268-80. Cited by Luce, p. 172.

93. Pindar, *Paean* IV, 27-44. Cited by Luce, p. 120. The speaker Euxantius is refusing an invitation to rule over a "seventh part" of Crete because of his "portent" of that land's destruction.

94. Josephus, *The Jewish War*, p. 199 (3.6.2; 123).

95. Luke 21:29-33 "does not belong to the Eschatological Discourse proper." Paul Winter, "The Treatment of His Sources by the Third Evangelist in Luke XXI-XXIV," *Studia Theologica*, vol. 8, fasc. 2 (1954), p. 153. "Luke 21:34-36 are clearly a Lucan addition based on the eschatological exhortation of the Hellenistic church, as the numerous parallels to I Thes 5:1ff show." Gaston, *No Stone on Another*, pp. 357-58.

96. Gaston, *No Stone on Another*, p. 11.

97. In preparing the following division and source-analysis of Luke 21:8-28, I have drawn especially on four resources: 1) Gaston, *No Stone on Another*, pp. 355-64; 2) Caird, *St. Luke*, pp. 227-32; 3) Fred O. Francis, "Eschatology and History in Luke-Acts," *Journal of the American Academy of Religion* 37 (1969), pp. 49-63; and 4) Paul Winter, "The Treatment of His Sources by the Third Evangelist in Luke XXI-XXIV," pp. 141-55.

98. Gaston, "Anti-Judaism," pp. 140, 143-44. I list all sixty-four references here especially for any reader who wishes to go through the consciousness-raising exercise of looking them up, thereby seeing a revelation of the Lucan testimony to Jesus' support among the Jewish people. In the course of such an exercise, one begins to understand why Jesus was accused by the Temple aristocracy of being a revolutionary (Luke 23:2). I include the birth narratives as important traditions that testify to the same truth of popular support. An especially helpful resource for distinguishing Special Luke in categories 1 and 2, and for comparing Luke and Mark in categories 3 through 6 (and indeed, for any study of the synoptic gospels) is *New Gospel Parallels: Vol. 1, The Synoptic Gospels*, ed. Robert W. Funk (Philadelphia: Fortress Press, 1985). 1) Pro-gospel "people" (*laos*) references in Special Luke: 1:10, 17, 21, 68, 77; 2:10, 32; 3:15, 18; 7:1, 16, 29; 18:43; 19:48; 21:37f; 23:5, 14; 24:19. 2) Pro-gospel "multitude," "crowd," "people" (*ochlos*) references in Special Luke: 3:7, 10; 5:1, 3; 6:19; 7:9, 11, 12, 24; 8:19; 9:11, 12, 16, 37; 11:14, 27, 29; 12:1, 13, 54; 13:14, 17; 14:25; 18:36; 19:3, 39. 3) Pro-gospel "people" references taken by Luke from Mark: 22:1-2. 4) Pro-gospel "people" additions by Luke to Mark: 3:21; 6:17; 8:47; 9:13; 20:1, 6, 9, 19, 26, 45. 5) Pro-gospel "multitude" references taken from Mark: 5:19; 8:4, 40, 42, 45; 9:38. 6) Pro-gospel "multitude" additions to Mark: 4:42; 5:15; 22:3-6. Given this Lucan evidence of popular support for Jesus, it is

therefore all the more "astounding," as Gaston puts it, to encounter Luke's "reversal of the role of the people in the passion narrative." Gaston, "Anti-Judaism," p. 144. The reversal has theological motives similar to Matthew's in his dramatization of the cry from "all the people."

99. On the women of Galilee, see Luke 8:1-3, 23:49, 55-56.

100. Joachim Jeremias, *Jerusalem in the Time of Jesus* (Philadelphia: Fortress Press, 1969), pp. 116, 112.

101. Martin Luther King, Jr., *The Trumpet of Conscience* (New York: Harper & Row, 1967), p. 60.

102. David J. Garrow, *Bearing the Cross: Martin Luther King, Jr. and the Southern Christian Leadership Conference* (New York: Williams Morrow, 1986), p. 580.

103. King, *Trumpet of Conscience*, p. 60.

104. Ibid.

105. Garrow, *Bearing the Cross*, p. 593.

106. King, *Trumpet of Conscience*, p. 62.

107. Ibid., p. 64.

108. Philip H. Melanson, *The Murkin Conspiracy* (New York: Praeger, 1989; second revised edition, *The Martin Luther King Assassination* [New York: Shapolski, 1991]).

109. "Who Killed Martin Luther King?" aired on BBC television in September 1989 and on U.S. cable television in March 1990. The film's producers, John Edginton and John Sergeant, wrote an article based on the information gathered in their investigation: "The Murder of Martin Luther King Jr.," *CovertAction Information Bulletin*, no. 34 (Summer 1990), pp. 21-27.

110. Melanson, *The Murkin Conspiracy*, pp. 32-38; *King Assassination*, pp. 32-38.

111. Jules Ron Kimble admitted his involvement in the King assassination while being interviewed at the El Reno Federal Penitentiary, El Reno, Oklahoma, in June 1989 for "Who Killed Martin Luther King?"

112. Isaiah 7:25, 10:6, 16:5; Amos 5:27, 6:14, 7:17; Daniel 12:7.

113. Gaston, *No Stone on Another*, p. 362.

114. Ibid.

115. Caird, *St. Luke*, p. 232.

116. Gaston, *No Stone on Another*, p. 356.

EPILOGUE

1. *Arab-Jewish Unity: Testimony before the Anglo-American Inquiry Commission for the Ihud (Union) Association by Judah Magnes and Martin Buber* (London: Victor Gollancz, 1947), pp. 44-45.

2. Ibid., p. 10.

3. Ibid., p. 42.

4. Ibid., p. 48.

5. A third factor in this revolution, growing in prominence since my conversation with David and Hava Hammou, will be the eventual rebellion of Soviet Jews from their new role, upon immigration to Israel, as

surplus labor, a pool of unemployed; this is now mostly Oriental Jewish, as the territories' Arabs provide cheaper labor and thus get jobs. But if you prepare to expel the Arab workers (together with the non-working Arabs, indeed all those in the territories), you need to replace them, while at the same time enlarging the labor surplus by importing a considerably important *foreign yet Jewish* population surplus; not just a small, containable surplus but one that will be beyond the country's ability to absorb economically. Only thus will management in a formerly socialized economy be able to keep the upper hand. Only thus can the Ashkenazied establishment keep the upper hand over a 65-70 percent-strong Oriental Jewish majority. (Maxim Ghilan, "The Big Swindle: Histadrut Elections and Soviet Jewish Immigrants," p. 12, emphasis in original; as reported by *Israel & Palestine* [October 1989]: published by *Magelan*, 5 Rue Cardinal Mercier, 75009 Paris, France.)

As Soviet Jewish immigrants are forced to join the present Oriental Jewish surplus labor force, they will recognize their common cause in Israel with Oriental Jews and Arab Israelis, and in the Occupied Territories with Palestinians.

6. David Hammou, "An Oriental Revolution in Israel," *Israel & Palestine* (October 1989), p. 15.

7. Josephus, *The Antiquities of the Jews* 17.10.5 (271).

8. The description of the events in Saffuriya on July 15-16, 1948, has been drawn from three sources: Benny Morris, *The Birth of the Palestinian Refugee Problem, 1947-1949* (Cambridge: Cambridge University Press, 1987), pp. 200, 241; Nafez Nazzal, *The Palestinian Exodus from Galilee 1948* (Beirut, Lebanon: The Institute for Palestine Studies, 1978), pp. 74-79; and Dr. James Strange, Professor of Religious Studies at the University of South Florida and director of a United States archaeological team at Sepphoris, who gave me the twenty percent casualties figure for the IDF (as told to him by the former IDF commander) in a phone conversation on January 5, 1990. I am grateful to Dr. Strange and to Mr. Ariel Berman, Inspector for Antiquities, Lower Galilee, for enriching my visit to the excavations at Sepphoris with their knowledge of the site.

Approximately two thousand Arab Israelis from Saffuriya continue to live together in nearby Nazareth and elect their own mayor for their displaced community. That they were not expelled, with other Arab citizens, from Nazareth as well may have been due to the courage of a Canadian Jewish IDF officer, Ben Dunkelman. The story is told by Simha Flapan in *The Birth of Israel:*

On July 16 [1948], three days after the Lydda and Ramleh evictions, the city of Nazareth surrendered to the IDF. The officer in command, a Canadian Jew named Ben Dunkelman, had signed the surrender agreement on behalf of the Israeli army along with Chaim Laskov (then a brigadier general, later IDF chief of staff). The agreement assured the civilians that they would not be harmed, but the next day, Laskov handed Dunkelman an order to evacuate the population. Dunkelman's account of the incident casts light on the policy of the IDF: "I was surprised and shocked," he wrote. "I told him [Laskov] I would do nothing of the sort—in light of our promises to safeguard the well-being of the town's population, such an action would be superfluous and harmful."

When Laskov realized that Dunkelman did not intend to carry out the order, he left. Two days later, Dunkelman was transferred from Nazareth. "I felt sure," he wrote, "that this order had been given because of my defiance of the 'evacuation' order. But although I was withdrawn from Nazareth, it seems that my disobedience did have some effect. It seems to have given the high command time for second thoughts, which led them to the conclusion that it would, indeed, be wrong to expel the inhabitants of Nazareth. To the best of my knowledge, there was never any more talk of the 'evacuation' plan, and the city's Arab citizens have lived there ever since." (Simha Flapan, *The Birth of Israel: Myths and Realities* [New York: Pantheon Books, 1987], pp. 101-2, citing Peretz Kidron interview with Ben Dunkelman, *Haolam Hazeh*, January 9, 1980.)

9. For a full development of these themes, see Richard A. Horsley, *The Liberation of Christmas: The Infancy Narratives in Social Context* (New York: Crossroad, 1989).

10. Henry J. Cadbury in "Note XXIV: Dust and Garments," a discussion of Acts 13:51, Matthew 10:14, and Luke 9:5, in *The Beginnings of Christianity: Part I, The Acts of the Apostles*, ed. F. J. Foakes Jackson and Kirsopp Lake; *Vol. V, Additional Notes to the Commentary*, ed. Kirsopp Lake and Henry J. Cadbury (London: Macmillan, 1933), p. 271.

11. Elias Chacour with Mary E. Jensen, *We Belong to the Land* (San Francisco: Harper Collins, 1990), p. 183.

12. R. Scott Kennedy, "Special Delegation, December 6-15, 1989, Mid East Witness," "Monday, December 11, 1989," p. 17; from Middle East Witness, 515 Broadway, Santa Cruz, CA 95060.

13. I have supplemented his account of the *intifada*'s beginning with details drawn from Naim Stifan Ateek, *Justice, and Only Justice: A Palestinian Theology of Liberation* (Maryknoll, New York: Orbis Books, 1989), p. 45; and from Ann M. Lesch, "Prelude to the Uprising in the Gaza Strip," *Journal of Palestine Studies*, vol. 20, no. 1 (Autumn 1990), p. 1. Lesch's article goes on to emphasize that "the groundwork for the intifada was laid in the [Gaza Strip's] social transformations of the 1980s and the heightened activism of 1987" (p. 21).

14. Psalm 90:2-3. Rabbi Steinsaltz's translation brings out a dimension of the text which is absent in the renditions of the *Revised Standard Version* and the *Jerusalem Bible*.

15. Rabbi Adin Steinsaltz, "Repentance, Necessity and Choice," *The Jerusalem Post International Edition* (week ending October 13, 1990), p. 16A.

16. Gila Svirsky, "Women in Black," *Reconciliation International* (Summer 1990), p. 13. The article was originally published in the bulletin of the Jewish Women's Committee to End the Occupation (JWCEO), Suite 1178, 163 Joralemon Street, Brooklyn, NY 11201.

17. Ibid.

18. Jeremiah 2:07. I have filled in some of Professor Leibowitz's shorter remarks in our conversation with statements from two of his articles, which he gave me that afternoon: Yeshayahu Leibowitz, "Jews and Arabs in Israel," *The Jewish Spectator* (Winter 1986), pp. 11-13; Yeshayahu Leibowitz, "Against a Greater Israel," *Jewish Chronicle* (May 22, 1981), p. 22.

19. Ezekiel 33:23-26.

20. Professor Yeshayahu Leibowitz, *Notes and Remarks on the Weekly Parashah*, trans. Dr. Shmuel Himelstein (Brooklyn, New York: Chemed Books, 1990), pp. 186-87.

GENERAL INDEX

Scripture Index